Christ's Messenger to Romania

Romania

The John Dolinschi Story

With love to
read it from
John Dolinschi
to
Lance & Candy
Omarek!

Christ's Messenger to Romania: The John Dolinschi
Story

Cover Graphic Design by Jeanine Giuffrida

Cover photos courtesy of:

João Cabral and Pixabay/Tudor44

Edited & Published by Joseph Giuffrida Jr.

For editing & graphic design services, contact Joseph Giuffrida Jr. at: jgiuffridacoach@gmail.com

Available @ Amazon U.S., Amazon Europe, Kindle, and hardcopy.

ISBN- 9798603404240

Contact John Dolinschi at: jdolinschi@aol.com

FORWARD

The adventure in ministry of John and Viorica Dolinschi in Romania is another chapter straight out of the book of Acts. The God story of the miracles the Holy Spirit performed is faith building and inspiring. Having known John as a student at Christ for the Nations Institute in the '80s and being with him at the beginning of his missionary journey establishing Bible schools in Romania, is a miraculous story for which I shall continue praising the Lord.

For anyone who wants to see how God is building His church around the world in countries that have been or are dominated by brutal dictators, using ordinary "nobodies" who have faith to move mountains, the Dolinschi's testimony is a classic example of God's faithfulness to anyone who will step out of their "boat of comfort" and trust God to walk on water.

Dennis Lindsay
President, Christ for the Nations Institute

TESTIMONIALS

I first met John Dolinschi back in the mid-nineties while on a teaching assignment in Timisoara, Romania. It didn't take long for me to realize that John was no ordinary Romanian citizen or Gospel minister. In fact, after spending a few days with John, I felt honored and humbled to be in the presence of a true national hero and authentic apostle.

For years I have encouraged John to write his story. I believe the world needs to meet this man, who not only risked his life to escape the grip of communism but had the courage to return to his homeland with a vision of freeing others and spreading the Gospel across the nation.

I further believe the faith of every Christian minister and believer will be strengthened by the courage, faith and determination of this great apostolic leader.

Dr. Larry Pyle, D. Min.

Author, *The Dynamics of Being the Church*

Founder, The Journey Church

Russellville, AR

John Dolinschi's life of faith has inspired me and my family for over 22 years. I consider him a modern-day Moses to the people of Romania. His sacrifice and faith have made its mark on the people throughout Romania and in America. As you read this book, put yourself in his shoes as you take this journey of faith with him.

Mark Duke
Pastor, The Rock Church
Brentwood, CA

It was shortly after the collapse of the Iron Curtain in the 1990's when I began hearing of the ministry of John Dolinski through my friend Wayne Crimm of Birmingham, Alabama. Wayne was working in Romania, and he began telling me I needed to come to Romania to help train the Pastors working under John's leadership.

I began traveling to Romania to teach leadership seminars which John organized, beginning a wonderful relationship with a true apostle. Over the years, we have covered almost every part of Romania with pastor training seminars, and what a wonderful blessing it has been. I have met wonderful men and women of God from across the nation and have developed lasting friendships which have enriched my life.

I thank God for the day I met him and for all he means to me personally. He is a spiritual father to so many Christian leaders, and his godly character and integrity have brought countless blessings to his native country. God bless you, John, and may the story of your ministry continue to bless others.

Dr. Dale Yerton
President, The Living Faith, Inc.
www.daleyerton.com

Our church has supported John Dolinschi's ministry for over 25 years. John is a man of faith, vision and integrity. I had the opportunity to travel through Romania and see first-hand what God is doing through his ministry. John is the mentor of a new generation of Pastors and Christian workers who are breaking new soil through evangelism, discipleship, and church planting.

Through the years, John has been a welcomed guest in my home. During each visit he has shared parts of his life's story with our family, reminding us again and again, not only how much it can cost to follow Jesus, but how God is so faithful to those who are willing to commit everything to Him. I've been waiting for John to write this book, and I know it will be a challenge and encouragement to many.

David J. Markey, Jr., Th.M.
International Board Member, The Fellowship Network
Senior Pastor, Good News Church
Quakertown, PA

I have known John for many years. We have worked extensively together. John is a man of integrity. His family is the same. For a faith-building experience read his book. You will be blessed.

Morris Sheats, D. Min.
Leadership Institute Inc
Founder/President

John Dolinschi is one of the great ministry leaders of our time. He is without a doubt a modern-day Apostle who is selflessly giving his all to raise up men and women who are equipped to carry the Gospel to the country where he was raised, the former communist nation of Romania.

Under the communists, John suffered for his faith. Today he lives to reach the many people of his nation who need Jesus. It has been my privilege to minister there on many occasions and personally see the work that he and those he has mentored are doing for Christ. His commitment is without question and his integrity is unquestionable. John is the real deal!

Dr. R. Heard, PhD
Senior Pastor, Christian Tabernacle
Houston, TX

The story of John Dolinschi's life is one of those rare experiences that begs to be told. Serving as a minister of the Gospel during the communist rule of Romania, John has seen and experienced real persecution. I highly recommend this book - your perspective of revival and the miracle-working power of God amid trying times will be changed!

James R. Bond
Senior Pastor, Revival Tabernacle
Watsontown, PA

ACKNOWLEDGMENTS

Here from the very beginning, I want to give my heartfelt thanks to the following world and church leaders for encouraging me to "put my heart on paper."

Dr. Dennis Lindsay, President of Christ For the Nations.
Dr. Dale Yerton, President of Living Faith.
Dr. Larry Pyle, President of Successful Living.
Dr. Richard Heard, Bishop of Christian Tabernacle
Dr. Charles Flowers, Pastor of Faith Outreach Church
Dr. Morris Sheats, President of Leadership Institute.
Rev. David J Markey Jr., Pastor of Good News Church
Rev. James Bond, Pastor of Revival Tabernacle
Rev. Mark Duke, Pastor of the Rock of Brentwood Church
Rev. Harley Fiddler, President of International Focus,

Pastors and individuals who've supported us both on the ground and from afar:

Dave Love	John Ortega	Mondy Cano
Ray Kline	David Humphries	Earle Farwell
Eugene Seibert	Mathew Anderson	Harold Maxey
Tom Lowe	Gerald Ripley	Rafael Guitterez
Stanford Williams	Robin Steele	Don Grosvenor
Gerry Menke	Mike Barbera	James Alexander
Gary Kauffman	Aline Mosteller	Paul Bauer
William Patton	Jason Zimmerman	Mary Anderson
Mathew Schroeder	Ronald Stoehr	Robert & Betty -
- Alexander	Dale R. Landes	Lyle B Goracke,
Terry D Rabon	Presley Duke	John Stocker,

James Roam,
Rusty L Bowles
Milton Spears
Curtis G. Lengefeld
David J. Markey
Mark Duke
Robert Alexander
Allen Wholwend
Joseph Ruiz
Julie Glimour

Don Johnson
Norma Lineberry
Ed Huie
Harry Fiddler
James Bond
Scott Olsen
Ethelynn Sherwood
John Stoian
Dorel Micula
Duke Thietje

Tony M Abram
Philip Hoss
Jason Samusi
Dorel Micula
Charles Flowers
Dale V Clark
Gail Hogan
David Teran
Joseph Samusi

I would like to thank from the bottom of my heart, the key leaders and Pastors in Romania who have sown their lives and the lives of their families into the work of the Lord:

Milo and Nina Novacovici
Laiko Veres
Relu Paraluta
Florin Scafariu,
Stelian Turbatu
Şerban Daniel
Mircea Zavalean
Leonard Gurgas
Sorin Croitoru
Daniel Engelman
Ignat Gigel
Sprincenatu Marin
Raducan Florin
CocilnauAlexandru
Cimpoeru Nicolae
Baran Cornel
Vasile Bostiog
Lautaru Ion
Grigore Vasil
Fotache Marius

Laurentiu Popescu
Sandu
Dorel Tudorache
Mitru Teleaga
Alexandru Badea
Sîmba Marin
Costel Iancu
Marcel Lelcu
Nicu Gatea
Petrisor Staicu
Ignat Alin
Feca Viorel
Grancea Felix
Ochea Mircea
Baran Daniel
Tavy Bruma
Lautaru Marian
Petrisor Staicu
Nicu Gramesc
Stefan Nadrag

Constatin Gramada   Loredana Gramada
Rebeca Luisa Bostiog   Anna-Maria Bruma
Dan Sandu   Nicolae Cretanu
Petrica Coman   Iuliu Centea
Dumitrica Nicusor

In remembrance of those who were great spiritual fathers to me also urging me to write this book:

Bishop Jack DeHart, former Pastor of Heartland Church
Dr. Ray Freeman, former Pastor of Christian Heritage Church
Dr. Randy Bozarth, former CFNI Vice President and Teacher

I want to express my gratitude to Joe Giuffrida Jr. for his tireless and quick work to edit and produce this book. Joe improved it with the right structural and creative additions. His meticulous work was greatly appreciated. I've enjoyed working with you, brother!

I want to also extend my personal thanks to Jeanine Giuffrida, our graphic designer who designed the book covers. Jeanine, without your imaginative mind, this project wouldn't have been possible. You've helped all of us see what God has done, by encouraging the reader to open these pages and read this story.

DEDICATION

I dedicate this book to my wife, whose name is often recalled in this writing. Viorica chose a life of valleys and mountain tops, of danger and beauty, of crazy ideas and the sweetness of unburdening me every step of the journey.

To my children: Alina, Nadine, Nathan, and Christina. You are our precious treasures. Just being your dad brings me the greatest joy and reward, for you bring light to my days.

And to my parents: Vasile and Agafia. You freed me into the hands of my Creator, to reach the world for Christ, while praying daily that the love and fear of the Lord would always be with me.

CONTENTS

Chapter One

Early Years

When I was still a baby, unable to speak much less describe what I saw, something happened which I will remember for the rest of my life. One morning I awoke alone in my bed, as my mom was outside doing some errands. As I looked outside my window, there was a large bull with long horns staring hatefully at me and madly trying to get inside my room where I was sitting on my bed. I remember this as if it were printed on my mind and heart forever. And just before I was able to call on my mom to save me, I felt a comfortable hand wrap around me, keeping me safe and whispering in my ear, "My baby, do not be afraid of this evil one. I am here to care for and protect you. I'm your mommy's helper and I'm the one who cares for you, not only here but all the days of your life." This vivid account has stayed with me throughout my life. In fact, even though I was only two years old, it was one of the only things that stayed inside my memory and spirit.

The second thing I remember very well from around the same age, was when my father came home from a State labor camp where he had been forced for six months to work for free, rebuilding the country roads and bridges which were destroyed in World War II. One morning, I woke up in bed hungry for food, waiting for my mother to come inside as she was working in the garden. She was trying to manage everything inside and outside our home, as well as obtaining some income, while taking care of her four little children. She did all of this because my father didn't get any monthly pay.

But while I waited for my mother to come in the house, my father entered the room. I remember well his sweet smile when he saw me, which melted away his tired face. He was so happy to see me that he kissed and hugged me. Trying my best as a young child to converse with him, I became frustrated with my inability to make him understand me. Later on in life, he would rehearse this account, saying that I just sat on my bed still sleepy and smiley, bumbling about with my bottle, trying to talk with "milky words." As for myself, I told him that I remembered those moments so well, like it had just happened the other day.

How is it possible to remember events from such a young child's age? I don't yet know. But I imagine our minds can print the most impactful information in our hearts, which then replays in our memories. Certainly, these two events were the most impressive and were imprinted forever in my heart. It may also be because I was predestined to write these accounts for you today!

The Winter Angel Visits Our Home

While I was a pupil in the primary school, the Dolinschi family had a visitor from heaven during a very harsh winter period. My memory is still fresh as I can still see his beautiful face and clothes. He appeared to be a man in his early thirties. Now, this supernatural experience happened at a time when communist Romania was confronted with a lot of food and supply shortages, especially during this period. Sugar, oil and other basic products were not to be found in any State stores, and the Dolinschi family consisted of thirteen children.

But in the early 1960's, nine of us kids lacked basic food on the table. You see, we were in a state of winter hibernation, as there was not so much as a garden vegetable to be found on the table. We had only what was pickled in barrels, such as cucumbers and cabbage, with the occasional apple for us to eat. Most meals were cooked from corn flower, potatoes and beans, along with unsweetened teas. Let me just say that you don't need to pity me, as this turned out in my favor, for when I was a baby, there was another sugar shortage. And so, from my beginning I grew up not being used to sweetened food but got used to unsweetened milk. Later, when sugar was found and added in my bottle, I wouldn't drink it, but rather refused it. To this very day, I don't have a taste for any sweetened liquids or even solid cakes, which can sometimes even cause me to feel sick.

The appearance of the angel occurred during the winter of 1962-63 when outside there were two meters of snow, with high snowdrifts that created hills so tall that you could hardly see the surrounding horizon. We were stuck inside our home, but we could still use snow tunnels we created to move across the yard and feed the animals, as well as carrying the firewood inside.

Despite the limited mobility outside, we were surprised to hear someone knocking on our door. When we opened the door, a man entered carrying two large hemp-made bags hanging down from his hands. Today, it is hard to imagine anyone carrying these bags as they were so heavy. When he entered our largest bedroom, where we were all gathered, he greeted us with a smile and with the peace and love of the Lord. He said, "Greetings to you from our Lord Jesus Christ." Then he said, "Here is what our Lord sent for your own use, which by faith may be multiplied in your hands as you use it." Sure enough, inside the bags were a variety of crisis goods we were truly lacking, especially sugar and an abundance of fine spicy oil. After presenting us with the food and before leaving, he asked us all to pray with him, and led us in a time of thanksgiving. Everyone kneeled and thanked the Lord, our great Provider. As we stood up, he blessed us again and said goodbye. He was gone as quick as he came.

Now, all of us were bewildered at the identity of this man. He was a total stranger to us. After the prayer my parents wanted to ask him who he was, where he was from, and how he knew about us, but this encounter went by so quickly. What *was* apparent to us was how peaceful we felt, as though we had taken a drink of refreshing gladness.

After he left the house, we felt as if we had just woken up from a wonderful dream. We thought about the fact that it was so very cold outside, and that no one would be walking around out there in such cold temperatures as this could become deadly. It would have been impossible to make it over those snowy hills, especially in the ranching area where we lived. The high snow drifts would make it impossible for any sort of transportation to move about, and even more unlikely for anyone to be riding or walking.

Our mystery guest, upon entering our home, did so with only a light suit, shoes, pants, and a shirt with a festive but light coat. We initially thought that upon entering our home, this man had left a warmer coat in the corridor; however, not only

21

did we not find a warm coat hanging up in the corridor, he seemed to disappear when he left the house. – not even a footstep could be found in the snow! My older sisters and I braved the weather outside and began running around crazily climbing trees, lifting ourselves onto the wood pile just to see if we could spot the stranger somewhere on the road. It was all in vain, as there wasn't a person to be seen anywhere on the horizon.

Upon gathering back inside of our home, we knew this was an angel sent by God, as a human being could not have been walking around unless he or she had proper clothing and were skiing or sledding. Of course, angels can walk anywhere! This one seemed to fly right out of our sight! We felt sorry we didn't search the sky to see him flying up to heaven. But our parents explained to us that angels are spirits and can disappear into the invisible, spiritual realm at will. And at times, just like this one, they can appear like a human being. We were then sorry that we didn't keep him with us longer so we could ask him about heavenly things. Since this experience was so real to us children, there is not one of us who could be dissuaded of our Creator and His heaven, not by all the books on evolution and atheist teachers in the world! All it takes is one angelic encounter for our faith to be strengthened and our assurance bolstered, to become fully persuaded that God is real and with us right now.

Healing in the Dolinschi Family

Growing up, we were a very large family, and nutritional foods were not a part of our diet. We didn't know a thing about vitamins, and medicine was very scarce in our home. Antibiotics were almost never to be found. But despite all of this, I can't remember a single instance when we got sick, or had to stay in the hospital, with one exception. As a young boy, I was brought to a doctor due to a case of diarrhea. Since I was the only baby boy in the family, my mother was afraid and took me to see a physician. Upon examining me, the doctor decided to put me in the Radauti Hospital, which turned out to be unnecessary.

Today, all thirteen siblings are still with us and well – no one has gone to be with the Lord yet. As always, the Lord proves to us all that His Word is still alive and well, powerful and sufficient while we are on the earth living our lives. And although we now have up-dated medicine in Romania, it has become a fad-like substitute for a living faith. Many today have become too concerned with things that don't matter, as modernism has made us weaker and more worldly, causing us to depend too heavily on medication instead of God's healing.

In my father's case, he suffered from a bad heart. For days at a time, he would be bedridden with chest, arm, and muscle pain. He would slowly recover only to have the pain start all over again. This was compounded by laboring all day on the State farm near our home. Usually, the summer months would find him mowing dozens of acres with only a hand sickle. He worked some of the most grueling manual labor on the farm, just to provide food and clothing for his large family.

I can recall my father being bedridden when I was fourteen, forcing me to go into the field to finish his hard labor. There were times I felt like I was dying out there. Despite being so tired and thirsty, I kept working to finish my portion of the field so I could go to school the next morning. I knew the rainy season was coming and there was much work to be done.

When I was seven, my father's heart failed. He was wet from much sweating and was approaching a heart attack. My mom prepared him to see the community doctor in the neighboring town of Arbore. I stealthily ran ahead of them in the field, hiding myself along the path they would take. They moved very slowly. My mom held him as to not let him fall. He held his hand over his chest, in pain. The distance to the physician was over two miles as our small village had no medical doctor. From my hiding place, I watched until I could see them no longer. All I could think to do was to pray and ask Jesus to return my father alive and in good shape. I believed He would.

When my father stepped into the doctor's office, he suddenly passed out. They had barely carried him to a bed before his pulse stopped. The good doctor worked as proficiently on him as possible. He immediately gave him a cardiac injection to restart his heart. Within a few minutes dad's pulse and life came back. He was given a prescription medicine, bought from the local pharmacy, and in about an hour, he had enough strength to return home by himself. When I saw them return, I somehow knew my father would live a long life. I felt secure that I would not be left orphaned.

Years later as an American I made a return trip to Arbore, to marry my fiancée, Viorica. While I was in America, my parents moved from Bodnareni, Suceava, to Rachita, in Timis County about seventy miles from Timisoara. While in Arbore, I met with the same doctor who treated my father, who was now visiting Arbore as well. He asked me, "What year did your father die?" I asked him why he thought my father had died, when in fact, he was alive and well. He told me, "Your father is just a walking miracle, as he should have died decades ago. I never believed he would have made it even a few years after I treated him."

"John, his heart and arteries were so badly worn out, maybe only surgery could have extended his life; but you know heart surgeries are not performed around here. Now I do believe there is a God and it doesn't matter how weak and feeble we are: if we still have days to live, we'll go until our mission is over."

My father died when he was almost eighty-six years old. What's astonishing is that most of his healthier friends died before him, and younger than him; my father, being the weakest among them, had outlived them all. We have a great God! Isn't it the truth, my brothers and sisters?

Later on in my life, this experience with my father inspired me to find a way to provide the right medicine, including supplements and vitamins, for the good doctors to use in the needy areas of Romania, and distribute them directly to people in need. In addition to this ministry, my wife and I have assisted in building and opening medical clinics in localities that are lacking in medical care.

Walking two miles to the doctor's office while his heart was in such a compromised state, my father most assuredly should have died. The Lord decided to spare his life, and despite his weakened body, the Lord gave him length of years. One time, I asked my father why his weakened condition was not completely healed along with his heart. He told me, "This is all according to my faith. I didn't ask the Lord to heal my weakened body. I believed my heart would not be the cause of my death, and that my weakened body would be strengthened in the Lord. Do you know why I love praying?" he asked. "And why I am happy, and why I don't grumble when our brothers are coming for prayer time in our home, even though I'm busy working on something? When I'm praying in the unity of the church, I feel an electrified power surging through my entire body. I feel it in and around my heart, and then I'm refreshed and made stronger."

This is what is lacking in the lives of many people today. We need to include personal and group prayer into our corporate worship times, standing in one mind and one heart. We should not pray just to ask the Lord for the things which benefit us, but primarily to praise God with a heart of thanksgiving. Let us join with the assembly of the Lord and His heavenly worshipping angels, which will be enough to heal our souls and bodies.

Establishing Underground Prayer Meetings

In those early years, we had a house in the village of Bodnareni, which was used as a house of prayer, both day and night. There were people coming just for prayer time with other believers from our own village and from other towns and villages around Bodnareni. One hundred homes made up our small village, and over several years most of the people there were saved and became full-gospel Christians. "Pentecostals" was the name given to Christians in Romania at the time. Each home, except for a few, had at least one saved person in the house. Most of the homes were full of believers. In Bodnareni, we had a salvation revival without any special evangelistic meetings in our village. Instead, all believers in Christ were missionaries sharing their faith with their neighbors.

Fortunately, this village was a prayer center in Romania, and in this town, we had no police station or police patrolling our streets. Our home was a safe distance away from our neighbors, so we did not run the risk of disturbing them. My father, Vasile Dolinschi, had a peculiar prophetic gift – a mix of tongue interpretations and spiritual knowledge, as he would know intimate details about people around him as part of his ministry. Sometimes he just had a clear message from God, like a prophetic word. He was not a public preacher and a rather shy person you probably wouldn't notice in a crowd; however, when God moved through him, he became bold and powerful. In addition to him were a couple of other prophets there, including a lady named Agafia Bodnari. She sought the Lord daily and had a peculiar vision gift. She would reveal to people the issues of their heart as well as what was going on with their physical bodies. I remember a few times when the secret service officers visited her home, pretending to be brothers in Christ wanting prayer. She told them exactly who they were and why they had come to spy on her, and that God was angry with them for persecuting His church. They were completely silenced, scared, and never returned! Amazingly enough, there were a couple that came back afterwards, repenting and turning to God, who later became part of the brotherhood of believers!

There were times when the police from Arbore would come during the night, checking around our home to see or hear if any people were gathered inside. Some unknown informers around the village had notified the police that the Dolinschi's were holding nightly church meetings, which were illegal. The police confronted my father, admitting they had checked our home at midnight the previous evening for the purpose of confirming what the infomers had told them, but saw only our family inside. This had not been the case though, for on the same night, there had been dozens of believers jammed in our large bedroom! We had been noisy and loud, singing and praying. God must have blinded the eyes and deafened the ears of our enemies.

These experiences are necessary for believers to build them up in the faith for the miraculous. Some have even wondered if humans can be made invisible to the eyes of others. Well, it is true, even as God is true! At times when God deems it necessary, Christians may be covered by the hand of God, but to experience this, we need to be spiritually sensitive so that we don't miss it when it happens.

In one biblical passage, we see Jesus as He passed safely through the midst of a crowd who were about to stone Him – He simply walked away! Somehow, He just disappeared from their eyes. In another passage, Peter was taken out of prison by an angel who escorted him right through the main prison entrance where the guards were congregating. They didn't even see Peter, or the opening of the gates, even when he was right under their noses!

Rescued by an Eighty-year-Old Saint

When I was thirteen or fourteen, my father had a couple of bad days. The alfalfa grass was due to be mowed at the state farm, as the rain season was quickly approaching. My parents considered paying a day's wages for someone else to mow it. I knew money was scarce, so I decided to take a day off from school and try to do it myself. I began laboring on the farm, mowing the hay with a hay sickle that was too large for a boy. At first, I didn't think that this was a job exclusively for grown men, and I was determined to finish the job before darkness came. Now, it was late afternoon with the sun beginning to set but was still shining in the sky. There was not much left to cut, just a few furrows; however, my strength began to wane. Trying to finish was painful. What's worse, I had almost fainted of thirst as my water supply was gone. But I encouraged myself saying, "Even if I die here, I will finish this job." Of course, it went from hard to impossible as I could not take another step, my strength giving out as well. One moment I was mowing, the next I was stopping; mowing then stopping, mowing then stopping.

Suddenly, I heard someone approaching behind me. It was our oldest sister in the Lord, Paulina Bodnari, who lived by the edge of our farming village. In one hand, she was holding a bag, and with the other, she propped herself on a walking stick. She greeted me with, "The Peace of the Lord be upon you! May the Lord be your helper to finish your job well."

I asked her, "Sister Paulina, how did you walk all the way from your home to here, and what brings you to this deserted field where I am the only one at work? Did you do this for me? I'm not that important." She said, "My brother Johnny, here is a bottle of water for you and a half a loaf of bread. Drink some water first and eat some bread too as I know you are thirsty and hungry." I asked her how in the world she knew my situation so perfectly.

"The Lord called me," she replied, "to come outside my room, and take a long look at the field ahead. On the horizon I spotted a small feeble man mowing. Immediately, I understood the message. I knew for sure, up there must be a tired man who is out of water. And then I thought, you may need a piece of bread too, and I prayed that the strength may return back to you." She then said, "When I came closer, I had no idea who this little, tiny man laboring so hard here, might be. I was so amazed and happy to see you, little Johnny, our Christian boy. Because your father is likely sick, I'm truly blessed to be able to serve you here. My dear little brother, doesn't the Lord promise that we should be rewarded if we give a glass of cold water to the thirsty? Here, I had received my reward already. Now, my heart is rejoicing. I will fly back home in the strength of our Lord! Here, I let you finish the job as the darkness draws near, and while I walk home, I will be praying for you to finish well, and your father's heart to be healed."

We blessed one another and she left happily to make the hard walk back home. Suddenly, my strength returned to me, and the job was finished before dark. For sure, her water, bread and prayer helped me finish the job. It took two of us to finish this job, just like it takes two people coming together for Christ to be in their midst, which is the very definition of the church. An old lady had been transformed into an angel of God, who visited and brought food to a younger brother!

Both of us were happy and blessed, as this aged, eighty-year old saint had walked at least a mile and a half to reach me. What a missionary! What unsparing dedication! This experience made me realized how much my Lord loves and cares for me. His presence is with me all the time, rescuing me from the most difficult situations. What a lesson I learned that day, to follow the example of this saint of God. No one is too far away to be a lifeboat for someone in need.

The Little Student & the Atheist Professor

Starting in the 5th grade, I had to walk more than two miles a day from our village, to the next town, to attend school. In biology class, we had an atheist teacher who was always pushing the "truth" of evolution and the "evil" done by the

Creation story. We were taught the errors of religion, and that believing in a non-existent God just served the interests of those profiting from this delusion. He would speak of a life freed from the bondages of religion.

Our teacher would take a poll of the Christian students, asking, "Who considers himself or herself to be a Christian and still believes in a counterfeit God?" He'd go on to lecture us by saying, "I am not asking you about your parents' beliefs or religion. These are old fools educated by the capitalist middle class who oppressed and subjugated the poor people. Our younger generation will soon take over this country who will do away with all these crazy religious beliefs. I know some of you are coming from homes where parents believe this primitive stuff about God and his Son, Christ. The virgin birth is a crazy idea. You should understand that all of it is just pure fantasy. None of us should believe a bit of it. Modern science has the real facts as to how life came on this planet. It started from a little living cell which was grown through the process of evolution."

He would direct those who were Christians to stand up. I was among several who kept standing, as we believed in God and Jesus as our Lord. Next, his evil would manifest, and would begin interrogating us one by one. "Why don't you listen to what I'm teaching you boy? Who told you and forced you to believe you are a Christian? It was your parents, wasn't it? Tell me the truth, right here and now. Are they compelling you to believe this crazy stuff, requiring you to attend their crazy church gatherings, praying there to a fantasy-like lunatic? They are wasting your time, keeping you from learning modern science."

I would reply: "Not them, comrade professor. They are just too busy to provide and care for all of us. Personally, I believe in God. Jesus made me to believe in the Father God, and Jesus is very real to me." This made him even more furious. He rained curses on me, dirty words and blasphemies over me and my God. "You are a crazy, stubborn, little kid. Now, listen to me young man; if our great president was a god and gave me the authority to punish you, I would force you to dig a grave for yourself. I would throw you down to the bottom, pour gas on you and set you on fire. That is how much worth you have now. I would send you to your imaginary, heavenly paradise. You are not worthy of living here with your rebellious attitude against the people of Romania."

Over time, there were fewer and fewer students who dared to stand. We were made an example of and required to stay on our feet for a full hour in his class for expressing our beliefs. Only a few were brave enough to stand publicly for their faith. Others who sat down, secretly told us they strongly believed in God, but had been too afraid to take a stand.

I praised the Lord, when, one year later, he left the school. We were told that he had been promoted to a governmental position in Bucharest. He wanted to fail me; but I learned his coursework and passed with high grades. I was good at studies and had secretly prayed under the bushes along the road to school that Jesus would confuse him, and that I would pass his class. Jesus did this miracle for me! He can easily confuse the minds of the evil ones when He deems it necessary.

This is just one example of the socialistic dream that today's globalists have for the future. Unfortunately, some young people are fully deceived, believing this is the ideal future for our world's happiness. What a big lie has been sold to them! I'm afraid for this generation and for the one to follow! For me, all of this was coming together as a puzzle, while being trained in this harsh school of Christian life. Truly, there was a greater purpose planned for me in the future!

Evangelism, Authority, & Night Devils

As a young man, late in my teens, I was growing stronger in the Lord. I attended Elim Church in Timisoara, where Pastor Teodor Codreanu was a passionate evangelist and a peculiarly skilled preacher. Soon, Elim Church became the largest in the country. I had been with this church since its founding. I first met Pastor Codreanu on Mangalia Street where the church was housed in a large family home. In less than ten years, the church grew from a couple of hundred members to a couple of thousand believers. The secret of his success was motivational, evangelistic preaching. He taught a practical, shared life, lived daily for the Lord. We would not dare to let a day pass without talking to someone about Jesus. This might be through deeds, love gestures, or sharing our Christ-story. And this lifestyle became my passion.

I was heavily motivated to express Jesus to those around me, and was committed to attending underground meetings where we could freely pray. There I could study the Word and join outreach ministries around the city. At this time, I matured in sharing, preaching and teaching the Word at the secret meetings. I kept a low profile, staying away from any personal publicity, as this was my time to take care of the forsaken and the lonely. I visited little congregations, sometimes walking five or ten miles to do so. Moreover, I didn't run for leadership positions of any kind, and kept away from serving in large city churches where a flood of preachers waited for a platform. Instead, I trained others in the ministry to go out and lead outreach groups. Because of this, I became a focal point of Satan and one of his fierce enemies. Although he had plans to take me out, I beat him at his game. And through each trap, I became even stronger for Christ.

I struggled for months in the area of sleeping and dreaming. I would often be awakened by someone trying to crush and suffocate me. Sometimes these attacks happened while I was awake. I felt paralysis in my body so stiff I couldn't move. My voice gave out as well. I couldn't express anything vocally, only mentally. Now, my mind stayed focused on Jesus, His Name, and the blood of Jesus over me. The Lord would help me, and I would become completely free. I would begin to move parts of my body one by one, slowly regaining movement. At times, an evil spirit would take my breath away while trying to steal my mental abilities, too. But I would get the victory before any damage could be done. I'm a small man, but a tough guy resides within. I was not afraid of losing my life and I got used to this kind of spiritual fight. Later in life, fighting in the spirit became second nature. Though I knew this was not your typical way of living, I felt like I gained a spiritual benefit. Sometimes in my dreams, I was fighting a giant man whose intention was to kill me. If I ran from him, he would become stronger, but if I resisted him, he became weak and light as a feather. I would push him away like a balloon.

After a couple of months, I put an end to these satanic approaches. While in my twenties, I took a job delivery driving. One evening in particular I was extremely tired and fell asleep early. Just as I fell asleep, I was awakened by stealthy steps approaching me from a distance. Usually, if I was partly awake, the first demonic symptom would be a body tremor. I told Satan to get out immediately from the room, rebuking him; but the nervy, impudent spirit came back again. This time, he caught me unguarded, but I used my mental authority against him and slowly, he departed, but being irritated, I jumped out of the bed and rebuked Satan, "This is the last time you will disturb me in my bedroom and my sleep, you evil one, Satan! Right here and right now, it is over for you Devil, in the mighty Name of Jesus Christ you must leave and never return. Now, I have won the war and you just lost it…. don't you see? You are defeated forever. In Christ, I'm much stronger than you are!"

I then went peacefully back to bed. After a short time, I again heard a nervous rustling approaching, as my spirit began to wake me when Satan was close by. Immediately after I awoke to his presence, I heard a soft and sweet but commanding voice on my right side. This voice was now speaking to Satan, "Don't you see that John just defeated you, Satan? Your attack is over, and forever! John won the victory and has passed the test. From now on, your testing him in this thing is forbidden. Exactly, as he had ordered you, you must stay away from him."

I then heard a rumbling on my left, which sounded like someone was debating with Jesus to allow different kinds of testing on me; but then the voice of the Lord firmly spoke, "Now this is over, leave him and this place right away, he has the full authority against you." At that moment, I saw my apartment windows opened and heard a roaring wind. The curtains were waving as if blown by a strong gust, but it was something I saw with my spirit's eyes. I checked the window to see if it was open, but it was not. Satan had left and never returned that way.

From that time until today, I might find myself scared of some physical creature roaming the earth, but not Satan or any of his evil spirits. I have full immunity against the spirits of darkness. Let me put it this way: if I walk in a deserted wilderness and Satan shows up, I will just laugh at him and ask, "What in the world are you doing around here? What is your business? Did a man of God send you out here to get lost in the wilderness?" In this way, I have the victory every time!

Chapter Two

Military Life

I spent seventeen months in the Romanian army, which became the most useful yet dangerous mission field for me at the time. Although I was in a literal army, I was fighting a spiritual war. I was fighting both a physical battle as well as a spiritual battle, so I found myself on one side, and everyone else on the other. Considering the math, it would be hard to win this sort of conflict, but God made the difference.

I was drafted into the army at nineteen, a requirement for all young men. I knew some who refused to be enrolled because of their religious beliefs. They were sentenced to four years in prison. On my first day I showed up to be conscripted, all packed and ready to go. An army Major came from Campulung Muscel, a chemical research army base, and picked up me and thirteen other men from Timisoara. We rode the train to Campulung, and while riding the train, the Major was looking at each soldier's file. Suddenly, he became panicked and called my name. "Dolinschi, please come and sit beside me."

He then asked me, "Man, why did you declare here on your file that you are a Pentecostal believer?" I replied, "Because the application asked my religion, and I just simply answered the question." He continued, "Man, if somehow you adhere to the Christian religion, then you should have kept it to yourself. Never write it down or tell anyone — just keep it to yourself. The military is not permitted to condone your religion. Now, we will have to somehow change this wording. If you don't, you'll have a real hard time in the army. Now, let's try to change the wording. Here, we can say 'my parents' just before Pentecostal, then it will sound like you don't adhere to Pentecostalism, it's your parents that do. You know, we may believe in whatever our minds imagine, but we don't need to tell others what our mind thinks. I warn you, in the army you should keep any religion to yourself, understand? Now, let's correct the wording."

I bluntly told him, "Please don't do it, because I'm a Christian and I don't want to lie about it. Just let it stay as it is written." Here, he became nervous and concerned. "You're going to see for yourself," he warned, "You are heading for lots of problems." I just thanked him for his concern, and said, "I really do hope this will be just fine, because I'm a good patriot and soldier and want to defend my people from our common enemies." During this same year, the Major was moved to another army unit. But he was right, I had drawn much attention to myself. I was spied upon, followed, watched, and interrogated.

Despite all this trouble, I never regretted my good decision. In fact, for me it was the only choice. I am who I say I am, I won't cheat on that. After about three months a fellow soldier came to me and confessed that he was a Pentecostal believer as well. He didn't declare it or speak anything aloud for he was fearful. He appreciated my stand for God and the way I was manifesting my faith, but he was not prepared to stand up to this kind of confrontation.

I realized he was a little different from others in my unit. He was a good boy who didn't speak curses or dirty words. And there were others like him, friends who didn't know about what salvation meant, or about being a born-again Christian: yet they were good boys. As a matter of fact, though we rode the same train from Timisoara to Campulung, and I knew him personally, I never thought of him as a Christian until he told me to my face. After my time in the Army, I met him at his local church in Timisoara. Although he was a loyal church attender, our life interests were completely different. Because of my contagious Christianity, I was transferred to the Ploiesti base later in my military career, and then again to the Buzau base not long after. The truth is, I didn't miss this brother, for while at Campulung, he had stayed away from me, afraid to fellowship openly. He wanted to hide his Christianity from others and was not willing to count the cost of following Jesus.

While in the service I was a part of three different army bases, but everywhere I went, I was the only openly evangelical believer among the men. In fact, when I moved out to a new army camp, it was like a new, virgin mission field. God was sending me to the very needy and hungry souls to hear the good news of salvation, and for a living relationship with God.

Soldiers Hungry for God

My time spent in the military was very helpful to me in defining my faith as a Christian. I was either highly respected or hated. At times, I was even revered with a sense of awe. I developed a peculiar reputation with the soldiers, army officers, and the staff. As I was gaining popularity, I knew people were talking about me behind my back. People knew who I was, even though many had not even met me. Many of the soldiers were in search for the one true God, especially my comrades who would come to me to receive counseling and advise when problems would arise. They were on a search for a real God who actually existed and was caring, who would be present with them. Not a single day passed without me talking to someone about God and of Jesus' presence with us. I found that everyone around me needed to fill the emptiness in their souls. They were chasing and searching for the fullness of life. I believe that if I didn't open my mouth to help them, I would be guilty of a sinful crime. This would be a crime committed against God and His creation.

You see, the educational schools and society of the atheist, communistic system doesn't help anyone satisfy the void in their hearts. That need is made even greater when freedom of expression is suppressed, and when violators of the system are punished. I wanted to make everyone aware of this oppressive condition even though I wasn't in direct communication with anyone outside Romania. I didn't listen to *Radio Free Europe* or Western propaganda. I didn't read about what was beyond our border and could only guess what the Western countries' freedom might look like. However, I wasn't limited by a lack of knowledge; no one could fool me as to what real freedom might look like. This was proven true when I first entered a free country. It was as though I instinctively knew it was free, like I had already taken a tour of a free society in the past. I have come to believe that we are hard-wired from birth to know what freedom is and what it is supposed to look like and feel like.

The First Plot to Kill John Dolinschi

At Campulung, I was made to attend office interviews where the staff forbade me to speak about the name of God while on the military campus. They entrusted me, however, with all the sensitive jobs around the campus. My commanders discerned that once I earned a job, I would do it with excellence, meeting every deadline. The commander of the base sympathized with me, as well as told jokes and even asked me questions about landscaping. He saw that I loved to landscape and that I had an eye for it. When it was just the two of us, he asked me not to salute him as we were all supposed to do, and instead shook my hand when greeting me. I came to realize that great leaders love it when those in their charge live up to who they profess to be in their character. It would be good if our Christian leaders would respect and love those that they are leading as well, and not act like dictators who only appoint the one's they prefer to places of authority, though they may not be qualified and honest followers.

Now, our large dorm held about 30 soldiers, and while we were there we often talked about spiritual topics, including spiritualism, witchcraft, and evil spirits, as well as about God and whether Christianity was real. We usually talked after the lights were out when we should have been asleep. My comrades always insisted on talking about sensitive, godly subjects and often I was supposed to give a final word on these topics, making a final determination about such subjects as spiritism, religion, and God.

One night, they were talking about Christianity and the existence of God, and of their parents' or grandparent's spiritual experiences, and spent over two hours discussing the topic of God and Christianity. Finally, they demanded of me, "Dolinschi! You're the one to speak up about our question here on this topic of *miracles*." Despite their being other college educated men there, no one else was recognized as the final authority on biblical truth, but myself. In fact, almost half of that night's talking was done by me. At times, I found myself preaching to them the basic Bible truths.

Now, there was an older fellow soldier in our midst during this gathering. He was an expert about evolution and held a graduate degree at some university. Many times, he was required by the commander to teach the atheistic classes by himself. Though both of us were friendly to one another and often discussed the "Creationism vs. Evolutionism" debate, he confessed to me that he believed more in creation than in evolution. "John, I do this as a job – it's not my religion." Although he confessed this to me, I think I stirred up his jealousy against me, because on this night, I was the focal point of the group. They all listened to me and were impacted by the words which I spoke. This man was shut down before finishing his explanation of the universe's origins, with all his flowery language.

Because of these late-night meetings, I was summoned and interrogated by the assistant base commander with his head officers. They tried their best to shut me down from sharing anymore on the military campus. "No one should be talking when it's time to sleep," they said. I just told them, "I'm sorry, but they are the ones who kept me awake. I was so tired, but the soldiers in my quarters were shouting at me to answer their religious questions. I'm not trying to preach. But, honestly, I am simply answering their requests with what I believe to be true. They are demanding that I give my opinion on what my friend Popa had already said." Popa was a scholar and fellow soldier who made a lasting impact on the men. They warned me, again, to shut up and keep my religion to myself, or my life would be in danger. However, I would not cave into their demands without continuing to speak the truth of God.

Many of my military buddies befriended and appreciated my living faith in God. When I initially came onto the base, I snuck in a tiny New Testament; however, only those with good eyes could read the tiny print. Thankfully, all of us were young and could read anything very well. It was passed through all the dorms. Whenever I lent it out, I would hardly get it back. I think everyone in the dorm shared it. I watched as soldiers who before going to bed would read this Bible. There was such a thirst for God in our dorm!

One evening, a soldier who I believed to be a secret service agent, warned me, "John, we're going to have a thorough inspection here. You may be among the first to be checked. Please let me have your Bible to hide and keep it safe." I took it from my neighbor's bed and gave it to him. Sure enough, a major and a sergeant-major came to the dorm and ordered us into the aisle. Typically, when a bed was checked, the owner was called to come watch his luggage inspection. My bed and luggage were the fifth ones in the row to be searched. When all was said and done, they found nothing, and left looking disappointed. God used even this informer to save our Bible. People needed to read it!

After a couple of weeks, we were scheduled for target shooting in the mountains. Our commanders had to make sure the area was guarded so that civilians could not enter the shooting area. I was among the first to shoot and the first to get an excellent mark. The same major who checked our dorms was with us and sent me to guard a post on the top of the hill. There were other soldiers posted with me, and two others not too far from me. I was set up on a fixed post, close by a large pine tree. After about twenty minutes on the post, I heard a sharp sound — a flying bullet passing by my ear. It almost hit me. By what seemed to be a divine quickening, I moved rapidly behind the tree.

A second bullet passed close to my face. The leaves were rustling in my face as the third bullet hit the tree. By now, I was behind it. Two of my neighboring soldiers saw this happening and shouted at the shooter, "You're wasting your bullets, we're up here on the hill!" Immediately, I knew I was this person's target. It is almost unimaginable to conceive of the evil which occupies an atheistic mind. When we left the area, I heard soldiers speaking about a known military person who had shown up for some unknown purpose to us. He spoke to the major and then disappeared. Close to the end of our target shooting excursion, he returned for a little while, but nothing was said about his purpose there and he left shortly before we all returned to the base. The Lord made this excellent marksman miss his mark!

After a couple of weeks, I was transferred out of that military base. The reason: I had made too many friends there who were watching out for me and my religious convictions. When I left the campus, the same major was waiting with another service man. This time, he was poised to find my Bible, taking apart my luggage, piece by piece, until he found the miraculous little Book. He told me, "We were looking a long time for it. This will not leave with you. It is a forbidden book at any military base."

I told him, "I'm giving it to you as a gift – my present to you before I leave. I only ask that you read it from cover to cover. This book has blessed lots of people, including myself." It turns out, he was happy it was uncovered. I told him, "Once someone sets their hand on this little book of God, he must read it. It contains the power to create miracles in your heart. The one who rejects it is lost for this book contains both blessings and curses." When he heard this, his countenance changed. I can only hope he became fearful that he was making a mistake.

I was bold as a lion upon leaving this military base. A few of my friends witnessed this as they walked with me to the gate. By now, all of them understood why I was forced out. I looked back at them and felt sorry that I hadn't left them with the Bible. I was leaving my dear military home, which was filled with both good and bad experiences, both friends and foe. Still, this was my home and my family which I was leaving behind. I almost cried. I knew for sure many of these friends were sincerely chasing God and that I was instrumental in the heart-changes which took place within them. I'm sure I will see some of them in heaven.

A First Interrogation

After a few hours, I made it to my new military home. I was able to make a home out of anywhere I lived, as I knew it was just a new ministry field. This was a new day for me, as I was surrounded by a new batch of needy people craving to hear the Gospel. And once again, I was received warmly. However, it wouldn't take long till I became known as a black sheep of the army. Although my new base leaders pretended not to know anything about me, despite what they did know of me, they soon trusted me with timely and valuable jobs for which I was grateful.

I have found it impossible to have a living faith and then have people not start asking me about it. "What makes you so different? Why do you speak and behave like you do?" I tell them that only God makes us different. And we have all sinned and can sometimes even be religious to a fault; but it is God who transforms everyone who comes to Him, not religion. It is usually after these types of conversations that the Gospel begins to bloom like a beautiful flower in direct view of the Sun.

Here at this new base, which was smaller than the previous one, we had a good time, though the opposition was more severe than I experienced earlier. But speaking life into the lives of mankind makes all the difference, as we see our enemies turn into friends. It seemed like everyone was aware of my arrival, which probably added to the resistance I would experience. After a little while, the soldiers as well as the civilian staff working there were curious about me. Most people were asking questions about the reality of God, if God truly exists, and if we are important to Him? "Is there really an eternal life after this one? Is there a paradise or hell on the other side?" They did not know anything for in these southern regions of

Romania, there were no evangelical churches to be found. The names "Pentecostal" and "Baptist" were names not known to them. In the largest city there was a small Adventist church, and in Buzau a few evangelical Christians gathered in a little church room. Most of these people I was sharing the Gospel with at the base were unaware of what these denominational titles meant.

At this new base they tried to fit me into different military positions; for instance they wanted to train me to be a corporal. I practiced for several days in order to assume the responsibilities of a corporal. I commanded orders that were correct, but I was often too soft when dealing with the men's needs. My caring behavior was more like a merciful Pastor than a tough drill instructor. They gave up on that idea and instead set me up to be interrogated by high ranking officers, several of whom came all the way from Bucharest, as they were part of the secret service unit. With six base officers seated around me, all their eyes staring at me, they asked me many questions. It was in this meeting that the fires of opposition were being stoked.

Like in the Campulung base, these interrogating officers took time to just ask me about my faith and my personal experiences with God. It seemed plausible that among these soldiers were informers who would report back to the leaders of the base. Toward the end of the meeting, one of the officers asked me why I was so sure there is a God in heaven. "Did you see him?" he asked. I told him, "With the same assurance that I have knowing that you are here in this room, I'm sure there is a God. He is not only seated in heaven but is in fact here with us right now!"

I then showed all the men in the room an empty chair that was left unoccupied. Pointing to it I said, "God is *there*." They looked at one another and back at me not only confused but scared – because of me or because of the truth, I'm not sure. They may have thought I was crazy, or perhaps what I said was real. For a few moments, silence dominated the room. Then one dared to ask me, "Did you have any personal experiences seeing a figure of God, since you're so certain of His existence?" And I answered, "Many times!

On one occasion, I asked something impossible from God. And He made it possible right there! God also rescued me from many accidents. If his hand was not with me, I would be dead by now. But as you see today, I'm still alive!" Then the last question; "Are you fifty years old to have so much experience with your God? How long have you believed in your God?" I just replied, "I was practically born into divine experiences. But my faith has grown in God as I'm different today than I was yesterday. As long as I can remember, I've known God." Then, one of the officers concluded, "This man is beyond any hope of changing his beliefs. Let him alone." The commander of the meeting sent me outside and ordered me not to share my faith.

The Second Plot to Kill John Dolinschi

Ten days after that meeting, while we were watching a required government political program, the overnight lieutenant-major (who was one of the interrogators in the above account) showed up in the TV room. He asked for about ten volunteers to unload a freight truck. Most of us were bored with the show, so more than ten men volunteered. However, he called my name to join the unloading team. In my ignorance, I thought he might have a special job for me. The job was rolling barrels down from the truck, each barrel containing about 200 kilos of canola oil. Once unloaded, each barrel was rolled to the underground entrance door. I was appointed to the second work team. Our job was to guide the barrel down the steep stairway, about thirty-five feet into the deep underground warehouse. The barrels could not be rolled down as it was too dangerous. Instead we were guiding each barrel headfirst. Each barrel was fitted in a special slide to easily and safely slide it down. Our main job was just to slow the barrels as we walked in a stooped-over position down the stairs.

The rule for guiding these barrels down was that only one man at a time could guide the barrel down. And it was here that a trap was laid for me by the interrogation officer. All the others before me took their barrels and then waited at the bottom. It was my turn, and as I made my way down the stairway, about halfway down, I heard a loud noise coming toward me. At the same moment, a guy from downstairs shouted my name "Dolinschi!" However, due to the officer's orders, we couldn't look back up the stairway once we made our way down the steps. In that moment I was not aware of what was happening behind me; however, it was certainly something supernatural.

In that moment, a powerful hand lifted me up – this was the strongest hand I had ever experienced. The swift, strong hand lifted me up from holding my barrel, throwing me backward, and then holding me against the stairway wall as though I had been glued to it. I felt a physical, mechanical hand on my chest. While I was being held against the wall, at the same time the speedy jumping barrel rolled just past my toes. I felt the air rush by my toes and legs. For a moment I felt death, a strong smell of fresh blood, fill my nostrils. I felt as though I might be leaving this earth, as I tasted something bloody. I had almost said "goodbye" to the earth, but realized that whatever happened was over, and I was left gazing intensely at the scene, completely unharmed.

This miracle stirred up a small group of people within the base who wondered how I escaped. "How in the world is Dolinschi still alive?" They were asking me how I made that quick, backward motion into the side of the wall. "John, were you trained in athletics?" And after a few moments of silence, the lieutenant – who set this death trap in motion – regained his own composure and stopped all inquiries into this situation. Instead, he scolded the other soldiers to take better care. However, the downstairs team of men no longer wanted to work with the lieutenant's soldier – the one commissioned to kill me – for fear that something might happen to them too.

I knew I was targeted, and many others thought the same. They knew I was hated because of my faith in God. Everyone also knew that the soldier who pushed the barrel down intended for me, was army soldier informant. The other soldier was older, in his mid-20s. He was married and took many leaves from the army to see his wife and children. None of us knew for sure why he was enrolled so late in the military.

In conclusion, I did not speak or inquire anymore about this event. I accepted it as a normal occurrence for a Christian in a communist country. I didn't complain or accuse anyone. In fact, I loved the soldier and officer involved even more, because they didn't realize what they were doing. The Satan of atheism took them over. They were just helpless lost victims. Furthermore, I was not greatly moved by these events, as only God decides when we die and how long we will live. No man has that kind of authority over our lives. The offending officer witnessed this miracle and saw first-hand that man is not able to kill anyone unless God permits it to happen. I do believe that he was certain that his plot would succeed, and I would be dead. But instead he got a testimony to tell others, to his comrades and superiors. He heard my own confession in the previous interrogation, but now he experienced all the facts himself. My hope was that he might repent and, in the end, be at peace with God.

A short time after this happened, I was posted to a watchtower guarding the forest. And I remembered this clearly, as I looked up into the clear night sky that was filled with thousands of stars. I knew it would be better to die than to live. I said to Jesus, "Lord there is nothing left for me worth living for, here on earth, only you God. I don't expect anything from life, no fleshly pleasures or even to get married and have kids. I don't care about life achievements for myself. The only purpose of my life is you God. Please, if you feel it is my best time to meet you, then let me be with you. I'm anxious to be home. If you see that my spiritual life from here will go downward, better take me right here while I'm ready." I was not interceding or asking God for protection. If I'm still living today it is only by the grace of God, who despite my frailty, kept me alive through it all.

Maybe an uninspired man or woman may wonder if during this time I struggled with suicidal thoughts. The truth is, I didn't struggle with these things. On the contrary, I felt for the first time that I was the happiest person on earth, and most of my buddy comrades saw my happiness and wanted to share in my joy, gladness, and positivity! If you struggle with suicidal thoughts, God will forgive you, but know that the only consistent happiness comes from God and not from our surroundings. I do believe I was closer to God as I tasted His heavenly joy!

You may be thinking that I was spared from death so that I could be used in the future to build ministries – which I have done. However, I don't think this is so. Rather, I believe my calling and ministry has been for each individual person that I meet and helping each person find God in a personal way. For me each day of life is a significant day that is given to us, regardless if it is a weekday, weekend, or workday. Each man, woman or child counts to me, because each person is very valuable in the eyes of God!

About a month after the barrel experience, many soldiers and military leaders were drawn to me. I could hardly keep them away from me. They wondered about life, death, and eternity. Since the leadership couldn't get rid of me, they moved me away again. "Let someone else deal with this problem man," they said.

Usually in the army when a soldier is transferred, he is sent with two or three from his unit. But this normal routine didn't happen to me. Each time I was moved, no one else in my group was with me. They didn't want the new camp to know about me. But for me this was fine for it gave me a fresh start. Their strategy hurt their ideological religion and benefitted God and me. Each move brought me to a new and more needy mission field. It is amazing how God uses even the enemy to fulfill his missionary purpose on the earth. Even an enemy military base can become a mission field for the children of God!

I soon arrived at this new army base about 70 miles north of Ploiesti. Once again, the staff officers knew my file, and I believe they had heard about some of the miracles. Amazingly, a few of them were curious and sympathized with my way of life, as I became liked by many soon after. Before long I

63

became a popular person, which helped to popularize what I believed; for our time is short and God will not waste a second of it. There were soldiers as well as a sergeant who knew stuff without asking me a question, but also tested me to see if what they heard about me proved to be right. After a while, instead of giving me a hard time, one by one they stood with me behind the scenes and became my protective friends.

Targeted by a Psychopath

Now, there was a man named Ghita on this new base, who was a clinical psychopath. Many really wondered why he was enrolled in the army and not put in a psychiatric hospital. Other than his mental illness he was a good person; however, you never knew when he might become agitated and dangerous. At those times, while dangerous, he likely did not realize what he was doing.

One day we were working in a basement storage area with just a few other men, sorting potatoes and throwing the bad ones away. The corporal who was also there was sent to persecute me. Now, it's important to realize *how* this persecution worked in a communist society. The attacks on Christians serving in the army, for example, were not always obvious; they could be as subtle as a higher ranked soldier "accidently" allowing a Christian to work in a hostile environment, in which some sort of harm could come to him. This could be permitted to happen to someone whose theistic ideas they believed rendered him unfit to carry the communist cause. Then, the high-ranking officer could excuse any harm done to the Christian as simply a lack of discernment. This subtle face of persecution was what I experienced in the following situation.

The corporal decided that Ghita would work with me sorting potatoes. At one point I asked Ghita to help me carry a large basket of potatoes outside, when he suddenly became nervous. Without any warning he picked up a midsize rock and hit me in the head. Blood flowed down my forehead. He tried to hit me a second time, but I grabbed his hand and held it up, squeezing it until he dropped the rock. Then I picked him up by his waist, lifted him high, and rotated him around like he was a ball. While I was holding him, I asked him, "Do you want me to throw you out of this building? Are you now ready to fight me?" But now he was scared and began to plead, "No, no please, I'm your friend. I'm sorry! I was crazy to hit you!" I dropped him and immediately he changed. He even tried to wipe the blood off my face and care for my wound, all the while apologizing for his actions. It was as though my lifting him up delivered him! Now this man was a little taller and heavier than me. In the moment I didn't know where the Herculean strength came to do this, but I quickly made the connection. Like David fighting the bear, the lion, and the giant, so too for that moment of time I was operating in the spirit of David. The difference was that I didn't fight to kill, but to heal a broken relationship.

From this time on, Ghita was good and peaceful around me, a calm friend. He later told me that he was ordered to attack me. He then told me he knew it wasn't right to listen to the wrong people. Now all the other spectators were so amazed wondering where my strength come from. How was I able to lift him up and spin him around, like I was holding a puppet? Some thought it was an adrenaline rush that made me incredibly strong. But I simply answered, "God is the real source of our own strength because He knows best what we need at each moment. It may be just to work and finish a job or carry heavy weights when there is no one else around to help." From then on, I had great respect from all who witnessed this event. A couple of them were transformed from being my enemies to being my good friends. Satan had lost another hateful fight once again!

The Trooper Sergeant Major

The trooper sergeant major is a staff position in the Romanian army. He is the first army commander in touch with the soldiers, like the dean of a student body. The temporary sergeant whose name was Sergiu, was determined to get a promotion, so he picked me as his opportune target. He would do things like mimic me publicly and fire nasty words against me and my religious faith. One time, we were marching and singing patriotic songs and our sergeant, and the sergeant major were both present. I was singing loudly, but not as loud as he wanted. Sergiu called out, "Dolinschi you should be singing the patriotic songs just as loudly as your religious ones!" The next day during the morning square report, the sergeant major called out our sergeant and reprimanded him severely. "Why are you attacking Dolinschi with your malicious words? People should express their religious faith as they do their patriotism as all of us may believe in someone or something different. We don't mock each other. Sergeant Sergiu, I command you to stop doing it, and if this happens again then the next step for you will be severe consequences." In the moment I felt sorry for Sergeant Sergiu as generally he was not a bad person. Occasionally, he could be arrogant and show off, but this was the only time when he received a shameful public warning.

I felt good when I saw the Word of God publicly honored and defended, as I knew it was a sign that the favor of God was coming over this place. I knew beforehand that this superior, though hired in the army, had the fear of God residing in him. He believed that God was the creator of heaven and earth. After he got to know me better and my character was proven, he favored me above the others. But he took extra care not to draw attention or be too friendly to me so that the others would not become suspicious.

My Birth Defect Healed at Last

When I was about sixteen, I was medically checked when registered in a professional driving school. And for the first time, a doctor asked me about my heart. "Do you know that your heart is not right? You have a birth defect. Your heart is like a room split inside. This may be a life-long problem for you. This being the case, you must take good care of your heart. While driving, this condition may create a road hazard for you and others – your heart could stop. It would be better if you were trained for auto-mechanic work. For sure you need to take care of yourself, and don't take on too much stress by working hard jobs or getting too tired." I already knew I had a heart problem while I was doing the hard farming work. My heart felt painful and weak at times. But as an ambitious young boy I just didn't care; instead I went forward without being stopped by anyone or anything.

There at Buzau military base, they were training us by having us run for miles at a time. After more than a mile, I felt my heart bouncing out of my chest, and a fainting feeling overwhelmed me. After a couple of miles, the sergeant major saw that I suddenly became pale and weak. He closed in beside me asking if I was feeling alright. I told him my heart defect was hurting me, so he listened to my heartbeat and advised me to stop running, leaving me with a corporal. This puzzled me; why was he trying to save me when others tried to kill me? What a contrast this was in my world! This would have been a good excuse to let me die by natural death, but this man's attitude was totally different from that of the previous leaders.

Afterwards I felt a contradiction arise in my consciousness. I was presenting Christ to others, myself being a sick person, with a heart defect. All the while, God would send miracles to rescue me time and time again. This did not seem to be a positive witness. Then I prayed, "Lord this is it, repair my heart, I need a healthy strong heart!" After a while I felt my heart becoming stronger. When I forced myself to do heavier labor I was no longer fainting, and my heart was not bouncing out of my chest. From that time until today my heart has mended and has become normal. Not one doctor after this episode said anything negative about my heart having a birth defect. In fact, just a couple of weeks ago, I had a doctor check me in Romania. Each time, he makes me take an echocardiogram X-Ray, and each time finds my heart to be the strongest and healthiest organ in my body!

About a month after doing the long-distance run, our squadron had to run a second one. The same Major came to me and said, "Don't run too fast but go slowly behind us." I told him I will try to run the race as usual, as today I'm doing a lot better. Then at the end of the race, he came and asked me how it was that I did so well this time. I just bluntly told him, "The Lord healed my heart since that first race." Shaking his head, he said, "You're just a miracle man, aren't you?"

A Base Commander's Blessing

While at Buzau base, I was invited a couple of times to the commander's office, usually for interrogation meetings. There were typically a handful of officers asking me questions and ordering me to not speak of Jesus. The base commander was nice to me, however, and would laugh at my responses saying, "You're a funny man!" I do believe he was protecting me from the bad guys around him.

A day before I was released from the army, I got a notice to go to the base commander's office. I greeted him with the military salute, to which he stood up, came to where I was, and sincerely shook my hand. This was unusual for an army officer to do to a soldier of lesser rank. Then he asked me, "How does it feel to be released from the army?"

I answered, "It is a mix between joy and sorrow. I'm glad to be free to go anywhere I want; but I will miss the military order and strict scheduling. I have a love for military discipline. But most of all, I will miss seeing you and the other commanders, including my comrade friends." We had become like a family unit.

He was emotionally touched, and continued, "John, the first thing I want to tell you is that I will miss seeing you around here with us. You're a special person that anyone should be proud to have close by. And sincerely, my heart is happy when I see you around here with us. Frankly, I have a heart-felt love for you like you were my own son and have enjoyed hearing your name mentioned. I think your stories are wonderful. You're truly a daring and mighty man and the kind of person that this country really needs to have! What resides inside you is very special and it is real. The life-truths you carry around should be in all of us. But please receive my counseling as from a father; be more careful with whom are you sharing your faith as this is a dangerous world we're living in today. I insist that you care for your own life, because people like you are needed in our country. As for myself, I'm happy you are released safe and sound from your military term. Now, go home but be careful as life perils and battles will still be threatening your life, hiding here and there. Please consider your life to be precious.

I thanked him for his care and heart-felt advice given freely to me as though he were my father and wished him the best. Then we stood and he led me to the door, looked into my eyes and said, "John, you're going to have a good and safe life from here. You'll marry a beautiful blond girl with blue eyes, have kids and a happy family." He shook my hand and wished me safe travels back home and for the rest of my life.

While leaving, I couldn't help but think about the mighty people of God along with the violent men still hiding within the communist system. As for me, I never regretted revealing my faith, telling everyone the truth that they needed to hear. This is more valuable than one-thousand selfish lives that are lived on the earth. Why treasure a miserable, self-focused life in this sinful world when souls around us are dying and going to hell? From here on, I didn't consider anyone as a lost cause, whether they were the police, secret service, or an army Major. When it came to the Gospel, I treated them the same as I did with the common people around me. The fact is, God is not selective in the process of determining who needs Jesus. We may be capitalists or communists, Muslims, Hindus or Jews, evil or good people; but *all* people need to see and hear the Gospel truth which keeps marching on!

With a heavy heart I waved back to my friends as I left the base. A couple of them walked me to the train station as I left the military world. For me it was leaving my mission field that made me feel sorrow in my heart and filled my eyes with tears. I really loved my challenges and my friends, but especially the Lord's interventions during my time. Now at last my mission had been accomplished!

For a while after my release I missed the army life. I still sometimes wish that the army would hire me back. I would love to return to that world as a staff member, plowing and seeding God's fields, as there are a lot of spiritual needs in the military.

Communist Ideology in the Military, Romania, & America

In all three army bases, I attended an atheistic-evolutionary class praising communism as the way to fulfill worldwide transformation. This system would bring us into the paradise of a one-world government. However, because of my beliefs I was the most unwanted person in that class – everyone *but* me could ask questions at the end of the course. I was just an observer, not given the right to talk, but to be present and learn. Sometimes the other soldiers would tell the teacher, "Let comrade Dolinschi answer this question. Let him give us an interpretation of the subject we discussed today." However, the teacher held firm, "Best let soldier Dolinschi stay silent, think deeply and assimilate this lesson, and after he passes this class, then we will let him talk about this stuff."

The communists believed their socialistic ideology to be a passionate religion the same way a true Christian believes in God. In the same way that pastor speaks of worldwide domination, Christianity speaks of the same thing, only through the second coming of Christ who will reign over all people, languages, and countries. Similarly, the communist believes in a world transformation. In Romania, the new world order was the main topic of the day in the early 1970s. All state newspapers were required to deal with this topic. The main country newspaper called "The Spark (*Scanteia* in Romanian)" would dedicate the whole front page to this subject every Monday. It proclaimed the righteousness of communism and globalism, which was the second most talked about subject by President Ceausescu.

The teaching was that Globalism (as we call it in English) is a strong socialistic system; in fact, it is the perfection of the communist ordinance. communism is the latest world system claiming to perfect a new world order. In other words, socialistic communism is the father of the globalist order to come. As a result, those creating its reign should be proud that they are the first world leaders to lead the rest of the world into their reality. During 1972-73 most of the world leaders believed in globalism as the last world order on the earth. Each country's leader had an agenda to prepare the right steps of change and prepare their own people to be ushered into it.

Now, the only problem holding back communism from changing the capitalist countries is their backwards ideology. First, they insist on removing the capitalistic system which supposedly subjugates the helpless, poor, and working people. Second, they believe that religion is the worst stumbling block resisting communism. All religions, Christianity being chief among them, are enemies in this twisted ideology. The globalist's core message is contradicted by Christianity's claim that Jesus will return and be King over the earth. Therefore, Christianity must be taken out of the way first, which will make it easier for the other religions to follow in suit. This is a delusional belief spawned directly from hell! That's why I strongly believe the atheistic-socialistic system is a demonic ideology. They believe they are fighting for the good of humanity, but their struggle is a devilish plan that will lead everyone to certain death.

The first time I heard about the death of Christianity and the communist takeover of the world was around the years 1972-73. It was in communist seminars that I heard predictions that around the year 2015, the whole world would turn into a communist order, or be directly ushered into the New World Order. This prediction is still alive today in western Europe and America. Unfortunately, the globalist order has revived, mainly in the younger generation of America. But praise God it still hasn't taken over. Communism's prophets and their best predictions have failed, and this demonic system has weakened.

I can recall like it was yesterday, a puffed-up officer lecturing us soldiers, proudly stating: "American people believe that they are the only people helping the world. They just granted Romania with the status of the most favored country to trade with. But we're assisting them with the most important thing." Someone asked, "Please, explain what you mean by that, that Romania is helping America?" The lecturer continued, "We're assisting their broken educational system that is good for only the very rich and religious people. Their public schools are astray and split on the topics they teach. However, we're sending millions of dollars, investing in a socialistic educational system, as well as bonuses for teachers. Our expectation is that very soon the younger generation will rise and replace the older one. And this new teaching will change their hearts and minds. This upcoming generation will change their world, the same as we did here in Romania, Russia, China and all the other great, smaller countries around the world."

Now, this prophecy has somehow come true as I don't recognize the America I came to in the early 1980s. Socialist and liberal ideas are far more pervasive. If a miracle doesn't happen, the globalist agenda may soon turn America into a globalist, dictatorial system. Unfortunately, the mainstream church has not seen this coming, or they just don't care. Only the church can change this hellish trend. Let's pray, and speak boldly, telling the truth and not just Christian theories – let us live what we are professing!

Chapter Three

A Return to Normal Life

Once I returned to normal life in Romania, my focus was on practicing and growing in the Christian life. For a short time, I visited my parents in Suceava, celebrating the miraculous nature of my time in the military, where I was in fact serving the Lord first and my country second. I then returned to my second home in Timisoara, which was like an adopted home since I was seventeen. This was a special city to me as I grew up and matured in the Lord there, enjoying the most religious freedom of anywhere in Romania. Timisoara was the city where many Christian leaders were raised up and trained in the ministry more than in any other Romanian city. Both the underground and the open churches had a great missionary vision for the country and the world.

Timisoara's Underground Movement

The underground missionary community's foundation in Timisoara was laid by Costan Ianus, Grigore Talpos, and Nicolae Ciuruc, and then in a later generation, was continued by Ionel Blaga, Timotei Husu, Ioan Varadin, Ioan Talpos, and me. Here we practiced devotion to the Lord and group prayers, thematic Bible studies as well as services designed for missional outreaches in the surrounding areas. What's fascinating is that everyone I came across in this time, without exception, was enrolled in and attended this group. Each person would soon become a gospel messenger, a preacher, a teacher, a song writer, or a reciter of biblical poetry. No one was exempt from ministry – *everyone* was involved! I believe that this missional group was the most powerful underground society for the raising up of ministry leaders within the Romanian church. And this is where my maturity and commitment to the Lord saw the most growth.

Now, while in Timisoara, I started preparing for missionary work through the underground Bible studies, prayer meetings, and preaching at home meetings and small village churches. From these small discipleship meetings, our leaders would create outreach schedules and ministry itineraries in locations where there were only a few believers. This would all be done covertly as our entire operation had to be kept below the government's radar. Our goal was to evangelize and then disciple new believers so that we could start new home groups. We also went to existing home fellowships to strengthen and train them to witness to their neighbors and friends. This was a wonderful time of intimate fellowship with God and people. You may ask: "Did you have to work hard to get into the ministry? Did you have to pray, fast, or do some other spiritual discipline to fulfill this ministry?" The answer: No! It was already in me. Every spiritual discipline I performed came as a result of what God invested into my spirit, not by my own design or devices.

While on this adventurous spiritual journey in Timisoara, I began noticing someone following me during my evening walks, on the way to the underground church meetings. I would typically hurry to arrive there on time, not focusing on anything but the road ahead. But while I was focusing on the upcoming meetings, I heard a still, small voice saying, "Stop right here." I would ask, "Why should I stop? I need to go faster to reach my destination." Then, I would hear, "Look inside this window. There are beautiful suits in there, aren't there? But I didn't show you this for the shopping. Just look as I tell you. Enter inside the clothing store and check out what they have." Next, I heard, "Look behind you." And sure enough, someone was behind me, following my movements. After chasing and watching me for ten to fifteen minutes, he would leave, likely disappointed. The next instruction I heard was, "Go meet Me and your brothers now." The

I considered it to be a great favor from God that His presence would be with me and watching over me. Whether it was an angel or some other heavenly being, I do not know. I was just aware that God was teaching me how to hear His voice, as I was growing in sensitivity, and in spiritual awareness of the supernatural around me.

In this time, I became very mindful of the Spirit's leading, as I knew when danger was around, and when God was saying, "It's time to go!" You see, the Spirit's movements are often hard to understand, and can't be explained easily; however, what is clear is that He teaches us how to follow as we become in tune to the feeling of His wind which blows us wherever He needs us.

A Driving Job & A New Mission Field

While in Timisoara, I found a driving job that I loved to work. Most of my time was spent at the trucking base, working jobs for different companies who needed to transport their goods around the city. I began making friends with my co-workers and even those at the top of the business, similarly to the way I made friends with those in the military. All knew about my faith, as every day I shared Jesus. And just like the military, I had great experiences, enjoying both the opposition and acceptance of my faith; for the eternal beauty of being a witness is experienced after each encounter – good or bad.

My unit section boss repeatedly warned me that sharing Jesus around work was getting the wrong attention from the directors and even the secret service. He said, "There are complaints of people converting to your Pentecostal faith, and even *they* are complaining that you need to be fired. But as always, I'm intervening on your behalf as you are the most faithful driver we have around here. I tell the higherups, 'John is always on time and is trusted to do a good job with whatever company he is working with. He never gets drunk, doesn't smoke, and doesn't attend crazy parties. He is a part of a quiet church group. If he is fired now, I don't know what we will do without him. He is well liked and is a kind person.'" What a glowing recommendation!

At times, my section boss would ask me, "What church did you go to last Sunday? I'm not sure if you took the east or the west train." I asked him, "How did you know about that?" He said, "Understand, others are following you, and even know what churches you preach at. I told you to be more careful as you are a high-profile person around here." Another time, he told me in passing: "John, the other day we held a communist security meeting, and your name came up quite a bit. As you know, the shop's mechanical director is the party activist chief, and he was pleading with our company to fire you once and for all because of your daily witnessing." So, I asked him, "Is it final? Do I have to leave this job at last?" He said, "Not at all man. I was the first one to step up and plead with them to give you another chance. And more than that, I was amazed to see how many there like you, confirming that you are a good man who we cannot afford to lose."

After a couple of months, I went to the senior director's office to have a work order signed for a truck repair, as he was the only one who could approve of truck maintenance. But inside his office there were about six drivers who were being reprimanded for their lack of discipline, mixed with their apparent abuse of alcohol. Because I had an urgency to bring the work order into the shop, I knocked on his door, and he let me enter. However, once inside, he asked me in a loud voice, "John, I need your help here. Take these guys away from me and turn them into good Christians like you are. Nothing seems to work for them. It's either prison or church that's going to change them!" I smiled and then encouraged the director saying, "Your corrective lessons should work out fine to change these guys. If not, I will take over! And after giving them over to Jesus, they will become just like me."

I handed my director the paper pointing to the signature line and thanked him. He grabbed my hand like I was a friend and shook it before I left. Now, when it came to Christians in the communist workplace, they were noted by many communist leaders as being honest and hard-working. As a result, it was difficult for some bosses to fire a believer for being open about his faith. Many under communism who did not share in the Christian's ethical mentality, would lazily go about their workday, unless of course the boss was watching. And, since everyone was paid the same salary, there was no incentive for non-believers to work ethically, as the Christian had. I just thought of myself as a black sheep to some and a white, shiny sheep to others. Either way, I'd pray, "God, open their eyes to see you!"

The Political Director Hears the Gospel

Early one Monday morning, I was among the first to show up at our trucking company. The reason was that the previous night I was riding the train from the Oltenia southern region, arriving early in the morning at the Timisoara station. I figured that I didn't have enough time to go home and change, so it made sense to go directly to my job. You can imagine how tired I was as I didn't take nap during my nightly commute. I was just carrying on with my team as well as sharing the gospel with my fellow travelers. But I was satisfied and full of joy as our ministry in the most barren southern regions of Romania was powerful with heavenly favor, people becoming believers, and the sick being healed.

However, after I entered the gates to my job, the main offices were still closed as it was before seven in the morning. It didn't matter, as I was just walking and quietly singing a melody, fully happy. Suddenly, I was confronted face to face with the political director of the party, who was a cruel man and persecuted me often. I just greeted him, "Good morning Mr. Director, and may God bless you and all of yours!" Now, the last part of my greeting was unintentional; however, being full of joy, I was happy I said it. He looked at me with angry eyes and said, "Are you daring to witness to *me* too? Don't you have any limits?" I didn't want to withdraw what I said, so I doubled down and continued with the gospel message. I answered, "Sir, do you really have no need for God's blessing in your life? Is everything in your heart so right that you don't even need God? I know for a fact that there is a hopeless case in your family that no doctor can solve. But God can! And now, right here, you should ask for help!"

Now, he became quite defensive with me, responding, "Dolinschi, what are you talking about? Are you really going to disrespect my authority by attacking me with your religion? Are you trying to convert me to your faith?" But he was simultaneously looking around to see if others were overhearing this conversation. In fact, he seemed intimidated by my boldness. And as he attempted to leave in an agitated state, I said in a loud voice, "Director! I will tell you something you should remember in the future. Sooner or later you will repent of your sins and will come to Christ for salvation. You and your family will serve the Lord!" Now he was really dumbfounded, looking back in fear, all the while trying to hurry out of sight. I don't think he ever complained to anyone, not even his superiors, about this incident. And after about a week I heard from his nephew that his daughter was sick with leukemia. I believe that this situation made him consider whether God could rescue her.

Years later, after I returned from America, I met this man's nephew again, as we were always friendly to one another. I asked him, "How is your uncle doing?" He replied, "John, he retired and moved into the country. But I've got some crazy news you're going to want to hear: he became a Christian!" With excitement I asked, "What kind of Christian is he?" He then said, "Man, I think he is just like you are. His whole family was water baptized, and I actually heard that they are speaking in some foreign tongues and are talking about the Holy Spirit a lot."

God is not into favoritism. If anyone repents and follows Him, that person will be received. And through faithfulness he or she will experience the fullness of His presence!

A Dream & A Mission Fulfilled in a Day

It was late one Saturday night when I returned home from a long-distance drive from the southern city. Due to a delay in one of my shipments, I didn't arrive home till about 3 AM Sunday morning. A little bit later that morning I needed to get to the train station in Timisoara to meet two other friends. From there, we would decide where the Lord wanted us to go – a town or a village that may need our ministry. We found that God's guidance was especially clear during spontaneous outings.

Now, after I arrived home in the wee hours of the morning, I fell asleep in my bedroom, until the alarm sounded at 6 AM. I only had about two hours of deep sleep. As I stood up beside my bed, my knee gave way and I fell to the ground. I felt dizzy, tired, and too weak to get up. Momentarily, I weighed my options as to what I should do. I concluded that going back to bed was the best outcome. Just then, my memory replayed a dream I had just before the alarm sounded.

It was one of those dreams that feel so real, like you are asleep but awake at the same time. I saw myself walking down a road beside Jesus. It seemed so natural to be walking with Him. In our fellowship with one another, we didn't use any audible words. And yet, we communicated very clearly to each other. His love inspired an assurance within me that took away any need to ask Him questions; I was fully satisfied knowing Him so well, even as He knew me so well. Because of this inner knowing, there was no point in speaking out loud!

While walking side by side, we arrived at a young fruit tree orchard. Many had been freshly planted; others were already blooming with flowers, and a few had small fruit showing. I looked but didn't see any ripe fruit yet. He told me, "John, work here in my garden." And joyfully I did! I took care of it, working and doing something with each tree. It felt good to work in this orchard.

Then, the Lord of the harvest came to me and said, "Let's go labor in a wheat field. And remember I am with you!" So, we continued to walk along the path, stopping on the edge of a farm field. Jesus pointed to the wheat field where we stood. He gave me the power to work on this field too. However, the work on the wheat field was hard, as the wheat specks were a mixture of thorns and tares. I was really sweating while laboring, and even blistered my hands and feet. But later, when I looked back at the work, I felt satisfied. In that very moment, my alarm clock went off and I woke up. After falling to the ground, I realized that Jesus had called me out of my house and into the world. So, I refused to stay.

I took the train to meet brothers Ilie and Traian, and from there we decided what villages to reach. We then bought train tickets to the towns of Igris and Periam, two locations we had never ministered in. As we made it to the small home church in Igris, there were twenty-five women and only two men occupying the room, all singing to the Lord. When they saw us enter the doorway, we were shocked to see them stop singing, as they began to kneel and thank God for sending laborers. This made me think about who we were to them. The important thing, however, was *Jesus* and not us. Later, we heard that the Holy Spirit had promised them special messengers to strengthen them by the morning. And when we found out that the two men attending were visitors who had not yet received Jesus, we recognized the significance of us being there. The ladies were not preachers or teachers – they simply encouraged each other in the Lord. And like a river out of my mouth, the words that needed to be spoken just flowed uncontrollably.

Considering these divine events, the ladies decided to extend the morning service another hour so we could teach the Word. The result was that tears of joy began to flow, and everyone decided to dedicate their lives more seriously and follow Jesus more closely, the unbelievers becoming believers. After service, we were invited to have lunch with their families, and so that we might be able to reach individual homes with the gospel, we were split up into three different groups, one preacher per group.

After eating lunch, and after the husbands received the gospel, the ladies took us to the neighboring homes in order that we might share the gospel with them too. Finally, by 4 PM, all of us met back together in one home so that we might give testimonies. The women were empowered with a fresh faith and more organization. They certainly had more passion than any other church that we had ministered in. We prayed over them blessings of deliverance and abundant life, salvation for their souls and healing. Then, we laughed with one another saying, "Hey you! How does it feel being exploited by the Lord, just like in a forced labor camp?" Of course, being a "slave to Christ" has none of the bad side effects that communism does! No one in our group got sick, overtired, or lost their voices. And what's more, it felt like I had slept for 2 whole nights straight, despite the only two hours that I *actually* slept! This was just pure grace!

In the late afternoon we walked a couple of miles, then crossed the large river of Mures by way of a primitive ferry boat, in the town of Nadlac – a little place by the border of Hungary. We then made it to the main city church for their evening service. There were about eighty believers singing and worshiping. It was a rather large church for that time. One of the church leaders came to us and asked if we were preachers or teachers. I told him that we were gospel messengers and members of the Elim church located in Timisoara. The pastor set us up to preach. Each one of us went to the pulpit to deliver a message from God to the church.

Now, you might be wondering, "If you were first-time visitors, they wouldn't know who you were. The only information they had to go on was what you told them. And if a church wanted to know more about a new person, they should use discerning of spirits and the word of knowledge provided by the Holy Spirit. This way they can know for sure if the new one should be allowed to speak." But in those days, it was common practice for most free-minded churches to just ask the visitors if they had a word to speak, because during the reign of communism, it wasn't wise to pre-schedule individuals you didn't know, as there was always the possibility that they could be secret service members spying on the church. Also, it was common for secret service members to integrate into the congregations. They could then take notes on any new speaker coming in and write reports as to the messages being preached.

If something went wrong in the presence of a secret service member, the pastor would be responsible. Of course, this practice of letting visitors speak is biblical and therefore can be done regardless of the political state of a country. This way of doing ministry was viewed as a right in the constitution of open-licensed churches. The communists used this loophole too, however; for instance, in the religious department of the secret service, officers were trained on how to preach a sermon. They would come in as "wolves in sheep's clothing," pretending to be brothers. But in a positive sense, this practice of letting guests speak allowed for disciples to be identified and raised up without a legal license or ordination.

Now, returning to the church in Nadlac, the evening service was unlike the morning service. Because this was a more traditional church – it dealt in legalistic practices. Before going to the pulpit, the pastor would warn us to be careful not to speak too long and would even scrutinize the teaching we had prepared. "Just stay in the Bible and quote verses, rather than getting into contemporary living," was a typical admonition. And while each of us spoke, they watched us attentively, word by word, to make sure we didn't make any mistakes or misalign with their regulations. They made sure we didn't trespass their traditional boundaries, including their dress code.

All of this made us feel like we were back in school, being tested and graded! We felt spiritual opposition and a need to put up a fight in the Spirit. We then asked the Lord, "What is your exact message for this church?" And as we preached, the words we spoke were being ordered by Him! it was as if the spiritual doors were opened, and the people were being led into the spirit with approving "Amens!" and "Hallelujahs!" At last, the joy of the Lord settled over the congregation, as smiles and tears began appearing on people's faces, although, a few of the traditional men didn't like to lose themselves in the Spirit, keeping a sober, stone-faced look on their faces.

What's fascinating is that, while the legalists in Nadlac were hard ground to plow, it caused me to remember the dream I had the previous night. The Lord spoke to me about the different soil types – good fertile ground and fallow, which is packed down and needing to be plowed up. And this was all fulfilled in one day! I told the dream to my fellow ministers on the train ride back to Timisoara, and all of us praised the Lord that the dream was fulfilled step by step.

From this point on, I was much more aware and sensitive to the Lord's voice. You see, He looks for someone to listen and obey His voice. He wants to send us to His harvest fields, because the harvest is large and there are only a few laborers willing to go. We must remember that He is the Lord not only of the harvest, but of our schedules, ideas, and planning. He owns it all! We are just vessels to be filled by Him. And this is how we bring glory to our Father; by being tools fit for the Master's use, and not because of our own, legalistic attempts to please Him with our good intentions.

Chapter Four

The Great Escape, part 1

Ultimately, we discovered that the Lord's way of maturing us was by sending us out, sometimes away from our own family and country. Did I ever consider leaving Romania for good? I had considered it but did not want to leave my people. In fact, I advised my friends against leaving, typically saying, "Hey friend, you were born here for a reason. You've been divinely designed and appointed to bring the gospel to this atheistic, communist country." I had to practice what I preached, however, as it was especially easy for me to leave, being a freight truck driver and oftentimes driving right by the border of Serbia. It would have only taken a one-minute push to drive over the border, a short run, and I could have found myself on the other side. I simply refused to do it.

But while approaching the year of 1979, the Lord started to challenge me, and changed my heart regarding travel. This conviction came to me in many ways, speaking to my heart directly or through dreams and prophecies. I would be given clear confirmations, silently telling me that this was God's will for my life. For example, when I heard a plane flying above, I instantly felt like I was born to fly, feeling an assurance that I would be traveling on many planes.

I would also have reoccurring dreams about being hindered from getting to Bible School, that I was registered to go, but could never get there on time, and that it was too far for me to attend. I would continually run into roadblocks that delayed my ability to make early morning classes. I should also note that in my dreams, the school buildings in which I attended missionary school looked different than the ones in Romania. Then, in the Spring of 1984, when I arrived at Christ for the Nations Institute in Dallas, everything about the campus felt familiar, like I had been there before. I would frequently remind myself of these dreams in order to encourage myself that I was in fact in the right place.

As my heart was slowly changing regarding leaving the country, we had a distant, older relative from northern Romania, in the city of Suceava, freshly converted to the faith. He visited us in Timisoara, with the understanding that he must defect from Romania. He convinced my brother-in-law, Nicu, to do the same. The two came and asked me to join them, revealing a detailed plan on how to escape. I told them in no uncertain terms, "I don't feel like this is the right time for me to go. However, I do believe a time may come for me to do so. But for now, I am positive this is not the right time." What I really needed was to get alone with God and know His will for sure. If this was part of His destiny for me, the roadmap needed to be clear and coming *only* from Him.

The truth is that I loved Romanians and felt that my work was not finished with them. But next came Constantin and Nicu to convince my two other brothers-in-law – Peter and Gabriel – to join them. They all came to me to convince me to take this flight with them as a team. They were displeased to find out that my heart was not united with theirs in this endeavor. They repeatedly tried to convince me that the five of us would be unstoppable, and that I was necessary for them to succeed. I became a bit confused that, although I told them I felt I was supposed to stay, I really didn't know exactly what my mission was here. Finally, I committed to pray for direction, and include the four of them in praying for me. We decided that all of us needed to be convinced of the way forward.

We located an underground church group where prophetic ministry was present. I received two words worth mentioning here. The first was an admonishment not to rush the will of God in my life, though the time of my departure from this city was imminent. The second was from a renowned prophet who had a vision while praying for me. He saw a road map being placed in my hand. He described it like today's GPS. My path was marked in red, and indicated a journey filled with rigorous bumps and turns, leading toward my destination – a glorious mountain top.

The prophet then interpreted the vision saying, "In front of you is a Christ-like cross designed to be carried for a season. This may be a troubling time for you, but you do not have a choice. It is a required part of the path laid out for you. However, at the end of this perilous road, you will end up in victory. I even saw a shiny white flag blowing high in the air." He continued, "This will be a baptism by fire for you, preparing you for the exploits God has in store for you. The Lord's destiny map is a great plan for your ministry. You might be asking, 'What must I do?' But there is nothing else to do, except for you to pray and fast as God will bring the next step for you. All that's required from you is to stay faithful to the end."

Later on, I would truly understand what this prophetic word meant, as it began the day I made my attempt across the Romanian border.

My First Attempt to Escape

Constantin, Nico, Gabriel, Peter and I boarded the train riding toward the Serbian border, in our daring escape mission to flee Romania. Upon stopping right before the border police checkpoints, we passed by the little town of Carpinis, and made our way toward the border on foot. Most of our walking for this two-day trek occurred at night. During the day, we stayed hidden in a hay-barn outside the town. However, we were not familiar with the area right at the border, except that we should keep moving southwest according to the map we checked before leaving Timisoara. We had no map with us, nor did we have much money, as it was dangerous to travel with anything that would make us suspect of trying to escape.

At last, on the second day at midnight, we miraculously reached the barbed wire fence at the border. We pulled up on the ground level barbed wire in order to crawl beneath it. This wasn't easy as the wire lines were dense and wound tight, the fence standing up about seven feet off the ground. I offered to keep the bottom wire lifted as each of the four were able to make it out. After each man got out, Peter turned back to hold the fence for me, and while I was on my chest, I began my crawl to get free.

Now, Gabriel was moving toward a brook of waste-high water that was just on the other side of the fence. Suddenly, he tripped on a security alarm wire that was laid as a trap. The alarm triggered what sounded like a few gun shots. Gabriel, now limping due to injuring himself on the wire, panicked and turned back toward me, along with Peter. In a frenzy to get beneath the wire, they were unknowingly crushing me as I was pinned down in the spot they were using to crawl back. I didn't realize what happened till after, as the noise of bodies and barbed wire was deafening above me. I thought that a soldier might have spotted us and shot his gun off. I then decided to crawl back with my companions, as I didn' t want to be captured still stuck on this wire.

While racing back through a freshly plowed field, I saw two men up ahead running fast and away from me. They stopped and look back to see who was chasing them, not realizing that I was behind. I called out, "Stop! I'm not your enemy. It's me!" When I caught up to them, I saw that it was Gabriel and Peter. Out of breath, I bent over to catch some air, and then asked, "Where did the border guards go?" they told me, "We didn't see any soldiers around." I then wondered what happened to Nicu and Constantin. They described what happened, that between the fence and the river, there was a trap laid in the grass, which was triggered by Gabriel's foot. And by the time the alarm had sounded, Nicu and Constantin made it across the river toward Serbia. I then said, "That was the easiest way for us too! Forward, not backward!" I pleaded with them, "My brothers! Let's return to the border as we are very near crossing it. Let's get up and go. There are no noises around us, just silence. This is the night especially prepared by the Lord for us to be free. This is the hour of our victory."

They firmly decided that it was better to not return to the border and be arrested, or worse, killed. They said, "It's better to return to our families." For me, this was the hardest choice I ever had to make. It was not in my DNA to side with a defeated team. I knew that I was built for this sort of challenge – go till the end regardless of the peril. However, I decided to go back home with them; yet inwardly, I vowed to God that I would be returning this way very soon without these men.

Beaten in Prison, Protected by the Lord

The prophetic road marked in red was just starting to develop in front of my eyes. I knew I needed to meet new people for the next leg of my journey. We made it to the Carpinis train station as we were going to board the train back to Timisoara. Just before the train arrived, however, we were picked up by three border guards who were on patrol. After a brief interrogation of Gabriel, they found out from him that we tried to cross the border. We tried to play it down, saying that we had a mind change and wanted to return to our families. But our interrogators branded us as traitors and placed us under arrest. For the next two days we were held in the torture wing at the Jimbolia police building.

Usually, the cruelest soldiers were chosen and trained in the art of torturing those who were caught sneaking over the border. Many people who were caught and tortured were beaten without mercy, to the point of death or to the point that their internal organs were damaged. Others were just killed in their attempt to escape and buried by the border line. Finding out that we were Pentecostal believers meant that these soldiers would try even harder to make our lives a living hell. But remember, we had God's protection working in our favor.

And I was set on sharing the Word of God to these miserable soldiers who both cursed God and us. Immediately, I sensed that we entered a mission field and there was a task for me to accomplish.

They started blaspheming Christ and making fun of our faith as if what we believed was a fairy tale. Then, they started pushing and hitting us around the room so that in the chaos of blows, we wouldn't know who hit us, attempting to make us feel like miserable slaves in some labor camp. But inside me rose a voice that spoke of the mighty power of God. I spoke boldly to them, warning them to be careful about blaspheming God who is the mighty Creator and Father of us all. I mentioned that He made us in His image, but that we rebelled against Him and went astray. "Moreover men," I continued, "Jesus came to earth to save us, and I am sure He is present with us. He hears all and sees everything. And the angel of the Lord is preparing a record of what is said here. You may curse us, but do not curse God. If you will continue in this folly and not repent, you will have to give an account to Him. And you will pay for each evil word you speak against this mighty God."

They were shocked at first, hearing my proclamation, but they didn't even try to stop me talking. But as I concluded, a couple of them became furious at me. "Now who are you and why do you dare confront and rebuke us like this? Are you trying to convert us to your faith? You better keep it to yourself. We're not interested!" However, the others were confused, and afraid of what they had just heard. This group suddenly softened toward me, coming to my defense. A couple of them who were somewhat superstitious were moved by what they had heard and stood up like bodyguards to protect us!

At last, all of them had agreed to set up a pulpit for me to preach. It looked at first to be a joke, but a few of them were very serious about hearing more. It was as if a reverent fear accompanied the words I spoke about this God. Later that night, I felt sorry for Peter and Gabriel who were working hard to clean the bathroom floors. Despite these rough conditions, I shared the Word to everyone who wanted to listen, introducing them to the real Jesus who is alive and well among us. A few of them tried to intimidate and interrupt me by throwing in dirty jokes, but others told them to be quiet. Finally, the sergeant ordered them to shut up, as the favor and grace of God began falling in that place.

Then, one of the guards asked me, "If what you say is true about God, why didn't He protect you from this terrible place?" I told him so all could hear, "The Lord gave me notice before coming here that this is where I'd end up. However, this is because He loves you and has allowed me to come here and bring this message to you." I went on to share a couple of the miraculous experiences I encountered with God. After sharing these things, anyone who wanted to beat on me was immediately confronted by another who would come to my defense. It felt like the angels had become my physical bodyguards, taming all the angry "lions" just like the lions in Daniel's dungeon.

I prayed for my two companions who were given to harsher treatment, both of whom received double the physical blows that I received. But I was sure the Lord was protecting us all and that the angels were guarding us on every side. One of the high-ranking officers started to hit me with a rubber club, while I was speaking about God's blessings that were upon him and upon all the military barracks. Immediately, one of the higher ranked officers who was sitting in the corner, ordered the one hitting me to stop. And I took this as a sign of heavenly protection, that God was paralyzing their hate toward us. We were standing on His Word, and therefore had a stronger authority than that of any worldly institution.

Now, on the third day, they put us in an army van to take us back to the Timisoara's militia headquarters. To my surprise, both Gabriel and Peter were released to go home. I, however, was kept in prison as the Lord wasn't finished with the red-lined road that was prophesied to me – I needed to follow my spiritual GPS till the very end. While in Timisoara, I was interrogated again by a very high-ranking police officer. While questioning me, he was shocked by the contagious atmosphere of love radiating out of me. I was not shy about asking questions concerning those who were lost surrounding us, nor of talking about the matters of life with him. He was open to answer all my questions. But one question I didn't ask: "Why were the others freed and I am still here in jail?" I refrained from asking this because I knew that my relatives, like Gabriel and Peter were not divinely inspired to finish this work of ministry. This grace was given to me. To this day, I am in awe at how much peace was upon me during this time. It's as if I didn't have a care in the world! Perhaps this is what Paul was talking about when he spoke of the "madness" of Spirit-life, where we don't consider the perils of this life anymore.

A friendly lieutenant colonel voluntarily told me that because of my contagious faith, I would continue to get in trouble, especially in Romania. He continued, "Moreover, you should know regarding your young age – you already have a large tracking file attached to your name which will give official services all the ammunition they need to continue investigating you. We cannot hold you here any longer either, as a member of the staff militia will come from Suceava to pick you up and return you to your place of birth. Only there can your sentence be finalized. Lastly, you may need to stay there, so they can monitor your movements more closely." Now, it was a kindness for this man to share this information with me, as it was above his paygrade to give me insight into what the future held for me. But I understood why, as Suceava is right on the border with Russia and would keep me within the iron grip of communism. There, the secret service would do a much better job of investigating me.

By the end of our talk, he was practically consoling me saying, "Mr. Dolinschi, be assured that I will write a good report about you, that you are an honest and straightforward man. You have a better attitude and character than most people I know. You have been a hard worker and very dependable, your managers trust that your work will be done right. And despite proving yourself to be this kind of person, you are somehow still a dangerous individual." Now laughing, he continued, "But you are still a man of integrity, willing to help others more than yourself. Just between us – if it were up to me, I'd let you go! I do hope the authorities in Suceava will see what I've seen and release you. Now, here is some advice: stay as positive and well-mannered as you have been here with me. In the end, the justice court over there will decide your fate; however, I will be doing my part to write a glowing recommendation for your release."

This was truly a God set-up for me to speak with a secret service police officer like this. Before leading me to my cell, he asked if I needed any food. I told him that I would like some bread, salami and cheese if possible. He then did something unexpected and offered to walk side-by-side with me to the grocery store so that I could buy these items. I was able to walk out of my cell and toward the local store without any handcuffs, just like a free citizen. What amazing grace! While shopping, he asked me if I had enough money to buy the food I needed as he would be able to help. I kindly thanked him while making the purchase, and we made our way back to my cell.

I was held in Timisoara jail for about a week, when I was moved to a larger cell room with another nine men. Here again, I had a great ministry time sharing the word of God with these precious souls. After a little while, my cellmates declared, "Hey John, since you've been here with us, the atmosphere has completely changed. Sadness and depression have left the room. Somehow, you became an inspiration to us, as you are always believing in hope. We are glad you have come to stay with us." This was a great encouragement for me to see another table upon which the nutritious bread of eternal life was set for us to eat. Truly, I started to identify myself with those poor prisoners, though some were thieves, rapists, including those who committed crimes worthy of long jail sentences. But regardless of their status and sins, I prayed without any judgment. If anyone asked for personal prayer, I did that too. I was blessed there, especially after a few of them confessed Jesus as Lord of their lives, wanting a complete change.

From Timisoara Jail to Radauti Prison

Two policemen from Suceava county arrived to take me from the west side to the northeast side of Romania. I discovered that one of the men had served a long time in my native town of Arbore. I knew him from a distance, as we greeted one another when occasionally visiting from Timisoara. However, he told me that he knew quite a bit about me, more than I realized. It was required for policemen to know about the town's people; however, he knew my parents and would occasionally warn them when not to have church gatherings in their home. This was because on certain nights there would be special police patrols from the county sent to check on believer's homes which were under security watch. There was a real godly quality about this man which I appreciated greatly.

The other policeman didn't know me as he was from Radauti. But both men treated me with respect and told me with all honesty that the Timisoara Militia sent a very fine report about me. And, in turn they trusted me because I was a man of honor, so they didn't handcuff me as was the requirement by law. They said, "John, don't try to run away from us as that will worsen the situation for both of us." They walked besides me like two friends, riding the train from Timisoara to Suceava, a trip that takes about thirteen hours. However, shortly before entering the Militia headquarters of Radauti in Suceava county, they handcuffed me as it was required by the jail to which I was going.

It was truly amazing how much favor I had received so far, and the bitter road I walked upon kept getting sweeter. I do believe I had received favor and grace because I accepted God's plan for my life. Whether in a cell or out of one, in Romania or America, it just doesn't matter. What matters is to be in the center of God's will.

For the first couple of nights, I stayed in a cell by myself. At first, I felt a bit lonely and discouraged after all I had been through, like I was being buried without anyone attending my funeral. But it was in this lonely cell that I become more aware of God's presence, as I gave myself to prayer and meditation of His Word. And then, amazingly, I started rehearsing scriptures without a Bible in my hand. I used this time to recite passages I knew and memorize those I never memorized before. Mostly, I was reminding myself of the Bible texts which I had read. It was like the Bible's pages became vivid to me. My inward sight suddenly came alive, and then amazingly, I could memorize and recite the scriptures coming to my mind without having a Bible with me.

During these first days in Radauti, my mother came to see me, as my parents were living about ten miles away. But while in the jail cell, I was unaware that she tried to see me at all, as the officials were blocking her access to me. Then, on a certain day after she was blocked from seeing me, she left the station and made her way to the home of an old widowed saint to hear a word from God. This lady was about ninety-three years old, blind and living alone in a humble little apartment in a Radauti suburb. However, she was a renowned prophetess, gifted with the world of knowledge and vivid visions, even though her natural eyes were closed. My mom just knocked and entered without saying anything of her situation, only that she needed a word from the Lord. The old saint stood up and began speaking with authority. She said, "My dear sister, I can't see what you look like because I am blind, but my inner eyes are wide opened. I see your heart is melted down with sadness and desperation. You are really troubled and broken. I saw in a vision that there is a young man beside you, who is locked in a small, dark room. And by the Spirit, I know this is your son who you're concerned about. First, I saw him sitting down, lonely and discouraged but praying. Then, a large, beautiful, white dove spread rays of light onto him which began filling that room with a divine light. And then I saw that bird feed him living bread."

She continued, "I then saw this young man stand up very happy and strengthened, to the point that you could visibly see his muscles growing and becoming bigger. Now, I am commanding you my sister to not be sad or broken, to not worry anymore as the Holy Spirit is covering your boy from head to foot. I'm telling you he's in the safest place, more than if he were here, as the Lord is leading him toward his destination. Now, you just go back home and be happy, relax while praising the Lord." Upon hearing all of this, my mother went back home with her faith strengthened, being comforted and reassured in the Lord. However, my parents still had a fear that I would have to spend many years in prison.

It was around the time my mom received this prophetic encouragement that I felt strengthened in the Lord. And on the third day, the prison warden came and opened my cell door, asking me to pack up and move to another cell. I thanked him, saying, "I know the next room is a better one, right?" He said that in the next room there was a depressed man who begged them to let someone stay with him. And I took this as favor from the Lord, knowing that it would be another opportunity to share Christ with a desperate soul.

After I moved in, I immediately made a new friend. Vasile was in his early forties and with tears in his eyes, told me that he had a wife and three kids at home, but was sentenced to spend about seven years in prison. I asked him, "My friend, what crime did you commit that you would be sentenced to such a cruel stay in prison? You look like a nice, educated man." He then introduced himself as a large store manager, who was negligent in his job, losing money by lending it to the wrong friends who didn't return it. He also had other con men who stole possessions and money from him. "John, you should know, I was very naïve. But my heart is good. These so-called friends badly cheated and hurt me. Although I was loyal and active in the Communist Party, I was arrested and sentence for this long prison term."

It was now my great privilege to introduce myself as the free slave of Jesus Christ. You see, although I was locked in a prison cell, I had inner freedom which the world could never take away. I expressed this to Vasile, who then said, "You are just confirming my thoughts about you when I first saw you. . When you entered through the door, I was shocked to see your smile, and the joy on your face which was so visible and sincere. At first, I wondered if you were serving jailtime, or if you were just a spy or psychologist tasked with finding out more about me." Next, Vasile asked me to pray for him to have the same joy and freedom I possessed. What followed was a spiritual time of prayer on the small spot between the two beds, where my prison-mate received Christ and decided to follow Him all the days of his life. From that point on, his depression lifted and was replaced by a joyful spirit of hope that was visibly expressed all over his face.

Then, Vasile told me one of the most moving stories I'd heard. "John, so far I've never heard this salvation message which you presented to me here. I didn't know about this kind of living Christianity which you possess. I've never been inside a church, but I do have Pentecostal friends. They never gave me this message. Now, I can hardly wait to get out of here and attend a church. Please teach me the laws of your faith as I have never felt so happy and fulfilled as I am right now. I don't want to lose it — I will treasure it! Please train me up to be a real Christian who will follow this faith in Christ. I promise you that when I get out of this prison, I will continue in it, teaching my family to live the same principles of this faith."

Now, I felt a bit offended when brother Vasile told me he was going to ask the judge to let me join him in Doftana prison. Doftana town and prison was not too far away from Radauti city. Moreover, he told me that I would be sentenced about the same amount of years as he received. For me, seven years of prison was a lot, however not too much to do with a friend. Then, I thought to myself, "This guy's heart is still unchanged and selfish, caring only for himself more than for a fellow brother." But I understood he was a former communist leader and was newly converted — a baby in Christ. But I knew as well that communist members could receive any of the favors they might ask for. But what Vasile didn't know was the persecution he would likely suffer now becoming a believer.

I was ready for whatever might come my way, whether it be favors or persecution, prison or freedom. I just wanted to continue down the road God set before me. I definitely wasn't happy to hear Vasile's gloomy prediction of an impending sentence like his. Furthermore, I was a little suspicious he might be recommending my sentence to his former comrades; but I was willing to accept whatever came from the hand of the Lord, and for Vasile as well, as I could be a needed ally in his new-found faith. I joyfully imagined us joining forces to reach other precious souls in prison; however, I didn't pray for it, or to be free for that matter. I didn't pray anything but the perfect will of God to be done.

Chapter Five

Standing Before the Judge's Seat

On a certain morning, I was led by the chief guard to a large hall still inside the police station, above the jail rooms which were on the underground floor. I was seated and told to wait. In front of me was a stately judge's seat, like the throne of some king in a movie. Shortly after, a tall, good looking and well-dressed man in a black robe came into the hall. I observed that beneath the robe was a police officer's uniform. I thought this might be a secret service prosecutor or judge; however, he looked rather young being around the age of forty.

He began questioning me as to why I was there taking up his "precious time." I said, "I'm so sorry. I am not very sure how to answer this question. But it might be about what has already been written in your file report, as well as my experience at the border, I'm not sure." Then he became hostile toward me saying, "How in the world don't you know what you did wrong? First, don't you know that you're one of those fantasy preachers exalting your own religion above everything else? Aren't you always trying to convert people to worship your God, who may not even exist? Don't you know that you are on a twisted path of pure enchantment and mind-fantasies? Second, don't you know that you are a traitor who tried to abandon this beautiful country, and this is probably because of your crazy desire to join the imperialistic religion of America? Now, if you can't tell me your faults, do you at least acknowledge that you are speaking about your faith and trying to convert anyone and everyone who will listen?"

He continued, "Doing all of this, you are betraying your patriotic party, standing directly against the beautiful people of Romania. In all of this, you have made yourself an enemy of our people and culture. Why in the world would you want to leave this prosperous country including your friends and family? Maybe you want to join the vagabonds of New York City and become like so many who don't have a roof over their heads? This is because they work hard for the wealthy who don't care about them and use them as slaves to enrich themselves. And if you think you want to preach to them over there, you should know that they are as religiously brainwashed as you are, believing If they are good enough, then Jesus will let them into an imaginary world after death."

After spending all this time with me, not only did I like this judge, but really loved him, especially his exposition of religion which I had heard many times before. I found him to be a jealous preacher who tried to give me a religious, social, and political lesson, all of which I had already heard in public school and at the military base. I answered him, "Your honor, I do love all people, even these miserable, enslaved street people from America. Besides, we must love the religious deceivers as well. I love my family and the atheists from this country equally. With God who is just, it doesn't matter if someone is a communist who professes to be for the people, or a capitalist – the Lord loves all people the same way. And He desires all of them to repent and return to a relationship with their heavenly Father, because with the same hands He created us all. Certainly, someone needs to love these precious street people from New York the same as we love Romanians. Jesus died for us all! Whether black or white, it doesn't matter."

Suddenly, he became angrier. With his voice raised, he said, "Who in the world do you think you are, telling me these things? Do you not realize that you're going to be here for a long prison term, and that you are the most broken and miserable person in the world?" But my eyes were fixed on him with mercy and love, as I knew *he* was the one who was broken and needy. Next, he almost jumped up from his chair, shouting at me and asking, "How in the world are you still happy and smiling like nothing happened? Where does this crazy joy come from? Tell me now, if we have a madman here or maybe you are just trying to irritate me some more?" This was the first time a straight question came out of him; and he needed a real answer! So, I prayed and humbly said, "Your honor, I am sorry if I created any offence for you, as I didn't mean to offend you at all. But you are seeing the real me, the way I am all the time, no matter if the circumstances are good or bad. And sure, I understand this is a tough time for me, but I can't help showing the joy that is in me like a rushing river. I may be a bit crazy in my faith, but I fully realize where I am, and what may be in store for me. Still, I'm happy because I know God is in control even here in this building. But I will affirm that, like you, my love is for the people of Radauti city."

Suddenly, the judge went from being a furious lion to a calm little lamb. Lowering his voice, he asked his next question. "Now, besides preaching, what else in the church are you doing? Are you singing? Playing music?" I answered, "My apologies sir. I'm not well gifted in the area of singing as my voice is a bit hoarse. I do enjoy singing in a group setting. My parents were poor and too busy to train us to play music or have instruments. However, what I am doing besides preaching is reciting the Bible by memory. I am working on memorizing the stories composed in prose, as well as poetry." He then asked, "Do you remember any by heart? If so, which ones?" I silently praised God that I would now be able to minister to this man. The passage I recited was about Jesus, as He prepared Himself in prayer, took on the Cross, and died for our sins. We call this piece of poetry "Gethsemane, Jesus' Prayer: Defeating the Devil Just Before the Cross." It would be well-known in Romanian culture.

"Gethsemane, Gethsemane flower ripped from the eternal cluster. The fierce battle won on bowed knees. One hour of prayer without any similarity. A dropping perspiration of a tense fight. Awhile the starry skies were filled by rustling commotion. Here the human's eternity is set on the destiny balance. On one scale is condemnation, on the other one is a full cup. A full suffering cup was set before Jesus' eyes. And the King's face and heart were terrified. Here men's sinful nature must be absorbed by God's Lamb. And then followed the heavens and the earth battle, a battle between heaven and earth, between evil and good, darkness and light, and ends up with a full victory on the cross, death and resurrection, as the whole universe was filled up with joy and singing as Satan was defeated scared off into the hell while Christ took over dominion over the humanity back since Adam's fall."

After this recitation, I continued, "Jesus, on the eve of His great passion on the Cross, was strengthened by the Father during His Gethsemane prayer, so He could suffer for all humanity and bring them back into relationship with the Father. He would go on to die for you and me, despite all the spiritual forces fighting around Him. He was strengthened by angels, while Satan tried to stop His redemptive work on the Cross. Then, the miracle of resurrection took place where all of heaven and earth were joined to celebrate Life together, worshipping with praises and thanksgiving to the Lamb who was slain. Hell was terrified! It was bad news for Satan, who hates all humans made in the image and likeness of God. Now, the salvation of mankind has been completed through the God-Man, Jesus Christ. Today we enjoy a full relationship with the Father, and all of heaven stays open to those who repent and receive Jesus' sacrifice for their souls."

It took me at least twenty minutes to recite this piece of poetry and conclude with my message of salvation. He listened with a reverent look on his face. But around halfway into my speech, his head dropped onto his desk until the very end. I made sure he heard me say "Amen!" so he knew when I was finished. Then, he lifted his head slowly and I detected tears in his eyes. With a soft voice, he uttered my first name. This was unusual for an authority figure like this to call someone by his first name, especially in a communist system. "Johnny," he began, "Now I understand you! When I was a small boy, my grandma had taken me to a Baptist church where she was attending. But these hostile times have plucked out that little bit of faith that was within me. My friend, I will do everything I can to get you out of this place. My hope is that you will go free from here." And this is exactly what he did, as on the next day he took me to the district civil courthouse. Once inside, rather than having me present my case, he went in and presented my case for me!

How he represented me inside that courthouse, only God knows. After he came back, he said to me, "Johnny, you can now rejoice, for you are a free man. Let's go back and pick up your luggage and leave right away so you may see your parents. I heard your mom came to see you but she was not allowed." I thanked him for his goodness in helping me get out of that place. He replied, "It was my pleasure to work with you. But truthfully, you must know, your God was good to you. Treasure your faith but just be more careful."

My next step was to take the last bus going to Arbore, and from there, walk about three miles to my parent's home in Bodnareni. I got home late, just as they were preparing to go to bed. When they opened the door for me, they were shocked and couldn't believe their eyes. Praising God, they told me that their first thought was that of the apostle Peter escaping out from Jerusalem's prison. Just as Peter knocked on the door to his friend's home during their nightly prayer. My parents had *just* been praying for me right before I knocked on their door! Along with siblings and parents, we had a wonderful time celebrating the Lord's victory together. I told them that God had done this as a result of Him changing the heart of a high-ranking communist officer. As the Word says, "If two or three are gathered together and ask anything from the Lord, it shall be done for them." This is the place where the impossible becomes possible.

Legally speaking, the sentence requirement stipulated that if I was released from prison, I was to return to Suceava and not go back to Timisoara. But I presented a reasonable case before the judge, that the best place for me to live was Timisoara. I mentioned that my long-time company job had put me on a list to receive a subsidized apartment. Also, I could get married if I lived in Timisoara and not in Suceava where I would be blocked.

Now, while my information was being processed, I was able to talk about faith in God with the official presiding over me. And by the will of the Lord, my case passed with ease, and I was able to return to Timisoara. Certainly, this was the favor of God for my life. To this day, it makes me tremble to think about the way God has miraculously provided for and protected me on this journey. Sometimes I still wonder if it was all just a dream, or had it all actually happened, as what took place went beyond my natural comprehension.

To conclude this account, the legal requirement in my case was for me to attend a special meeting in my native town of Arbore. My case was to be presented to the local Communist Party leaders in the City Hall meeting room. It was here that my legal benefactor – the honorable police judge who presided over my case in Radauti – made an eloquent case in support of my good character and loyal heart. This came as a shock to his audience. However, either because he was their senior officer, or by their own conviction, they all affirmed that I must have been a great guy. A couple of them even took turns speaking good things about me and my parents. I didn't understand this procedure very well, for I was just surprised to be attending a meeting like this at all. For me, it seemed like a church disciplinarian meeting, where the congregants had come into agreement with the senior leader of that group. The main difference is that in a communistic system, the physical authority figure is like a god who must be obeyed no matter the circumstances.

I recall when the Arbore communist members saw the prosecutor-judge, they ran over to him and bowed down as though worshipping him, with a military salute. The judge looked at me with a friendly smile and said, "Hello Johnny,

127

how is it going with you? How have you been treated by these guys? Well I hope?" The contrast between how he treated me and their treatment of me astonished their communistic minds. Perhaps they thought it was like a king making a pact with some violent outlaw. But I considered us to be equals, captains of two different spheres of influence; he was over the physical political world, and I over the spiritual realm. When we offer God our loyalty, honoring Him above all else, there's no telling what kind of favor we may experience in the world.

Before leaving for Timisoara, the judge and I met once more in private. I was amazed to hear from his own mouth, "Johnny, soon I do see that you will leave this country. But right now, I am asking you a favor: wait at least one more year before you leave. Do it for me. If you attempt to cross the border before the year has passed, then you may get me in trouble. I trust you as a friend. Do I have your word? I am telling you this because you'll be strictly monitored, and you'll have to be careful who you talk to, while in Timisoara." With my hand on my heart, I promised to do what he asked. I replied, "Sir, I promise that you will not get in trouble because of me anymore. I know I've created problems for you already, and I'm sorry. I promise that you will be in my prayers forever, and I hope to see you soon, at least on the other side of eternity."

This officer didn't attempt to make me an informer, or to sign any confidentiality papers. Those in official positions normally wouldn't try to turn someone who was as convinced of their faith as I was. However, I do believe that this man was convinced that he needed to trust God as I had. This is because all men are frail, and despite the kind of demonic pictures that are painted of evil regimes and world leaders, human beings are not without hope – they are not the devil. Indeed, there is hope for *all* humanity.

With a Christian that is convinced of his or her beliefs, the State might have only two options. The first is to deal harshly with them such as imprisoning them, hiding them, kidnapping them, damaging internal organs, faking an accident, or killing them. The second is to soften them as much as possible, giving them a bad reputation so that they could not be trusted by their brothers. In my case, putting me in prison was not the best option, as I was the kind of believer who others would, and did, follow. Nevertheless, the authorities would attempt to change the convictions of these types of prisoners, so they would become better citizens of the State. But in dealing with a true believer, they ran the risk of having these firebrands convert many to Christianity. You see, the communists believed that Christianity was closely associated with Capitalism, and that this dynamic duo was a threat to their slave-inducing governmental system. Consequently, free-market capitalism remains the enemy of the communist State, as well as any socialist country – freedom of choice is the enemy of these systems.

Chapter Six

My Final Year

By God's grace I made it back to Timisoara and was hired by Auto-base No. 3, a sister driving company to the company that I worked for previously. I had formerly worked for eight years with Auto-base No. 1, which was the main city trucking company that was used by all city businesses. It was 1979 and exactly one year before my next and final attempt to make it out of Romania for the free world. It was a wonderfully anointed time of ministry, sharing at the trucking base, and in church's all over Timisoara. This was also a busy time for me, driving all over, as we supplied freight goods throughout the state.

This final year of life in Romania was a time to embrace the Lord as my Guardian, as I had known Him to be my defense lawyer, prosecutor and judge. I sensed the Lord was always around me. This was also a time when I realized that a lot of people knew of my past, my strong beliefs and church activities, as well as my affinity to leave the country. They knew about my problems with the law, that I had been recently jailed and that I was well-known and closely followed. I also understood that the secret service informers were tracking my steps. I was reminded of the police judge who told me to watch my steps, especially the first year after my release, as the secret service would be tracking my movements. He warned me so that nothing worse would happen to me. If I got into any trouble over this year, I could possibly get a couple of years added to my sentence.

Later, I realized that it was the Lord who protected me. And though I was being watched behind the scenes, I was still feeling free. Besides, it wasn't good for me to become overly concerned with staying out of trouble, as it was better for the Lord to keep me out of danger. I didn't get a chance to preach at the locations lined up by the Serbian border. However, I made sure to make as many underground prayer and mission's meetings as possible. In this time, I also had developed a heightened spiritual awareness, which was stronger than any other time in my life.

While at my job, I took the ministry of sharing Jesus very seriously. As the Scripture tells us, we ought to be blessing our neighbors with whom we are in direct contact. This way, we can minister out of the everyday joy that emanates from our hearts and feel fulfilled as Christ rewards us on the spot. On the contrary, much of our unhappiness in life is due to us keeping silent about the Lord's goodness. It's like having a banquet table full of delicious food, enough for everyone we know, and yet we do not invite anyone to eat with us. Today's ministry outreaches are often misunderstood and treated like mere religious programs. However, we must see this ministry of evangelism as oxygen to our spiritual lungs – it allows us to live fully! And when it becomes as commonplace as eating or drinking, we will truly experience abundant life.

The Radical Repentance of a Company Thief

One time while I was in the trucking garage working on my vehicle, I saw a couple of my co-workers stealing some parts from another driver's truck. I told them that this was wrong, that they were sinning against their friend by stealing from him. I said, "The better way is for you to trust God for the parts you need and wait until that happens." However, it is worth mentioning that in a communist country, this act of stealing was not actually considered stealing another's property, but just taking something that is needed from someone else's supply. So, what I said to them went against the social norm of the time and was as productive as talking to the wall.

It is also important to remember that in times of national crisis, which occurred from time-to-time in Romania, truck parts like the ones these men were stealing were not available to buy at any parts store. Also, it was not up to us workers to buy what we needed, as that was the responsibility of the State who owned our businesses, and us for that matter. If a parts-order was filled, a worker might wait for weeks or even months before that order was fulfilled. The tragedy of stealing someone's parts was that the other driver would have a disabled vehicle; and if the truck was not drivable, the driver would not get paid at the end of the month. On the other hand, if you were the one who needed a part for your truck to be fixed, then stealing the right part from another vehicle would solve your problem. And, since most of the men had families to support, theft became a viable solution to keep food on the table.

Now, if you gave a fellow believer the kind of warning which I gave these men, you might find their reaction one of fear and trembling. However, asking a non-believer to stop stealing was never well-received. After a few days of me confronting these gentlemen, the battery from my truck disappeared! I came in the morning and found a dead engine in my truck, already knowing the two men I confronted earlier needed the battery. I did my own inspection of their trucks to see if they had my battery – and sure enough they did. I waited for the driver to return to the shop, and then asked him to return my battery as it had my initials on one corner. He angrily replied, "I didn't steal it, and I don't care if the battery of your truck is on my truck, because I didn't do it, and whatever is on the truck I drive belongs to me. And who are you to judge what is right and wrong around here anyway? Not only that, you're trying to sell your religion to us. We all know who you are and what you did to earn 'traitor' status." I answered, "My friend, I only ask you to return the battery to my truck. If you don't, I will do it myself. And in case you resist me, I will not fight you for it. But just know, the God who you despise is the only Judge."

The very next day, the Lord provided another battery for me to use. I happened to connect with a trucker friend from a sister company. He said he wouldn't need it for some time as his engine was being rebuilt. However, the quarrel with the former driver had not ended. About one week later I met Claudiu, the same man who stole the battery, along with Valer, who was driving another truck. We were at an industrial company unloading our railway freight, when both men came over to start trouble. They blasphemed God, while telling me "Who are you to tell other people what is right and what is wrong? We know the illegal things you are up to! We know you're going to different villages preaching your religion, and that you plan on taking it over the border. We know that you were in prison, and were trying to convert others to your faith, betraying our state and orthodox faith. It's only a matter of time till you are back in prison." I didn't expect what they said next, "*But*, we want to help you stay out of trouble." Then, Valer raised his hand and slapped me on my cheek. I thanked him for it, and told him, "You may slap the other one too, as I will be getting more favor from God that way!" I then said to them both, "I'm just asking God to bless you two so you can know Him – the one you're playing games with!"

About a week after this incident with Claudiu, he came up to me in the morning, greeted me kindly, and said, "John, please come by my truck to pick up your battery. I'm sorry I stole it from you. Forgive me!" I said, "Thank you. I've already forgiven you. In fact, on the same day you decided to not return it, I made peace with the fact that it was now yours." He thanked me, saying, "But John, I don't need it anymore. I'm just delivering this truck back to the company and then I will be leaving this place for good." I replied, "No! This is bad news to me. Why are you leaving?" He then said, "A little over a year ago I had been sentenced to nine months of prison time; and then, someone intervened for me. The prison term was then suspended so I could go free – like a probation of sorts. About a week ago, a judge took my case back, and decided that the nine-month sentence must be spent in prison instead. So, in a few days, I need to present myself to the Popa Sapca prison."

He told me that he wasn't the good person that I knew, prior to coming to work for this trucking company. "Previously," he continued, "I had stolen materials from a building warehouse. When the night guard caught me, I turned around and beat him up, so that he would stay quiet. I then drove off with the stolen materials; that is, until the police tracked me down." Claudiu asked me to pray for him to receive the mercy of God. He repeated his apology for what had happened between us. He saw this as the right time to straighten out his life. I prayed blessings over him with passion and tears in my eyes. Tears had begun to well up in his eyes, too. I asked the Lord to save and change his family, that his prison time would be easy, and that he would experience more of Jesus.

After several days, Valer came to say goodbye as well. I told him, "I am really shocked to hear that you're leaving this place. It will be lonely without you. I want you around here, man! You really did help me to get right with God." Both of us laughed, and he said, "Thank you sir. I especially came to apologize for slapping you on the face. I knew I shouldn't have done that. But John, understand, it was my zeal for this communistic regime we're living under. I have since decided to reject it as it leaves our hearts cold and unhappy. And the day I slapped you I received some bad news about my father." I said, "Valer, I forgave you the day you slapped me. And I really understand your emptiness. Now don't worry. I know you are a nice person inside, but it is God who is the one that is able to bring out the good inside of us." Valer then told me his story. He started, "Now, I have to leave this beautiful city. I'm forced to go back to my native village, which is about three hundred miles away from Timisoara, somewhere in Salaj county, because my father died of a heart attack and my mother is not in good health. A few of my younger siblings are at home needing a mature figure among them, and I have a possible job there to work on a farm driving a tractor. I also just found out there is a small evangelical church in my town. I found out when at my father's funeral. I also met a childhood friend who became a Christian, like you, and attends a church. I am going to visit it with him to see if I can make a deal with God! Please pray for me, for my mother, and for my family. John, I will tell others about you. And I will miss you too, as I always felt better when you were around. Your joy and positiveness are contagious around here. You have a smile that never leaves you."

I prayed right away with Valer for his family, gladly sending him out to his new-found church. I told him that our next meeting would be in a church setting. I haven't seen him yet, but I do hope to see him, either here or in heaven.

Mr. Dilimann's Shocking Demise

One of God's mighty interventions in human experience is the ending of a life. I can recall one such time this happened to a German man named Mr. Dilimann. When I first got to know him, he was working the same job and shift as me. But as he was approaching his senior retirement years, I felt so much love for him because had a permanently sad countenance and talked very little. I tried my best to befriend him, and to show him the love of Christ. However, he was a die-hard atheist who usually didn't respond to my sharing or challenges. As time went on, I discovered that he knew more about me than I knew about him, and I understood that he might be a secret service informant as well. But as I had already committed myself to be a living testimony of Christ to all mankind, it didn't matter who I was talking to – whether persecutor or friend. Instead, I saw all people on the same level, just needing to know God and to be saved. And so, I continued to share about the love of Jesus. Whenever I started to share with this man, he would immediately light a cigarette, continuing to smoke one after the other, hardly breathing, but exhaling his smoke in my direction. Despite this, I continued to share the whole gospel of love, which is made real and tangible once a person becomes a believer.

A few months before I left, Mr. Dilimann was promoted from a driver to a chief trucking manager due to his old age. At this time, I needed to deliver back my old freight truck in exchange for a brand-new one. Several nights before going to the main garage to fix my old truck in preparation for turning it in, I found that some of its accessories were stolen. The problem was that in order to receive a new truck, I needed to present the old one fully functioning. Because all the parts were initialed by the truck's driver, they were easy to locate. And when I found out who stole these parts, I confronted him. Instead of giving my parts back, he went to Mr. Dilimann, who was a co-conspirator in the theft.

While I was signing some papers in the company office, in the presence of the director, the secretary, the accountant, and a couple of drivers, Mr. Dilimann came to me and started spewing ugly, hateful words against me. He said that I shouldn't expect to receive anything from anybody, that nothing is owed to me, and that no one stole my truck's parts. He went on, "You are solely responsible for those truck parts, and I will not accept excuses as to why those parts are not there when the truck is returned. Everything must be in perfect condition. And if anything is lacking, you will be charged for what is missing." He said this, even though he wasn't the man to fire or give fines to anyone. But he proved by his own words, in the presence of all the other people in the office, to be an authority behind the scenes, so no one from the office said anything. Now, I was mostly listening, and asked nothing from the people in the office. He saw that I was not defending myself and was clearly immune to his hateful words. And so, he turned to my religion in order to further harass me and my God. He burst into a flare of blasphemies against God and my "crazy faith", saying that I was a fool for believing in something that didn't exist.

Then I began to plead with him, "Please, stop cursing God. Better curse me, just don't do it to our Creator. The God you're cursing is right here, in this place, and hears your words. Please don't speak about God like He is depraved and dirty. Mr. Dilimann, I just want you to be safe. Please do not anger God. Please, I don't ask for anything else. No parts at all! Just stop this fury against our Lord." He then threatened me, saying that in about ten days when the truck delivery was set up, he was going to make it very hard for me. I uttered my conclusion, "Mr. Dilimann, for you and me, tomorrow does not exist. The future is not in our hands. Do no boast like tomorrow belongs to us." At this moment, it sounded like he uttered something under his breath, although none of us in the room could understand it. However, everyone in that room had a look of reverence on their face, like they were convicted – not of what Mr. Dilimann had said, but of what I had spoken. It was as if they had been struck by a powerful vision. As for my words, they did not seem to come from my mind, but somewhere deeper. It didn't even feel like I was the one talking! I concluded by saying, "I would like to leave in peace. I have already forgiven whoever stole my parts. I don't want them anymore. I hope I didn't spoil anyone's day. Goodbye!"

On the second day, I hauled my disabled truck to the main repair shop. I parked the truck outside the main door and walked inside to schedule a repair date. In the early afternoon when I entered the main doors to the office, I met a co-driver named Greg who looked scared, saying, "John! Did you hear that our friend Dilimann was in a tram accident and in very critical condition?"

Now, before going on with his account, let me briefly explain where the accident happened. The major tram track line passed between our garage and the trucking office across from the freight warehouse. Over the years, thousands of people crossed these track lines and not one accident occurred. Because this was the end of the tram line, a single tram coming in at very low speeds presented no real danger to anyone.

Greg continued, "Mr. Dilimann began crossing, but wasn't paying attention to the tram coming down the track. By the time he realized it, it was too late. I heard this bad news just fifteen minutes after the accident happened. By this time, Mr. Dilimann was already in the ambulance and rushed to the hospital." When I heard this, I shouted to Greg, "I just can't believe it! This couldn't have happened." I immediately turned around and walked toward my truck, got inside and started to plead with God. "Oh Lord be merciful! Don't let him die. Give him another chance to live as you know he is still not at peace

143

with you. I worked so hard on him, but I will do even more. Lord, I don't want to lose him." For about twenty minutes, I was not able to speak to anyone, but stayed inside my truck praying and pleading, "No, no, no! Let him live!" Then I wondered, "Just one day ago, I had spoken those prophetic words to him. This must be *my* fault!"

After about twenty minutes, I went back toward the office. But just as I entered the doors, Greg was coming out in desperation and exclaimed, "John! Have you heard? Dilimann didn't survive the accident. He died before reaching the hospital." I shouted, "No, no! That can't be true. Maybe you received the wrong information. It's too early to know for sure." Then, he softly replied, "Dear John. I just hung up with our representative there at the hospital. And about five minutes ago, the doctor declared him dead. Accept it. Dilimann is not with us anymore."

Although this was not a positive outcome, these circumstances speak to all of us today. We *all* will die, and we all will eventually end our journey here on earth, and our deeds will follow us for eternity. I've always wondered if I did everything possible to help this man find salvation. Maybe on the way to the hospital he was conscious enough to remember my words, repent, and find peace with God. However, thinking back over my life, I can't think of anyone who's heart was as hardened as Mr. Dilimann.

Three days later, I went back to our main trucking office, and was greeted by those inside with a reverence, which seemed to permeate the whole room. From then on, everyone was careful to not allow me the space to give another prophetic word, as they remembered the words I spoke to Mr. Dilimann. Instead, they carefully listened when the name of God was spoken, which made it more acceptable for me to speak about the Lord with them. If someone did not believe what I was saying to be true, they stood silent without comment. The office director was very open to hear more about God, and was respectful to me, at times asking me questions about my faith. Occasionally, he would tease me about my sermons and demeanor, saying, "John, I know that one day, the Americans will be back here. You prefer them, right? Well, you won't need to go to America anymore because they will come here! And then, you can be the next director. If that happens, will you treat me well? Maybe do me some favors, and at least let me drive a new truck?" I jokingly replied, "Sure! If such a miracle happens, you can be my best man, my right hand! I'll let you keep the director position because you are a good man, well-trained and qualified. However, I am afraid the Americans won't let us use the same socialistic order we're used to around here. Instead, we should be the ones to initiate new enterprises, developments and investments. We will need to use our minds more and work harder. Otherwise, the society won't fare any better."

At this point, the door to share the gospel was wide open at work. But every so often I would be warned that others were closely monitoring me, even those of whom I was not aware. I needed to use discernment with what I said, where I went, and what I did. Nevertheless, most of my major enemies had either become tolerant of me or had left completely. In all these things, the Lord proved repeatedly to be my defender, guardian, and judge. He did it in visible ways, showing up right on time to give me favor, deliverance, and wisdom. I learned that He could be trusted without reservation, because he loved me beyond my imagination and comprehension. And so, the preaching of the gospel continued without fear.

Chapter Seven

The Great Escape, part 2

Toward the end of my time in Romania, the Lord's bell sounded loudly with the clear message: "It's time to go." And the closer I got to the end, the stronger my conviction was that I had the divine approval I was looking for. It was like an ambulance siren approaching from the distance, getting louder and louder. It was like everything around me turned into a voice shouting, "Get out! Go now!" And I heard the Lord say, "I am the Lord who is with you and goes before you. I am leading and protecting you, my son. And I will come to breech the impenetrable iron wall before you. Just trust and obey."

While my strength and faith began to rise, I was praying for the divine appointment to lead me onto the right pathway out. Then, one night, while returning from the underground missionary meeting, I met two other brothers – Ioan and Viorel, who were also hearing the word of the Lord to leave

Romania. The fact that we were on the same page and ready to be sent forward by Christ, not having sought each other out, was surely a miracle of partnership.

From this point on, the three of us asked the Lord to speak to us and confirm His perfect will concerning leaving together. Every night for about three weeks, in nightly underground prayer meetings and on long walks from town to town, our mission was confirmed countless times through prophets, special visitations, and dreams. Each one was a unique "Go!" that we interpreted as God giving us the green light. It was like God providing miracles even as He did to the Israelites before they left Egypt.

One of the prophetic visions I saw was that of a closed box. Inside were three doves, which were then set free to soar as an angel lifted the box lid. In another vision, an impenetrable steel wall was before three men, who bumped into it without any natural possibility of passing through it. With their hands lifted in prayer, a powerful angel with a sword in his hand, descended and cut a door into the wall, allowing the three men to pass through. A trumpet sounded to announce, "Victory!"

Besides us men, there was no one else who knew of our secret plan, not even close family members. This made public prophetic words even more accurate. They typically sounded something like this: "Here in our midst are three people who are united in one mind and heart, asking the Lord for one thing. And the Lord says that your request has been given to you. Rise up and go for the Lord is with you."

On one night, I had a dream that was a repeat from the past. I found myself walking toward the registration for Bible school, visiting places I had never been, in a foreign and unfamiliar land. With everything God communicated to me, I felt like my feet were hovering above the ground, like anything was possible. And I knew that Ioan and Viorel had the same faith. We were ready!

When we fully decided to make plans to get out of Romania, I went back to Suceava to see my parents one more time. This was a farewell visit, so I kept it brief. Once I left, I couldn't be sure when we'd see each other again. Now, I did not reveal my plan to leave the country with them. Little by little, I revealed that the Lord would soon be sending me away from Romania. Because of the hostile times we were living in, it would be dangerous to reveal sensitive information to anyone. Instead, we used a lot of discretion, keeping secrets between us and the Lord. However, once He told us to move, I told my parents that they would not hear from me for some time, but that I would be safe and happy.

I said, "Mom and dad, you don't have to worry about me. Just know that the Lord is my shield and I am moving by

His heavenly instructions." Of course, this kind of news was not received very well, as only a year prior I had my imprisonment for something similar. Finally, my parents said, "Then if you are so sure, boasting that it is the Lord who sends you out, and he will keep you safe, then let's go together to see the old, prophetess in Radauti." This was the same lady my mother visited when I was in jail.

Although we had already seen visions and heard prophesies that confirmed our move, my parents were not fully convinced. So, we walked to Radauti, entered the prophetess' home, and knelt to pray without letting her know anything. The prophetic word came first for my mother. "Woman, why are you still trying to possess my creation like he belongs to you forever? Don't you know that what I gave you to treasure was just for a little while? Why do you allow your mother's heart to stand against my plans for this vessel? Don't you understand that he is no longer in your hands, but Mine? And the time has come to send him out! Just trust me and do not worry, because after a short time you will see him again, and you will rejoice at what the Lord has done. Now, I am commanding you to release him into my hands for the place I am moving him to. Do not fear! I am his protector, and will pour my blessing over him, says the Lord."

Then the prophetess turned her attention toward me. She began, "Young man, my heavenly bell sounded for you to go forth. I am there to protect you from your enemies who are against you. Now, do not doubt because the Lord is your Shepherd, leading you into green pastures. My son, I am pleased you have heard my word and you are following it. Now you know my thoughts and plans for you. Just continue to trust me and I will take you all the way – till you reach your destiny! And I will keep my Word exactly as you heard it, says the Lord of hosts." It is worth mentioning that these kinds of accurate prophetic words were more prevalent when Romania was under the oppression of communism, than today.

Upon hearing the prophetess speak, my parents were convinced. Afterwards, however, they wrestled here and there with doubts as it pertained to the way I would leave the country. They thought it would be folly to go to the wall like I had in the past. They wanted the Lord to show me an easier, safer way to go. They released me to do what I was led to but were fearful that I may never be able to come back, once passed that iron wall.

My Second & Final Attempt to Flee the Country

When I returned to Timisoara, Ioan, Viorel, and I picked up our planning where we left off. Immediately, we set a date to go over the border. We felt that the best day to leave was a Sunday. As usual, on Sunday mornings the train station was filled with Christian groups, boarding trains to minister in small county churches or other new church plants. We planned to visit a couple of churches close to the border of Yugoslavia, in the villages of Cenei and Uivari. However, it was not an easy way to penetrate the military check points on the border posts. But in previous days we had prayed that the Lord would cover us with favor as we passed through.

It was Saturday night around 10 PM when the three of us were riding a tram back from a prayer meeting. When we reached the station named Timisoara Freedom Square, a good friend named Mihai boarded the tram as we were getting off. Bumping into each other, we greeted one another. Now, Mihai was living in Timisoara for years, coming from the village of Cenei where he was born. He repeatedly invited me to join up with him for a ministry visit at his home church. Mihai reminded me of this invitation, and gently rebuked me by saying, "Why in the world have you never responded to this invitation?" I exclaimed, "Here you are! You got on just at the right moment to see me. Tomorrow, we are scheduled to pay a visit at your home church, my friend." Although Mihai had been scheduled to visit another church in Timisoara, he decided in the moment to go with us instead. He said, "I will cancel my meeting tomorrow and join up with your team."

The next morning, we rode the train to Cenei. As we got closer, we had to stop a couple of times so that the border police could check us. The guards immediately recognized Mihai as he was from Cenei, which was the best thing possible, as it allowed us to pass quite easily. Mihai told the guards that we would be visiting his family, which we did after the church meeting was over. Truly the Lord was faithful to His Word!

We divulged our plan of escape to Mihai, who confirmed that it was the right time for us to go. He was considering doing the same, however, soon and not with us. He expressed some sorrow in likely never seeing us again. After we said our goodbyes, my dear friend returned to Timisoara. He never got the opportunity to sneak out, although he planned on it. About ten years later, I met Mihai back in Timisoara rolling around in a wheelchair. He shared his story with me, that after we had escaped, he mustered the courage to help others pass the border. However, a few of those people were caught, which led the police to discover the identity of their helper. He was on the most-wanted list, which produced a search for him so that he could be captured and interrogated. On a certain evening, the police knocked at his apartment door. Looking for a way to escape, he jumped from the second-floor window into the back yard. Sadly, he hit the concrete siding, which paralyzed him from the waist down.

On the evening we departed Cenei with Mihai, we rode the train about ten miles toward the Uivar church. All of us preached the message of "heaven on earth" both during the morning and evening service. What's amazing is that on our last day in Romania, we were able to spend the final moments preaching the word of God. Just seeing the great need for teaching in these Romanian churches almost made us want to call off the whole escape. In the end, we knew that our Shepherd had given us a mandate to go, and that it wasn't our own invention. We decided to follow the divine plan and not our emotions, as noble as they were.

While in Uivar, we happened on another miracle. An older brother in the service wanted to make sure we boarded the train back to Timisoara, as a kindness. He rode his bicycle close beside us the entire way to the train station. Now, we wanted him to stop following us, so we tried to turn him around, telling him we didn't expect this kindness. He looked rather old and feeble, and it was at least a two-mile ride back to the train station. However, we didn't succeed in turning him around. About three hundred feet before reaching the station, a providential miracle took place, as two men ran up to this old man and forcibly stopped him from proceeding. He tried to refuse their interception, but the two men insisted they needed to talk with him.

In front of the train station was a police border guard watching people coming in and out of the train. While the other people were busy getting onto the train, we hurried among the crowd and climbed inside. Once inside, we opened the door on the other side of the train, jumped off onto the tracks where there were no lights. Mihai took a seat on the train. Then, Ioan, Viorel, and I slowly crawled through the weeds and passed onto the other side of the tracks into the open field. We laid down, motionless, until the train left. From the ground, we saw the older man looking into the train to make sure we got on. Once he saw Mihai sitting down, he waved goodbye, looking satisfied that we were on the train as well. He then stopped to talk with the security guards. I suspected that he might have been a secret service informer working undercover.

We then made a stealthy approach westward into the darkness of night, struggling to orient our steps so that we were headed directly toward the Serbian border. If we could continue straight ahead, the border would have been around eight miles away. But we couldn't avoid walking in circles as we tried to navigate in the darkness and around the channels filled with water. During that season, we were supposed to have a large moon in the sky, but because of the cloud cover and rain, the night times were inevitably darker. At least that night it didn't rain. We were asking the Lord to guide us by the GPS of heaven. We were also able to keep positive, believing for the best.

One of the major obstacles we faced was a large sheep herd and their guard dogs who started to bark at us. We had to retreat quickly as far as we could to get away from them. A little later, however, we discovered that we were being tracked by the border guards. They were tracking us from a distance, and at times they shot lightning flares into the sky. After a couple hours, we figured we had either lost them, or they gave up. After about six hours of walking, we finally checked our watches and realized it was 3:30 AM. The youngest among us was eighteen, who pleaded with us to take a break, and lay down for about thirty minutes. We gathered dry grass and tall weeds to make beds, on which we agreed to rest, and *not* sleep. However, being late October, the cold climate was coming in and our resting time became a few hours of deep sleep.

I was the first to wake up and had realize that it was now morning and 7 AM. When I picked my head up to see the scenery, I was shocked to find that the border was less than a half mile ahead. There was a border watch tower there, with the army guard standing on the outer balcony. And still ahead on our right side there was another tower by the bank of the river. Moreover, a third tower was on our left side. And still, about a half mile directly in front of us I could see through the trees, the military border building, usually used as a dorm station where the guards would either be going on shift or being relieved from shift. And at this moment I realized: we have been thrown into the lion's den with enemies all around!

After about thirty minutes, Ioan and Viorel woke up. Like me, they wondered how in the world we were able to bump up right next to this military fortress. From our natural point of view, it looked like we had locked ourselves in with no way to escape from this geographic position. From horizon to horizon was the flattened plain of Banat, which made standing up, a tactical mistake as we could easily be seen from miles away. At that moment, our spirits were awakened to see something supernatural. The Lord had covered us with a cloak of invisibility even as He promised to protect us on this journey. He positioned us right in front of our enemy!

We could certainly hear the soldiers talking amongst themselves, and moving around, which confirmed the fact that we were being concealed; for they surely would have been able to hear and see us by now. We were able to see all their movements on the border, which made us the greatest border spies in Romania! Throughout the day we laid down on our bellies without moving, and then turned to rest on our backs. Our movements were made slowly and stealthily. Later, we realized that we were still small in the faith department, because we were trying to help God keep us safe, when He had already made us invisible!

But we would be tested even more, as a tractor came up behind us, plowing the land and being steered right toward our feet. We looked back and saw the tractor blades about ten to fifteen feet away from our heels and made sure that the driver would not roll over our legs. If he crippled us, he would sure get a good bonus! We could clearly see the countenance of his face. And to our surprise, his eyes were not toward us at all; rather, his eyes must have been blinded to us. We had become to him like three needles lost in a pile of straw. While this was happening, God was talking to us, working on our faith, and making us understand the miracle of blindness that was being done to our enemies.

The date was October 21, 1980, and the weather was beginning to turn cold, as it had already been cloudy and windy all day. We were still wearing our Sunday church apparel, with our suits and shirts on, and holiday Sunday shoes on our feet. We were laying side by side to keep warm as it was about forty degrees. And just before noon, we began taking turns being the one on the inside of the other two. This was a great experience to learn how God's immune system worked within us, and only by divine grace did we not become sick. We prayed that God would hold the rain as it was very cloudy and a little windy with some small raindrops starting to fall. We were untouched for the most part.

I then said something bold to my brothers, "Let's have a signal from God. If it starts raining, then we will stand up and walk toward the border, right through the midst of this stronghold." Then we just started wondering, "Why don't we just make the journey toward the border right now? Why are we settling for this cold, uncomfortable ground when we could just get up and go?!" Certainly, we had been obscured from their sight. Even to this day I still wonder, "Why didn't we just stand up and starting walking, waving at the guards as we crossed into Serbia?" I feel like our faith was too small and that we didn't exercise ourselves to the fullest. But perhaps this was God's plan, that we should experience all the ups and downs of walking in faith.

One positive takeaway was that we got used to walking through dangerous circumstances, as though it was normal. It became like childhood games where you play hide-and-seek; except we weren't around our friends, and there was actual danger all around. The fact is, we were not afraid. We were whispering and poking fun at one another. At one point I said toward Viorel: "Brother Viorel. You of little faith! You poor little boy. Stop shaking all over us here as you can be seen all the way over there! Why did you allow fear to creep into your heart? Are you feeling unsafe here? Just confess your sin to the Lord and He will forgive you and heal you of fear." The young man answered, "Oh no! I don't have any fear. I'm just cold man! You better keep me warm. And don't expect God to do it!" Then both Ioan and I replied, "Why are you not just believing Jesus to heat you already?" Of course, we did our best to create more heat for him, mainly by pressing our bodies against his. We also developed Bible subjects to talk about, just lying there in the cold, mainly on the topic of God's ability to sustain us in perilous times.

Truly, we had been covered by supernatural heat, as each of us only shivered once in a twenty-four-hour period. Today looking back, with everything we endured, I feel more fearful now about those events than I did then! But that is what faith does – it creates courage amid danger. How can we be free from fear when the situation looks dark? We simply need to act like little children, seated in the hands of our Father.

Now, it was the second night of Viorel, Ioan, and I, waiting in the darkness, when the clouds completely disappeared from the sky, and a chilly wind blew around us. There was a large, full moon brightening the night sky, and creating more light than we had anticipated. This would present our next test, as there was a denser group of patrolling teams along the border than in the daytime. Here we felt like the Israelites right before passing through the Red Sea, followed closely by the Egyptians who desired to recapture and enslave them. We had made a temporary home in that perilous spot, as it seemed very familiar after spending twenty-four hours there.

We were also hungry and weak as we hadn't eaten for two days, except for sharing a few tiny chocolate squares. We decided to take a small nap, hoping the moon would set lower in the horizon, at least dimming a bit, giving us the opportunity to go under the cloak of darkness. At last, by Tuesday around 3 AM, we made a thanksgiving prayer and decided to stand up and make our way to the border while the moon was still shining in the sky. Our route would take us away from the border's house barracks, though we could still be seen for miles away. And just as we skirted to the left of the barracks, we came across a dried farm irrigation channel. These channels were typically dry in late Fall as the water was blocked. As a result, we decided to change course and walk along the bottom of the channel, parallel with the barracks. And although we were about a quarter of a mile from the military barracks, some of the dogs must have sniffed us out, and began to bark nervously. Immediately, a couple of the guards came outside to inspect the area. We just kept our heads down and stayed between the channel banks. It was clear that the Lord was present, as both the dogs and guards were confused, ultimately leading the men back into the building.

Cautiously, we headed slightly south until we came across another water channel that was filled with water, flowing directly from the Bega river, toward many Romanian farms. Unfortunately, this mainstream of water was too wide and too deep, as well as very cold. Since it could only be crossed by swimming, we had to make a quick decision. Instead of crossing it, we started walking along the channel bank, now to the west toward Serbia. Once again, we were walking close to the military barracks, and the dogs started barking. Border guards came out and this time, shot a few more light flares into the air, lighting up the whole area. We laid on the ground, barely breathing, whispering prayers to see deliverance. We believed that like before, these men would experience confusion, laziness, and sleepiness. Sure enough, they went back inside, and we were able to continue our walk.

Soon after, we arrived at the large river's bank, and were able to cross it by way of a natural clay bridge. This allowed us to pass over the flowing water channel, bringing us southwest by the Bega River's bank. After walking about one hundred feet, we came to a passenger cable bridge set across the river. And as we looked at the other side, it felt as though we were in a beautiful dream as we were surely about to cross into Yugoslavia. But since we were still close to the military building and watch towers, we remained quiet – just whispering to one another. "Is this a God-miracle or what?" I said, "It's like God built this bridge just for us! Let's cross it." The bridge was supported by four steel cables and a wood-planked floor. However, it looked very old and rusty, even missing some steps. We decided to proceed one after the other, as we did not want to make too much noise and wake up the soldiers. What was amazing, and another likely miracle, was that there were no soldiers posted at the entrance of this bridge. It's as if they had fallen in battle, and we just walked past their dead bodies.

Everyone wanted to fly to the other side of the river. But first, we needed to use caution and walk softly across, just in case there were any traps on it. Viorel was the first to step on it, but the noise made was too loud. We thought it might be heard from a mile away. Ioan stepped on it, deciding not to wait any longer because of the soldiers who had already come out twice. And after I heard the initial noise, I made it onto the bridge as well.

The bridge began rocking back and forth like a boat on turbulent water and was about seventy feet long. We made it to the other side and hid behind some bushes to see if the noise we made alerted the soldiers. Amazingly, after the bridge stopped swaying and making noise, we saw no movement from the barracks – not on the Romanian or Serbian sides. And while praying and resting, we felt a freedom in the atmosphere for the first time. Somehow, we knew that we were out of Romania. We praised the Lord's great name, and His miraculous deliverance, for blinding the enemy's eyes, making their ears deaf, and giving them deep sleep.

Chapter Eight

A New Day in a New World

It was still the second night when we passed into Serbian territory, as the morning light began to burst through the eastern sky. We started walking behind a village, through a field of corn, and stopping by a power pole, we looked to see what language was written on it; sure enough, it was written in Slavic letters. We thanked God again and made our way deeper through this new country to put as much distance between us and the border.

As we continued to walk through the corn field, brother Ioan began complaining that he felt tired and weak, and that he couldn't carry on anymore without resting. We stopped for a moment and I stretched out my hand to feel his forehead. To my surprise, it was as hot as a radiator, and his face was a deep red color. The previous day's cold weather had caught up to him, and he had developed a severe fever. We had no doctor, no medicine, but humbly knelt and prayed for the mercy of God to heal him. Praying less than five minutes, Ioan jumped to his feet, praising the Lord and exclaiming, "I feel better!" I felt his forehead again, and sure enough, it was a normal temperature, with the redness on his face completely gone as well. He was healed. It was our mistake for not stopping a while to thank God for His deliverance, after we crossed the bridge. We just kept running like the Israelites who made their way to Canaan. But God, who is rich in mercy, heals those whom He leads, keeping them from harm, and covering them with favor as they approach their promised land.

From the border, we walked west, through the wilderness fields of Yugoslavia. If a person was caught in this land, it was uncertain whether they could keep going west, or if they had to return to Romania. It reminded us of how Satan tried to make the Israelites return to Egypt, choosing slavery over freedom. It is in this wilderness spot that so many Christians give up and turn back to their old lifestyles. Some people just want new experiences to tell their friends about, but never end up developing in character. They are still committed to Satan – their former, Pharoah-like boss. But faith must stand its ground, and keep taking ground, until we arrive at our destiny.

On the first day, after we departed the border, it was a bright and sunny afternoon, which felt like a generosity to us after what we had just experienced. We laid on the ground, truly resting in this comfortable heat. We felt not only refreshed after our sleep, but as though we were recreated and given our bodies back. For several days, however, we fasted as we hadn't had a meal since the previous Sunday's lunch back in Romania. We simply drank whatever water we could find in the streams or the farm wells. We didn't want to complain because we knew that water would sustain us even without food.

On the fourth day, we traveled toward Zrenjanin. Along the way I found an onion which did not make the harvest and began eating it. It was sour and filled my eyes with tears, but at least it gave me some nutrients. My brothers did not want any; however, I felt more strength in my body afterwards. On the fifth day, we moved closer to Zrenjanin city, and were able to eat some grapes that had also been left after harvest. This time, the earth had truly offered its best!

A funny thing happened as we continued walking. We came across a pig farm late in the evening. We needed a warm place to lay our heads, and so we made our way outside the main farm building where there was an abundance of straw prepared for the animals' winter bedding. After we found the right pile of straw, we climbed in and covered ourselves to keep warm, as well as to hide from anyone passing by. We made separate piles but stayed close to one another. I said, "Sleep well. I do hope to see all of you come the morning!"

As the morning came, Ioan popped his head out of his straw den, and we talked quietly as we heard the morning workers doing their activities. We started to look for Viorel, but after much searching, there wasn't a trace of him to be found. I joked and said, "Either the rapture has just happened or Viorel looked attractive to one of the farm girls! But we should keep looking just in case." We started to dig around, calling quietly, "Viorel? Viorel?" Now, we were afraid that he might have buried himself to the point where oxygen was cut off. "Oh Lord!" I exclaimed, "Don't let us lose our friend!" And finally, as we dug in one spot, there was Viorel completely covered up and just then waking out of sleep. With a lazy roll of his eyes and a smile on his face, he said, "Hey! Why are you waking me up? Let me finish sleeping. Go back to your bed and take another nap. What? Are you guys late for your jobs back in Timisoara?" I replied, "Hey man! Stop it. You already scared us. Now it's time to get up and get out of here and back on the road, sleepy head." We prayed and thanked God that we found brother Viorel. Afterwards, we left our lovely little straw motel.

Priests, Police, & Serbian Precincts

After we entered Zrenjanin, a rather large city, we had a money exchange with a Serbian man. We gave him a small amount of lei – Romanian currency – for dinar currency. I'm sure we made a bad deal, but at least we could buy something. We went to a store and bought a couple of bread loaves and two boxes of matches. This way, once we began our travels to Austria, we could have the ability to light campfires for food and warmth.

Upon leaving Zrenjanin, we started to walk besides a main highway, when we heard the loud, screeching sound of tires. Looking up, we saw a big truck making a sudden and dangerous turn onto the overpass ahead. Right after the truck passed us, we observed a police car parked on the right side of the road. Out of the car came three policemen running toward us. I asked my friends, "What to do, should we run away?" They said, "Yes! We'll run." I replied, "Then just start running!" However, they didn't move; they just stood there and so I stayed still as well. I figured if it was God's will for us to run, they would start running first; if not, we would then just surrender. The next moment, I said, "Let's walk toward the policemen." I started walking in their direction, my friends following.

The police asked us to show our identity cards or our passports. We just said, "Nema passapoarte" (which is "no passports" in Serbian). They then asked us to lift our hands so they could search us. They found nothing – no knives and no guns, except for a couple of matches, little Bibles, and small song books in each of our pockets. Relieved and smiling, they asked us, "Are you priests?" (They spoke in Serbian which we didn't quite understand; however, since we were taught Russian in primary school, we understood a small bit). I replied, "Yes sir, we are priests." Of course, this was true in the sense that we were part of Christ's priesthood. From that moment on, they treated us very well.

We were put under arrest, however, because they viewed us as priests, they didn't bind our hands. They did wonder why we had come on the same day that the Romanian president Ceausescu just arrived to meet President Tito in Belgrade. We pointed up, "God knows." I said, "We are here according to God's schedule, *not* Ceausescu." As they talked amongst themselves, I understood some of what they said. Ceausescu was making a deal with Tito to return all the border traitors back to Romania. The soldiers seemed concerned that this would affect us. They signaled for us to get in their car, saying, "You just behave and be nice! We will drive you to Belgrade. From there, you'll go to Austria and then America." We just said, "Thank you for the ride!" God was good to us, knowing we needed a break from walking as we were tired and hungry.

Now, instead of going to Belgrade, they took us back to the Zrenjanin courthouse, and presented us at the office gate. They gave us a good report, saying we were fine, valuable men of honor. We knew they wrote a positive report about us as we were peaceful in our surrender. They then waved to us "goodbye." Later in the day, we stood before a judge, while someone translated for us. We were asked a few questions about who we were in Romania, including the reason we snuck out, and if we killed anyone at the border. The judge simply sentenced us with these words: "It is our law that once you violate our land without a passport you will spend twenty-one days in jail. Then, you will go your way." He didn't say where we would go and didn't ask anything of us either.

For the first part of the sentence, we were placed in a small jail cell with three tiny beds and some blankets.

Compared to the journey we had been on, this was heaven! The food, however, was hell. At times, after the meal, we were still hungry but at least we weren't fainting. One of our dinners was a giant pig's ear just lightly boiled. I refrained from eating any of it, whereas my companions ate a small portion. The best part of our time was consistently praying, believing, and preaching the word to one another. We were even singing at a low volume. It was like a church service! A prison guard who spoke Romanian would occasionally come by our cell, open the window and tell us to stop carrying on about God. We told him that if he were in our place, he might be doing the same thing.

There were some days when they took us in for interviews, interrogating in order to understand our motive for leaving Romania. They'd ask about schooling, jobs, religion, and our faith, including if we had committed any crimes in Romania. They wanted to know everything, even what we ate on our way out. Considering that this was also a socialistic country, it had a lot more freedom than the closed communist camp of Romania. However, we could tell that these men had the same mentality as those in the communistic system back home. So, we were careful not to express any hatred for communism.

One night the Lord spoke to me while in our jail cell, in the form of a vision. I was leaving Yugoslavia into Austria with five other men who were all strangers to me. It was a vivid vision as though it were real life. I had seen the exact faces, the buildings, and the scenery both of Yugoslavia and the Austrian border. Now, I kept this revelation hidden from my brothers, as I feared if they knew, their faith in this mission would diminish. But I did tell them that the Lord showed me that everyone of us would be free, and that we shouldn't worry about making it.

On the twenty-first day spent in Zrenjanin jail, they took us to a large refugee camp in Padinca Skela, by Belgrade, to await the trip to Austria or Italy. But after arriving there, we heard that some of us would be selected to return to Romania. In those years, the Yugoslavia government had a deal where fifty percent of the refugees would be returned, and fifty percent would be helped to freedom. However, those who would be returned typically were sent straight back to Romania and did not linger in the refugee camp. You see, the Serbians were cunning as they knew how to please everyone, while also making money. Their deal with Romania was to get a wagon of salt for each person they returned. And for each person set free, the UN and Western countries would pay them currency.

Austria, My Dream of Freedom Fulfilled

When we arrived at Padinka Skela, each one of us was interviewed again, and then taken to a very large auditorium which was filled with beds, some sleeping two on a mattress. In that one room there were about one hundred men, with just one or two small windows. Oxygen became a necessity. There were also a lot of men who smoked in the room. I felt like I was breathing more smoke than oxygen, which made conditions worse. It was also a locked facility, which made us all as good as prisoners. From my previous cell to this, it felt like I had come from paradise and descended into the hallway of hell! But I was able to comfort these disparate people and make some friends as well.

That first night's sleep in the refugee camp was deep and restful. The next sound I heard was early in the morning when the room's alarm bell went off and all the lights came on. At the door stood a few of the uniformed officers, shouting out, "Anyone who hears his name called out, come to your new room!" I didn't realize there was another section for refugees. My name was called along with around forty people. But when I began walking to the next room, my two friends followed me closely expecting their names to be called out as well. But an

174

officer stopped them and asked for their names. Upon looking at the list, he said, "You two…you're not on the list. Back off!" With sadness in our eyes we waved goodbye. The officers didn't realize they had just separated the greatest team on earth.

Then, I had much relief when they took us downstairs and told us that we would be taken to Austria soon. We each received a lunch package and were instructed to eat it at lunch time. In the afternoon, we would receive a dinner package as well, along with an announcement about our travel schedule. We then boarded a rather attractive visitor's bus. I had never ridden in a more comfortable bus than this one. Everyone felt safer now that we were going to Austria rather than Romania. But I heard some men still doubting, not sure what they would do with us. But this bus was proof enough to me that we were going in the right direction. And as we drove away, we were in fact going west, and not back east toward our former country.

Before evening we arrived in Maribor City. The bus driver was making good time as we only stopped for a short lunch break, and a couple of bathroom stops. Upon arrival, we were herded into a large waiting room – a police station or army base by the look of it. Then, an officer came and instructed us to hand them any Serbian papers or documents written in Serbian. The reason for this was that the Serbians didn't want us to have any proof that we stayed in Serbia. The officer continued, "When you report to Austria, don't tell them anything about the Serbian prison or any of our official state buildings. Report only that you succeeded to sneak out through the Yugoslavian territory without being caught."

This gave me the impression of a mafia network, teaching us to be good liars, in the same way socialists and communists tended to be. And as the darkness of night began to cover the land, they started to split us up in about three or four groups. Each group was boarded into a van or little bus separately and then driven away. I was waiting in the holding room for my vehicle to arrive. Right before midnight, the officer came and asked us to go outside, and I boarded a small terrain van, with two officers up front. They drove us onto a highway out of the city, where we observed some gates up ahead with cars lined up. This was the customs border service which was a routine stop where people and their belongings would have to be checked. Our vehicle was stopped about a half mile before getting to the waiting line. We were then instructed to get out of the van and walk onto a nearby field which led toward a steep mountain adjacent to the gate; the idea was that we would walk around the check point.

It was already snowing, and the ground was covered, which presented a problem for many of us who only had light shoes on, snow easily getting onto our feet. This looked a very treacherous path as we had to climb alongside the mountain's steep slope. We then started saying to one another, "Why are we taking the hard path? By now the customs guards have seen us as we're within a couple hundred feet from them."

So, we then made our way straight for the customs gate. However, the officers who dropped us off drove up right next to us in the van and cautioned us to go around, telling us that we would be sent back to Romania for sure if we went through the checkpoint. We heeded the warning and went around to where the gate fence met the mountain. However, since there was a large rockface blocking our way around, we went through a small hole in the fence. Soon we were about one hundred feet inside this new territory which was officially Austrian land. We made it! And my thanksgiving went out to the Lord for this promised land!

If you recall, God gave me a vision during my stay at the Zrenjanin prison about what I would experience concerning my freedom. And as I was now in the land of my freedom, I remembered the vision! Like that supernatural encounter, there were *five men walking besides me*, whose faces were just as I remember them. Also, the surrounding scenery was just as I remembered it. For a moment, I wasn't sure if I was still dreaming or if this was happening. It was so surreal. I hardly communicated with those around me, as I was lost in the goodness of God for me and my journey.

And while walking through the fresh Austrian snow, we saw several apple trees, with large, healthy fruit hanging which were left from the previous harvest. In Romania, we could never find apples neglected like this – I felt sorry for them! We were very hungry, as the last time we ate was lunch; the officers had not handed out dinner food as there was no time. But we didn't complain, because we had our freedom. We picked the apples and hungrily ate a couple of them, storing a few in our pockets, not knowing where our next meal would come from. I must have lost at least fifteen pounds since leaving Romania. The people of Austria would certainly be impressed with our tiny physiques – a testament to how wonderful life is in a communist country! No chance anyone could become obese, which will keep you in great shape!

At last, we got to the edge of a small town, with the sign on the road saying "Gendarmerie" pointing to the left. So, we took that route which led us right to the Gendarmerie building. The time must have been around 2 AM. We knocked softly at a large gate, which prompted a sleepy policeman on the third floor to signal with his hands something like, "What is up with you?" We cried out, "Romanians are here!" Now, the Austrians generally understood the fugitive problem. These people did not seem happy to see us at first as we were bound to make lots of work for them to do. However, one look at a bunch of skinny, hungry guys prompted compassion from them. I'm sure they had no idea what we had been through. One of them actually went shopping for each of us, buying us sandwiches. We were just amazed at how nice they were. And sandwiches after midnight? This would never have been available in Romania. Then, by the late morning they drove us to a large city, named Gratz. Here we waited in a large room with other refugees from Bulgaria, Albania, and mostly from Romania, including those from other dictatorships.

On the same day, we all boarded a special bus that took us from Gratz to the refugee camp of Traiskirchen, thirty kilometers from Vienna. After a couple of weeks, Ioan and Viorel made it to Traiskirchen as I expected they would. At last, we were all safe and free, ready to go to America. Today, both of these precious men live in California.

As for the Serbian advice that we should lie to authorities about our journeys, I decided that whether I spoke with the Austrian or the American authorities, I would tell the truth exactly as I wrote it here, without exaggeration. I trusted that the Lord would continue to protect me. And as I look back at the whole experience, I can still feel the tangible freedom in the Austrian atmosphere. Even the trees and plants seemed to be dancing in this freedom. I believe that there were angels assigned to cover that country. In the words of David, the psalmist: "Even when I go through the valley of death, I will fear no evil, for you are with me; Your rod and your staff they comfort me" (Psalm 23:4).

Chapter Nine

The Year I Made it to America

After I crossed the border, stepping into Yugoslavia, I turned back toward Romania, waved a sad farewell, and with a crying heart I said, "Goodbye my dear country! My time has come, my work is finished, and may Jesus free you from the evil grip of communism. I am sorry for my family and friends that you must stay. I am sorry to all of you atheists who I was not able to share the gospel with anymore!"

I took a deep, painful breath once more, waved goodbye to my dear country, and committed myself to follow the Lord wherever that obedience would take me. I then turned away from Romania, faced the west, and made another vow: "As I journey west, in whatever country I make my home, whether America or another one, I will never denounce that place or look back in nostalgia. Even if I am enslaved and yoked to a plow in their fields, I will not have any regrets about leaving Romania. I am committed to this new path."

After my departure, I spent almost six months in the little town of Traiskirchen where the Austrian refugee camp was located. After a couple of interviews while in the camp's quarantine, I received political asylum. This gave me the ability to live and work in Austria indefinitely. I received my identity card and was legally hired by a furniture company. What's more, I was able to ship special food and clothing packages to both my parents, as well as a few gifts to my fiancée Viorica. But the most blessed thing was the little Romanian church where I became very active in the ministry of preaching and teaching. What a blessing to praise the Lord amid His people!

Now, I was a part of this small church when it started in the Ungheanu's large family home, right on the premises of the refugee camp's family apartments. From there, we moved into a large back room of the City Hall. What made this time special is that I didn't need to impress anyone with a polished image or preaching; I was simply glowing with God's presence which originally came upon me as I crossed the Romanian border. The theme of my preaching was that life should be lived in continual awe, for *nothing* is too difficult for God! I was flying high in the Spirit! I remained in the atmosphere of God's presence just as I had experienced across the border. My Austrian brothers would continually remind me that I was "flying and smiling." And when people heard me preach, they understood that the miraculous I spoke about from my past was not simply a past event but should be happening every day. We are, after all, called to supernatural living.

Work, Ministry, & Life Begins in America

A few months later, I got the appointment scheduling me to go to the American Embassy in Vienna. After only 10 minutes of meeting with the chief counselor and two of his aids, they quickly concluded with these glowing words: "John, you are good to go! America needs you. You will be receiving the flight schedule very soon. For now, Welcome to America!" After a period of about a month and a half, and in April of 1981, I was on the flight to New York. From there, I flew to Portland, Oregon where I would reconnect with my brother in law, Nicu Giurculete. This was made possible by my sponsor,

Pastor Nicu Pop, who led a Romanian church in Philadelphia. He was a wonderful brother whose church was ready to help anyone in need! In fact, before I landed in America, they were already planning to bless me and sow seed into my life. My first financial seed in America came from this church, where I received one hundred dollars.

Shortly after arriving in the U.S., I found a job with a German carpentry company in the Portland area. While there, I had to communicate mostly in German, thankfully learning some of the language when living in Austria. I made some Romanian and American friends, too. Eventually, a group of us young people came together with the purpose of moving to Houston, Texas, where the job market seemed better than in Portland. Nicu, my brother-in-law, joined up with our group; however, by the time we made it to Houston, the job market was beginning to collapse, as America was entering into the '80s depression. For three months, we didn't find any available jobs around the Houston area. Instead, we just worked odd jobs here and there.

What happened next was unexpected and began to make sense of why I moved to Houston. I found myself in the beginning of my first Romanian church plant, which would become the main ministry to follow me throughout my life. Around the year 1981, more Romanians began moving to

Houston, which caused the church community to grow rapidly. Our first church meetings were held in people's homes, and after a little while, the Sunday main church service was moved into an American church building, the leadership allowing us to utilize one of their auditoriums. It was during this period that I was involved in preaching and teaching the Word of God in earnest, preparing myself for a life of ministry.

Now, I landed a job as an industrial painter in Wako, Texas. The Marta family lived there, who were natives of the Cenei border village in Romania. We had visited the church in Cenei the same Sunday we left Romania, so we were already acquainted with their home. Back in Romania, Elijah Marta tilled the state farms on a tractor around the border line of Serbia. He was familiar with the area, especially the dangerous passages. Back in Waco, Elijah asked me if I could recall the border we crossed when we had fled. I could describe it to him in detail as though drawing a map. Elijah was shocked to hear it, as he remembered the danger of this passage. He shouted, "Are you a crazy man?! How in the world did you make it across such a hot spot?" I replied, "It wasn't us leading the way, but the Lord who led us to that spot. We didn't have a map or any other guide to get us over the border. Yeah, we were a little crazy for doing it! But God loves and uses the crazy ones who are willing to trust Him no matter how unusual the situation."

Elijah continued, "Anyone who has have lived in that area of the country would say the same thing; *no one* has ever passed over that part of the border. And if they did by mistake, they would surely be caught and arrested by the officials." Elijah went on to recall a time when, while working the field by the border, he asked a border soldier if anyone comes by to pass in this location. The soldier's reply was, "Not really. Only if they are extremely unlucky!" You see, this was a private pass which served as a military throughway where Romanian and Serbian soldiers would communicate. And there was a border post guarded by two soldiers at the bridge separating the two countries.

But the Lord instructed us beforehand that we were going to hit an impenetrable wall made of iron without any doors to pass through. And as we were faithful to be led by our King, an angel descended from heaven, using his sword to crack open a door right in the middle of the wall, ushering us through it. Certainly, this was not a easy thing for me to decide to do – to sneak out of Romania without anyone's help, maps, or money. I only had the clothes on my back, shoes on my feet, and a little Bible in my pocket. Upon exploring God's Word further, I realized that my actions were based solely on God's grace and mercy within me. And what's more, I wasn't surrounded by encouraging people, nor the right events to launch me out; on the contrary, I experienced only adversity. But regardless of the natural circumstances, it was sufficient for me to fulfill God's plan for my life.

Constantin the Defector

One of the major obstacles to freedom for the Romanian people, was a man named Constantin from Suceava, who became a propaganda tool for the communists. He snuck out on his first border attempt, and made it all the way to Detroit, Michigan. But after almost a year living in America, he returned to Romania to be with his family. At the time, the Romanian embassy was elated that a defector decided to renounce the West and return to the "socialist paradise." They were so pleased that they didn't even imprison him for defecting. I am certain that upon returning, they used him to discourage others from leaving the country based on the Romanian socialists' perceived superiority to America. I don't think Constantin's role in discouraging people from leaving was necessarily wrong, as I had engaged in similar activity to make the risks of defection known; however, what was important was making sure those wanting to leave sincerely believed that God had called them to do so. Only then would there be the kind of safe passage that I and many others experienced.

Now, just a couple of months before I fled the country, I visited Constantin in Suceava. It was there that he tried to convince me to give up any plans to leave the country, arguing, "It is not worth risking your own life for a little more than we may get here. In America, you work harder than here to make ends meet." I didn't quarrel with him but rather listened and made my own conclusions about what was true. Besides, at this crossroads in my life, I was hesitant to reveal to him that I was going to leave the country no matter the cost of leaving, or of starting over in America. The truth is, he did not discourage me from moving forward; in fact, I only felt a stronger resolve to leave Romania behind.

The funny thing is, I could see that Constantin was already regretting his return. He was not a happy man but came across as fearful, like a man who had realized that he landed back into slavery, even as the Israelites would have had they returned to Egypt from the Wilderness. I am certain that Constantin had been placed on the police's security watch, which meant that every step he took and every word he uttered would have been monitored. This is because the communist state is intimidated by those who venture beyond its iron walls. He was likely distrusted by the secret service for the fact that he might have become a spy for America. This suspicion would have branded him for life.

Now, Constantin was very close to retirement age, and it would have been difficult for him to start a new life in America. What he failed to see was the benefit he could have passed on to his children had he stayed. However, he would have been waiting for a long time before his family could join him in America. Nicu, my brother-in-law who crossed the border along with Constantin, waited for three and a half years before his wife and four kids were able to join him. The communists made it very hard for my sister Silvia to unite with her husband in Portland, Oregon. She was often advised to divorce him instead. A couple of times she was enticed with marriage proposals from handsome men she didn't even know. They would address her kindly, ask for her hand, and vow to love her and her own kids. The communists tried hard to make her divorce her traitorous husband.

For me, my illegal crossing adventure wasn't an easy thing at all, but meant risking death from a bullet, being beaten to death, imprisoned for years, or separated for a long time from loved ones. Over the years, tens if not hundreds of thousands attempted it, with thousands paying for it with their lives. As for me, I didn't leave the country for a better life, neither for better economics, but rather for a spiritual purpose – it was time to step into a new dimension of living.

Back in Waco...

After I found my industrial painting job in Waco, I moved there for work but commuted back and forth to Houston so that I could continue ministering in the church plant. Shortly after, we started a home church meeting in Waco as well. Here, I was preaching quite a lot with an older brother who was a retired pastor from Jimbolia. In a short amount of time this home meeting began to grow significantly.

While in Waco, I purchased and began riding my first ever bicycle, getting me back and forth to work, church, and the local stores. A few months later, I bought my first car – a white Mercury Cougar, with an 8-cylinder engine! God was good to me as over a three-month period I could completely pay off the car. Although my job was paying me around $3.75 per hour, the owner and the manager liked me and added another 25 cents per hour. Of course, they wanted me to keep this a secret from the other workers! My salary was raised from $3.25 to $4.25 by the time I left the company.

At this time, there were two mid-size Romanian churches in Houston. Ioan – one of the brothers who crossed the Romanian border with me, moved to Waco from Detroit. It was a joyful reunion as we shared a joyful history together. We ended up moving to Phoenix, Arizona, where we stayed with our friend Crisan, who was from a Timisoara suburb in Romania. Crisan snuck over the border a couple of months after we did. Despite being married with a few kids, he mustered the courage to do it, after he heard that I snuck over the border successfully. We ended up meeting at the Traiskirchen refugee camp in Austria.

By early June of 1981, Ioan sold his old car and joined me in the Mercury Cougar as we made our way to Phoenix, Arizona. Although we had jobs working outside in the hot summer climate, we enjoyed it; in fact, we enjoyed *everything*, both good and bad. Our new-found freedom was such a blessing which created such positivity, especially looking back at what we had to endure and overcome by faith.

Once in Phoenix, we began attending a Romanian church, and as soon as we started attending, the church leaders expressed a need for our ministry, like hungry men needing fresh bread. We were called upon regularly to deliver Bible messages during each service. Also ministering alongside us, was another brother from about forty miles northeast of Timisoara, Peter from Arad. We helped this small, Elim Fellowship church grow quickly, and as the people multiplied, it became a large church in the city with three new midsize churches branching off from the original plant.

Passports, Arabia, & Richard Wurmbrand

While in Phoenix, we often ministered in the Romanian churches around Los Angeles, California. The Romanian community in Anaheim was larger than the one in Arizona, as Romanians had been moving to California for a long time, whereas they just started moving into Arizona. One time while at a prayer meeting in California, an unknown prophet spoke of a spiritual vision he saw concerning me. In his vision, I was standing by the edge of a large body of water with a baited fishing rod waving in my hand. I was catching a lot of big fish with it. I believed this vision was a confirmation from the Lord that I was called to catch the souls of men with the ministry He had given me.

Back in Arizona, I found a landscaping and general maintenance job working with some of the richest people of Scottsdale and Paradise Valley. They scheduled me one day a week for each home, and all of them were willing to assist me in starting a professional landscaping business. They offered to help me purchase my own truck and equipment, to secure my services indefinitely. But I found myself unsatisfied with this new-found success. And even though I made good money, my heart did not find happiness.

This was contrasted with my life In Romania, where I experienced inner joy despite a very hard external life. While in Phoenix, though I was very involved in the church ministry each week, I had a heart-cry for something more, as the presence of God did not seem that intense. The American dream with its liberties and financial opportunities didn't give me a sense of fulfillment, certainly not like the constant challenges and persecutions I experienced in Romania. In the U.S., I had to fight to keep my inner life alive. I craved more of His presence, to feel guided step by step by the Spirit. In Romania, there were times when speaking to God was the main reason for my being alive; but here, my comfortable lifestyle with all its ease and abundance put my soul in what felt like a pickle jar. I reminded the Lord often that I needed Him and the challenges of missionary work.

Now, Ioan – the brother who crossed the Romanian border with me – was living in Arizona. After much prayer, we both agreed to do missions work in the Middle East. However, we were not yet U.S citizens, and so we were not able to acquire passports yet, which was necessary to get an appropriate visa for such a trip. But after a visit to the immigration office in Phoenix, we were at least able to get our temporary immigrant passport. Now, with our sights set on the Middle East, we drove to Los Angeles to obtain short-term visas from the Israeli Consulate.

The Lord saw our passion and heard our prayers with regards to Israel, and for the peace of Jerusalem, and allowed us to explore this desire. Afterall, this was our dream, that after we got freed from Romania, we could live a life of freedom while fulfilling our missional call. The Israeli embassy staff were impressed with the two Romanian men standing before them, and immediately issued us three-month visas. To this day, I am still holding onto this passport.

At this point in our lives, we were moving with intense boldness planning to cross national borders. We were filled with excitement at the idea of being spies for Jesus' kingdom! The plan was to pass illegally over the Israeli border into the Jordanian and Lebanon countries. We would learn the Arabic language in order that we could be long-term missionaries in those lands, trusting the Lord to protect and lead us. We didn't care about the risk of being arrested or even killed; for us, that would be considered *normal* Christian life.

After we got our Israeli visas, we made an appointment to see our Romanian-Jewish brother Richard Wurmbrand who was living in Glendale, California. He was a native of Romania, who spent about fourteen years in the cruelest prisons in our country. This man truly suffered for his faith. His Calvary started right after the Second World War when Russia invaded and occupied Romania, acquiring this land and shortly after turning it into a communist state. We believed that Richard was the best man for us to receive counseling from as well as prayer and a blessing for our lives and mission. After arriving, we openly confessed to him all our plans, particularly our desire to enter Arabic countries as missionaries. But after talking to him, we felt like we had made a mistake meeting him, because of his discouraging reaction to what we had planned.

Richard firmly discouraged us not to act on our plans at that time. He said, "My dearest brothers, I am treating you like my own children. Now, please don't be naïve! First, become as fluent in the English language as possible. Next, go and study at a Bible school here in America. Then, after you have become U.S. citizens, go your way to the lost world. Just be certain that before leaving, you pray and make very sure this is God's plan for your lives. I love you my brothers. John and Ioan, you remind me of my passion when I was young. I now pray God's blessings on you as you go your way and do great exploits for our Lord Jesus! You've got time and the rest of your lives still ahead of you. Be encouraged, full of passion and faith. For now, slow down a little, and then go and bless the people you're called to."

It is certainly true that while in Romania we used to listen well as God would speak to us through His saints. But in this situation, we felt that we were actually being blocked by this brother; yet we became fully convinced in our hearts that the Holy Spirit used him to guide us. We decided to follow the Word of the Lord's through our brother, give up on our current plan, and continue our lives back in Phoenix.

Saved from a Car Accident in Phoenix

A little while later, I got a job with a fitness sports club, managing the day-to-day supplies and maintenance for the exercise rooms and pools. While there, I believe Satan had a plot to kill me. While on the job one morning, I felt a grieving inside, a sort of suffering that I didn't understand. I thought, maybe I am picking up on a problem in my family back in Romania, with my parents, with Viorica my fiancée, or maybe with a friend who needs prayer. I felt led to pray in the Spirit so that He could intercede through spiritual tongues. I realized that I didn't know what to pray for intelligibly. And while moving about and working for quite some time, I continued to pray ardently until I felt a fresh release and joy returning to my soul.

Later that day, coming home on Central Avenue, I was driving about 50 miles per hour as I approached the city edge. A small sized bus was slowly backing up out of a home entrance gate, intending to turn on Central Avenue. It looked like the driver spotted me as he stopped momentarily. But as I got closer, he frantically backed up into the road so that he was blocking every lane. In that instance I knew that it was impossible for me to stop my vehicle before crashing into the side of the bus. I cried out to God – "Jesus, stop this accident!" My feet instinctively pressed on the brakes, to at least soften the crash if possible. Although everything happened so fast, I knew that I was in God's hands; whether He would save me supernaturally, or I would go to heaven, it was His choice.

In that very moment, I saw a big hand like a wall right in front of my car and heard a mix of skidding brakes with clanging noises as my car made impact. Amazingly, it felt as though there was a giant pillow in between the bus and my car. My vehicle spun around twice as if it were a toy car spinning and flying about, and then just stopped perfectly onto the driveway a few feet from the bus. When the dust settled, I looked out my driver window where my car hit the bus, but there were no scratches on the bus – it was completely untouched! At that point, I didn't even need to look at my car as I knew it would also be unscratched.

The driver of the bus got out of his vehicle in order to assess what had happened. Upon looking at his vehicle and mine, his face turned pale like a white wall as though he had just seen a ghost! He looked at me as though just waking from a dream, and said, "Are you okay? Did anything even happen here?" By now, he was speaking like a bewildered man, not knowing what to say. "This was my fault" he added.

Since the traffic was stopped in both directions, and the road completely blocked, I told him that we should get out of the way. I drove slowly and very closely behind the bus driver to the side. After we parked again, I said to him, "Everything is good, Sir. God was with us, wasn't He? We were spared and rescued! Let's give praise to our God! Now may the God of heaven bless you, Sir, and give you a great day. From now on, just make sure to take a second look when backing up out of your driveway." And while I smiled, waved to him, and drove off, he stood in the same spot as if paralyzed. I don't think he had quite digested the sort of miracle we had just witnessed. As I drove off, I came to realize that this man might have been an innocent victim of the devil's attack against me. But I also recognized the importance of my praying in spiritual tongues all morning. It is true that with God, *all* things are possible!

Beaten by Thugs, Rescued by God

A couple of months before leaving for Christ For the Nations Institute in Dallas, the enemy tried to destroy me again. On one afternoon, I was visiting brother Costel, who was going to attend CFNI with me. However, he was not home; instead, I was greeted by the children of the family who lived next door. Once they recognized me, they said, "Your friend Costel left home about an hour ago." I blessed them in the name of the Lord, and asked them if they knew and loved Jesus, or are attending a church. They said, "No, we don't know Jesus nor are we attending a church." I encouraged them to tell their parents to find a good church in the area and to join them during their weekly service.

I drove off intending to return by evening to speak with Costel about moving to Dallas. After leaving, I parked by my residence, and began walking to the building entrance. I was spotted by a few Spanish men who were drinking and chatting together by the corner of the building. One of them signaled the others in the group to attack me. A couple of them immediately approached and started hitting me using their fists and feet. I didn't know why they were doing it. When I fell, I shouted to God to stop them because they were beating me without cause. Miraculously, they stopped like they had all been stunned and forced to stand still. I was able to get up, run inside my apartment, and wash the blood off my face in the bathroom.

At some point, someone must have seen this incident as the police had been called. The policewoman sent to investigate told me that I was lucky because one of the men came out of his apartment holding a knife in his hand, intending to hurt me. But somehow, he bumped into the stairway and fell, cutting himself with his own knife. This was likely reported by the same person who called the police. I saw the man's hand which was bleeding profusely. But I knew I wasn't lucky – God intervened and wounded their leader, disabled him and his team. The police could attest to the wild nature of this whole situation. And at the end of it all, there was more blood coming from the knife-wielding thug than from my own nose.

After the event, an assault report was filed with the aggressor's names on it, while a couple of them were fined and placed on the police watch list. The police asked me if I wanted to sue them in court as they would gladly assist me. But I waved my right to do it, telling the police to let God be the judge because their souls were lost and needed to be saved.

202

Chapter Ten

Christ for the Nations

Before the opportunity to attend Christ for the Nations Institute came to me, I refused three other Bible colleges. The first was Bucharest Pentecostal Seminary in Romania, as I was recommended to go there twice. The first invitation came from Pastor Dragos from Arbore church, and second time, Pastor Clim from Timisoara Elim church. And although this was a comprehensive seminary with many young men desiring to study there, I declined them, as only fifteen students were accepted each school semester. I was also afraid that they would pressure me to cooperate with the secret service some of the time. This was a real issue in Romania. And I was unwilling to give them any opportunity to corrupt me for the sake of obtaining church leadership positions.

Next, when I came to America and was serving at a Houston church, Pastor Lucaci from Detroit came to see our church beginnings. He came specially to meet with me, asking for a partner in registering the church under the Church of God organization. And, as bonus, I was promised a spot either in a Tennessee Bible college, or in a German-based branch of the Church of God seminary. Of course, I refused as I don't participate in anything that comes as a compromise, especially if it is for the purpose of reaping material benefits at the expense of a church. As it turns out, the Houston church became a part of a large Pentecostal Fellowship instead.

After Ioan came from Detroit, we both moved to College Station in Texas, where a missionary pastor named Paul was living who knew us from a Romanian church in Traiskirchen, Austria. Upon returning to Texas from Austria, he purchased an old monastery at College Station in order to start a Bible school. Here, we were the first candidates to become students in Pastor Paul's missional Bible school. This was the third academic opportunity I was presented with. But God clearly spoke to us, saying that this was not the school He meant for us to attend. This is when I left that place and drove straight to Phoenix, where I had to wait for about two more years before ending up at Christ For the Nations. Now, it seemed to me that God was not in a hurry to lock me in anywhere. But at the right time, He would propel me in the right direction.

Initial Steps

As I continued to wait for God's will concerning my education, I became more interested and passionate to visit American churches, which meant that I would be skipping some Romanian services. This caused our Romanian brethren to reproach us, as they did not have enough teachers or preachers without us. However, we began to attend Echo's Gospel Church, where we made friends with the young people as well as the leaders, especially the youth Pastor, Gary Kinnaman. Later, Gary founded the Grace Church of Mesa, Arizona, a church that grew to a few thousand members. This would become the first church to sponsor me while I was going into the full-time ministry.

Among our new American friends at Echo Church, were the Lloyd family. They were especially kind, treating us as they would their own children – Gayle, Bonny, and Joy – who were all graduates of CFNI Bible school. We made other friends who were also former students at CFNI. It was in this congregation that I first learned of Christ For the Nations Institute. When I had first heard the name, something happened in my heart, as though I had been quickened to life. When I was first asked by the Lloyd family to consider attending, I was hesitant. The reason was because I felt inadequate to learn in a school setting due to my broken English. I thought I'd be unprepared to learn the Bible from an English speaker as well. However, Echo Church became a catalyst for me to attend, as my closest friends kept encouraging me and insisting on it.

Later, a CFNI graduate friend called me out on my hesitation. He said, "John, I am not just recommending that you go to CFNI; I believe you *must* go!" I asked him, "Can you tell me truthfully; are you speaking from earth's perspective or because you see a heavenly calling on my life? Is this coming from your mind, or from the Spirit?" He firmly replied, "I am speaking straight from heaven. And I'm telling you that what I am saying is coming directly from the Spirit. That is why I'm insisting you go to this school. I know the Lord has a great plan for your life, because you are on a special assignment. I just don't know what it is." The next words out of my mouth were: "Then, I will certainly go to CFNI. Yes sir! I'm going to study there as soon as possible." For me, when I make a promise like this, it is a done deal. I would surely end up in Dallas.

I didn't do anything else. I didn't call or apply to CFNI. It wasn't like today, where you can just go to a website and fill out some forms. All I had were a couple of magazine brochures laying around. However, after a couple of weeks from the point of my decision, my friend Bonnie came to me and said, "John, you are good to go! You have already been accepted to CFNI. This Spring you leave for Dallas and will start school during the Summer semester. We spoke *for* you and introduced you directly to the school president and academic dean, sister Freda Lindsay. All you must do is stop by the registration office, tell them your name, and you'll be good to go. Besides, you've already been approved for a full scholarship, which is a privilege given to only a few."

A Dream Fulfilled

In April 1984, after about three years spent in America, I began my drive toward Dallas to start my Bible school adventure at CFNI. Upon arriving, I stopped in at the registration office to discover that what Bonnie had said was true – my name was already on the list! The Academic Dean smiled and welcomed me, adding, "John, you're God's favorite around here. Our president Dr. Lindsay offered you a full scholarship. Why don't you come to my desk, brother, and we can have a chat over coffee?" There wasn't much more for me to do but praise the Lord, thanking Him and the CFNI staff as it was a great privilege for this poor Romanian fugitive to be loved and accepted. Certainly, it was wonderful to be received with open arms into the most wonderful missionary school in the world.

When I first got onto the campus, I was amazed at how familiar it looked to me. Here, my dreams would be fulfilled. This was the school for which I suffered so much, struggling for so long to make it in its appointed time. I began to realize that it was the Lord who was hastening my steps so that I could be here. It was my destiny! This was the beginning of further training for international ministry, to the Glory of God. The academic dean named Dr. Reents told me that I was the first Romanian to have ever attended CFNI. Since then, a couple hundred Romanians have graduated this school, and there hasn't been a semester where a Romanian is not attending classes.

The truth is, even during my college experience I still had the same spiritual river flowing through me as I did before. I felt a strong desire to exercise myself in the service of the Gospel right away after attending classes and hearing teachings and was not keen on the idea of spending a long time on the theological benches. What I wanted to do was go out and demonstrate what God had already put within. In truth, I didn't care that much for traditional Bible schooling, where the focus tended to be on getting a diploma to hang on your wall. Instead, I believed in a practical path where we let the Spirit lead our hearts and let our intellects follow. I also hoped that the Lord would not rapture His Church while I was sitting on some Bible school chair. How much better would it be for Christ to return while I was saving a soul who needed to know Him?

Where He Guides, He Provides

I arrived at CFNI about a month before the Summer semester. There were several students who stayed on campus during the break who were working a variety of jobs around the city so that they could make the money they needed for school. A few days after my arrival, I found myself working for a furniture moving company which hired many CFNI students. The great part of this job was being able to pick our schedules so that we could have the flexibility we needed with school.

Obtaining this job made me realize that my scholarship should be given to someone else, for I was already a legal citizen, and could work for my tuition. I spoke to the Dean's office about it, and although they were surprised to hear it, they agreed. Over the next couple of years, I was able to pay school expenses, tuition, food and board, as well as a trimestral package. Although the scholarship was still available to me should I need it, God's grace continued to supply all my needs until graduation. I never regretted my decision!

Adjusting to New Traditions

Throughout my time at school, I was often confronted by Satan in the form of temptation to return to Phoenix. I had a good job there which promised me a comfortable future. Also, I had some prejudice against the craziness of the worship music, as I was not familiar with it. People were clapping their hands heavily, bouncing and dancing around, and running around the auditorium – all of which was a little too crazy for me. At times, the heavy usage of makeup on the women and their general dress messed with me. In all fairness, the dress-code was decent, but I was just not used to it as this wasn't part of my tradition.

Unfortunately, I let it hinder my joy and worship of the Lord. Besides the laughter and joyful craziness, I had seen tears in some people's eyes, many of them lifting their hands with a spiritual tranquility about them as they worshiped. I immediately asked myself, "Am I the one who is wrong?" I then told the Lord, "Here's the deal. I have joined this group of worshippers and I will just flow with them in Spirit and Truth, praying and praising you along with them. Forgive me, as I will not manifest the way many of these people are, unless the Spirit moves me to do so."

After about five minutes, the Spirit began to move so strong in me that I spontaneously began lifting my hands, clapping with praise, and bouncing up and down with a heart full of joy! From this moment on, all prejudice left me. I was no longer influenced by my religious tradition. The outside appearance of things seemed to vanish. I was free! And I have stayed free.

My Healings at CFNI

During the first year, the Lord healed me of daily headaches. I hadn't noticed how or when this became a chronic issue. But after a while, I understood this to be a stronghold of the enemy meant to disturb my fellowship with God and His people, as well as to make me less receptive to learning scriptures. These strong headaches visited me each day for hours at a time, usually starting by the midmorning and lasting to about midafternoon, sometimes till the evening.

Now, when pain of any kind lingers in my body, I tend to ignore it and give it a license to continue. One day after the morning classes I went to the school's prayer chambers to pray. While there, I realized that it was harder to pray. It was in this moment that I became determined to see an end to this situation, as I was angry at whatever this thing was which hindered my study of the Word, my fellowship with the Lord, and with other people.

And in a holy moment, I commanded this headache to come out of me. I said, "Enough is enough! Headache which has been oppressing me, get out of me right away, whatever your root may be. I don't care if this ache is because of the colds I endured in Romania, or because of life pressures, or a thorn from Satan sent to torment me. I don't care about the details! Satan, take your luggage and leave my head alone right here, right now!" I then turned to Jesus and asked Him to fill the empty space with wholeness, health, and a sound mind.

Suddenly, the joy of the Lord filled me, and I stood up to give thanks to my healer. I felt what seemed like a heavy blanket lift off my head, chest, and shoulders, leaving me feeling unbelievably refreshed and light, without any headache to be found. To this day, I have trouble relating to people when they say, "I have a headache." This is not because I don't remember having headaches in my past, but because I haven't dealt with them for so long that I've forgotten the physical sensation. Jesus set me free and has kept me free!

By the second year of my schooling, while on a lunch break from our moving job, the company men and CFNI students were talking about my hand strength. Although small, I possessed strong muscles. One of my friends had large muscles and challenged me to a muscle test with him. We ended up wrestling in various positions. Now, my grips were better than his, so I was winning this challenge. However, at one point, I put too much pressure on my legs, and immediately felt a sharp pain go from my wrist down to my leg. For a couple days after, I continued walking with a painful limp that got worse with time. Finally, I said, "Lord, I'm sorry for playing games that appealed more to my vanity then for your glory. I won't go to a doctor because *you* are my only doctor. Here I am! Heal my back and my leg so I can walk and work for your glory. Thank you, Lord for your complete healing!" Slowly, the pain wore off, and as soon as the morning came, there was no more pain. It had disappeared like it had never been an issue. I'm here to tell you – you don't need a better doctor than this One!

A Quickening to Return to Romania

In a significant time of spontaneous prayer, I said to the Lord, "I want to build a Bible school like CFNI in Romania." I then started to praise Him with thanksgiving as I saw this desire as a lifetime dream that would be fulfilled. I prayed this repeatedly. And after praying, I felt a bit dizzy, a little crazy, and stopped to think. I reasoned, "What in the world am I praying for? Surely, this is impossible in Romania!" And since I left illegally, I would never be allowed to do anything if I returned. As a transgressor of communist law, I would become the enemy of the people, and if caught, the secret service judge would sentence me to a prison term. If you were part of the government and were caught, you would typically be sentenced to death. This is because a communist country made it their priority to keep their idolatrous image from being tarnished. They would even lie just to keep themselves appearing superior in the world. This is why I consider the atheist-socialist movement of today to be the most evil religion in the world.

However, with my prayer to start a school, I thought at least I was making the Lord laugh like a father laughs at his baby. But then I thought, "Maybe the Lord understands my heart and perhaps He will accomplish this, communism or no communism. Maybe it could be a strong underground Bible school that will penetrate Romania." I then began to reason with myself, "Why do I need to be praying about this stuff? It would better if I just stop it." But just as I stopped, I realized that my desire didn't come from the mind, but deep within my heart; my spirit just exploded! Naturally speaking, I knew this would be impossible. And a lack of faith entered my thinking as I thought that communism would never be defeated, at least not on this side of the Second Coming. Despite my own doubts, the Lord began to prepare my heart for a return trip to Romania.

We had a guest speaker from California named Chuck Smith who would speak to us for a full week during the 11 AM sessions. After each session he would call the students up and prophesy over each one. And with each positive prophetic word given, I found myself judging the people who were receiving them. I knew several of these students and felt like these friends did not meet the standard of holiness and dedication required to receive such positive words. Honestly, they didn't seem to meet *my* level of commitment to the things of God. Then, little by little, I understood that the prophetic ministry reveals what God intends for an individual, over time and through much preparation. Hopefully, we know that everyone in Christ is destined to be a winner, ministering God's oracles to people around them. The main hindrance will ultimately be me and you, as *we* may be the sole enemies of God's plan for us, through doubt and unbelief.

Seated beside me was a close friend who doubted his prophetic destiny. Despite feeling down, he mustered the courage to respond to Pastor Chuck's alter call. When he returned to his seat, he said, "John, this man truly speaks the truth of God over each one of us. The Lord just spoke to me the same promise I often heard in the past. I was reminded of God's master plan for my life!"

On Friday at 11 AM, it was the last session for brother Chuck to speak at CFNI before flying back to California. I finally decided to go up to the alter all the while reminding Jesus, "I am here for you God. But I have only fifteen minutes to pray before leaving for my weekend moving job. I know, I only have a short time. But if you see it is important to speak to me using this man, please do it!" Looking back, the chances of me being prayed over were slim as there were about one hundred and fifty people lined up to receive a word, packed all around me and in the very back. Humbly, I walked to the back of the crowd. After a few minutes, I heard nothing but silence, with my head bowed down, and eyes closed. Suddenly I heard steps coming closer to me. Next thing I knew, I felt two heavy hands placed on my head, and the voice of Chuck speaking forth:

"Young man, you are from a far east country. And you know I have guided you into this place. Now, I tell you again, you're not with your own people as you wish to be. But I am the Lord who is sending you back to your own people, and family, whom you were with before. Do not worry about how this will happen, or when it might happen; you know that I am the Lord who opens the closed doors. The same door you thought was closed, I am opening again. Those in authority will just usher you in without knowing what they are doing. Those who oppose Me will be taken down. Because I am doing a new thing over you and your country. Just

remember Me! I am the one who opens locked doors. No one will withstand or harm you in any way. And now, I have poured the anointing of favor over your life. And with a little spark in your hand, I will cause a national fire which will come upon the younger generation throughout your land. And they will come to me in the thousands, growing in their knowledge of me. Churches will thrive and be multiplied. And then I will raise up shepherds who will care for my sheep, and souls will be saved and blessed by me, says the Lord!"

This prophetic word came about five years prior to the overthrow of communism in Romania. And with such a powerful word still ringing in my heart and mind, there was nothing left to doubt. I found myself dumbfounded at the love of Jesus who had such wonderful plans for me and my people. I thought, "Who am I that I would be used to do such great things? Surely I am nothing without you Lord!"

The truth was that I had no idea how all of this would happen in Romania. The one thing I knew for sure: God was faithful to His word. After leaving the auditorium, I asked myself, "Does this man understand that my country is in the grip of communism?" It dawned on me that this man didn't know who I was or where I came from as we had never met. And besides, the student body at CFNI had about sixteen hundred students. I was calculating all this in my head to make certain that what I just heard from Pastor Chuck was from the

Lord. But of course, my intellect was just trying to catch up to what I knew in my heart to be true.

Soon after, during a national missions conference at CFNI, I met Ralph Mann who was the founder and president of Mission Possible in Denton, Texas. This ministry was smuggling Bibles and teaching materials into the Eastern European countries. I met with Ralph at his ministry's display table, and after my introduction he asked me, "After graduation, would you be interested in working with Mission Possible?" He then explained to me that since I knew the ins and outs of the communist mentality, I could be cleverer than those in communist governments. To which I replied favorably to the idea, stating my love for those countries still bound in communism. I mentioned my need to first become a U.S. citizen. I said, "If it is God's will, it would be an adventure and risk worth undertaking to go back to Romania and infiltrate it with Bibles."

Graduation & Visas

After I graduated from CFNI in May 1986, I immediately applied for U.S. citizenship. Miraculously, the whole process took only a couple of months. By the month of October, I was naturalized and handed my citizenship certificate. After five years of living in the U.S., I was finally in good standing – me, the traitor from Romania – getting the opportunity to be a part of the greatest country on earth. From now on, I knew that America would fight on my behalf should I need it. Right after, I applied for my passport which I received a short time later.

The next major step of faith was to mail my passport to the Romanian embassy in Washington, asking to be issued a Romanian short-term visa. My instinct was to make the main reason for my request, to see my fiancée Viorica. I believed it to be wisdom to not disclose anything about smuggling Bibles or launching underground church ministry. I put on my application that I intended on marrying Viorica. Because we had written hundreds of love letters over a six-year period, these letters reinforced to all the officials who would see them how much I loved her, and how much I would fight for her, and for our lives together.

I also included the International Marriage Freedom Act article number on my application. This Act was signed by our great president Ceausescu. He signed it into law, allowing every Romanian citizen freedom to marry a man or woman from any civilized country in the world. Since many people in Romania didn't know this law existed, I wrote the article numbers to demonstrate my knowledge of it, that I was legally able to see, and eventually marry, Viorica.

Because of the illegal way I left the country, I concluded my application by stating: "My intention is not at all to give our beloved country a bad image, as I know that would hurt us all; but instead, I am writing so that we may solve this issue with good will and peace. I'm sure you are willing to help us, and may God help you do it." I added this at the end: "I do hope that I will not be forced to read all of this correspondence between Viorica and myself before the U.S. Capitol, should my visa not go through." This I wrote as a subtle warning that I was prepared to go before America's Congress if Romanian law wasn't upheld.

The truth is, not many believed I would be given a visa, especially my Romanian brothers who told me, "No way will you get that visa! Think about it! Your name will be flagged in the system as that of a traitor. You'd be better off not going, because if you attempt to enter, you will likely be arrested. They could invent their own accusation against you, or just kidnap and kill you behind the scenes." However, I knew what the Lord told me, that He was guiding and guarding me. He promised that I would not be harmed in any way, and that the favor of God would follow me.

Marvelously, a couple of weeks later, I received my passport from the embassy. Before receiving it, I thought I might only be granted a one month stay; but it turned out to be two months. This was a miracle of favor, which my Romanian and CFNI friends could hardly believe. Now, I wasn't sure if I had already been sentenced for a prison term during my absence, or if they hadn't even noticed I left; either way, I didn't care. What I needed was a visa, and I got it! God's favor intervened as the Lord clearly told me that I would be back. I just didn't expect it to be *this* easy. It seemed that everything else came quickly too, as though God had accelerated the timing for me. Over the last six months, I graduated college, applied for citizenship, took and passed my citizenship exam, participated in the official citizenship certificate ceremony, acquired my passport, and obtained my Romanian visa.

I was also working hard over this six-month period, preparing for the expenses of the trip. I had some friends seek me out to give me small offerings. Others were afraid they would never see me again, that I might be killed while in Romania, so they came to pray for me. One such friend who was raised on the mission field, found me while I was praying in a classroom. He said, "John, keep praying but wait for me as I need to get something to give to you." After a little while, he came back and gave me about seven hundred dollars. "I went back to my family and raised an offering for you," he said. "I told them with tears that this man John from Romania is leaving and may never return. *Now* is the time to sacrifice with him." What a true missionary heart this young man possessed. He knew what missions really meant. It was a blessing to be knit my heart with these people.

Chapter Eleven

Returning to my Homeland

By the middle of December 1986, I flew from Dallas to Frankfurt, Germany. At the German airport, I was picked up by a Mission Possible missionary, whose home I stayed in for a couple of days. Upon going to the main European office for Mission Possible, we began talking strategies for how to implement an underground ministry in Romania. We decided that the best course of action to begin with was that I first go to see the actual needs inside of the country. It would also provide me with the opportunity to lay a foundation with the people I knew and trusted.

About a week before Christmas, I boarded the train from Frankfurt, to Timisoara, Romania. I was carrying with me three heavy suitcases, about seventy pounds each, as there was no weight limit for bags yet. In addition, there was no such thing as checking in bags before train trips; you were required to carry all your luggage with you, stowing it in either the hallway or the compartments where you were seated. This made my trip more difficult, not simply because of the physical burden this created, but also because I needed to make sure none of my things were stolen. So instead of sleeping, I ended up spending two days, through three countries, completely awake so that I could keep an eye on all my belongings before reaching Romania.

When I finally arrived in my dear country, I was physically exhausted. However, it made for a more adventurous and exciting trip. And now, I would once again experience the Socialist Romanian society. At the border of Curtici, the customs officers were shocked to find that a Romanian American man was trying to enter. And one with an American passport! They asked, "But you were born in Romania? What brought you back here? Did you leave Romania legally or did you defect? What are the contents of your bags? Bibles? Anti-communist propaganda? Weapons?" I then showed them my bags, as all I carried with me were clothes and sweet gifts for my large family.

They proceeded to tell me that I had too much luggage and so they would need to take me down to the customs office, where they would do a more thorough check of me, including examining my passport. I was placed in a private waiting room, where the officers spent an hour and half investigating all that I owned. As they finished up, I heard the train leave the station which made this whole situation even more tense; for I knew that there was no going back now. This was a good opportunity to trust in the Lord who was in control.

The officers inquired, "How in the world did you get a visa since you are still considered a traitor to Romania? You should know, when people have committed treason against a Socialist State, we suspect that their visas might be fake." They further instructed me that I needed to be held here so they could request that the Interior Minister of Bucharest confirm that my visa is valid. This meant that I needed to stay the night as the government didn't resume their duties till the morning.

It was now the second day, when at noon I heard another train make its way in and out of the station toward Timisoara. And here I was, still in my temporary prison, not able to board as they had told me that the Bucharest office placed a call to the Washington embassy and that they had to wait until Washington got back with them. Because of the time difference, they needed to wait until it was morning on the East Coast of America. I felt that this might be an excuse to discourage me from entering the country. However, through it all, I was not scared but encouraged, full of boldness toward these officers. I said, "Why in the world would you not trust the Romanian embassy in Washington? They answer to Romania, *not* America!"

After a while, a couple of the men who were in the office started to act friendlier toward me, treating me as an equal. By now, they were convinced that I was not afraid of them. The truth is, I didn't care about any threat they could make because I was in God's hands, not theirs. I kept reminding them, "I am a Romanian! Can't you hear my accent? Why are you treating me like a vagabond – worse than a foreigner?! If I am a citizen, which it clearly says on my passport, why keep me here? It's your problem and not the Washington embassy. They are kind people. Even the government of Bucharest, including President Ceausescu agrees with the embassy's judgment. International law is also on my side, allowing people all over the world to come and go back to their home countries. You guys are worse than centralized government!"

With this rant, the officers were a little confused as to why I was putting all of this onto them. I was bold! But I became sympathetic, and even started joking around with them. Based on their reaction, it was like they were experiencing the speech of a free man for the first time. This is exactly the kind of reformation in the body politic that the Soviet Union began to undergo with the *Perestroika* initiative. In the case of the Soviets, President Gorbechev was attempting to deconstruct some of the heavier, more totalitarian practices that crushed the people, so that individuals could exercise more freedom within the economy and other parts of the culture.

I realized afterward that my conversation with these officers was good training as I was gaining wisdom on how to reach the communist mindset with my newfound spiritual authority. Today, we could use a good dose of wisdom in an increasingly socialistic world, where the societal elites decide what the law should be; meanwhile, the actual written laws are hidden from the public's eyes. For socialism to work, a group of people must convince the rest of society that the means justify the ends, no matter how evil those means are. It is a system that depends on mind control. If a person finds themselves in a full-blown socialist society, he or she should be "wise as serpents, innocent as doves." In other words, the truth should be spoken of in parables, where what is right is hinted at instead of blasted on the rooftops. However, there are other times when we need to be bold as lions. I did this with the officers as I told them, "I am a native of Romania, as are you. I was born here so I should have all the rights that you do." I said this bluntly to make them feel a bit uncomfortable, and ultimately get them to be more favorable toward me.

I spent a total of 24 hours in the waiting room from the time I came upon the train from Germany. But I used as many opportunities as possible to witness to the men about Jesus and salvation. They dared to ask about American life, which led to their change of opinion on America in a positive way. What wasn't clear to them was why I would risk coming back to Romania. I thought about it and realized that whenever the devil wants you to believe you're on dangerous ground, you are probably in the right place. Before boarding my train to Timisoara, they had apologized for holding me so long. But jokingly, they said that I was the one who won this battle. After wishing me luck and safe travels in Romania, I departed.

Now, in the early morning I arrived in Timisoara station. It was three days and four nights since I last slept. I gave all the glory to the Lord who gave me Herculean strength in the process, keeping me awake and alert as I didn't feel sleepy throughout my ordeal. From the train station in Timisoara, I picked up a taxi ride to my sister Flory's flat address. And how miraculous an event it was to see her again! When I had assembled a small team of friends to begin some ministry in a certain town, she left to minister in another town. We unexpectedly reconnected on Sunday morning. And at last,

I was able to catch up on some much-needed sleep, right before making our way to catch the train to my parents' home in Rachita. From that point on, I had no more trouble readjusting to Romanian time. Thank God!

As I got reacquainted with Romanian life, I was invited by many pastors to preach in their services. I ministered to the underground meetings as well. Most church activity was done in Suceava and Timisoara, as well as around the country. My Mission Possible underground work was not known by anyone, and I had to make direct contact in private with the leaders of this movement. I didn't disclose this part of my life to anyone, not even my family. It was necessary for their safety, along with the safety of those in the underground network. Viorica knew about it only after we settled in America.

Beyond just Bibles and teaching materials, Romanians lacked medicine and nutritional supplements as most of these disappeared from the public pharmacies. Here, I saw a human crisis which required someone to do something. Basic food supplies were hard to find, like bread and milk, which were bought using ration cards. A few times I tried to buy a loaf of bread without a ration card with my name on it, but the cashiers refused to sell to me. The communist system was on life-support! While I saw people dying from treatable diseases, like basic infections and common colds, I was angry that there were little in the way of antibiotics and cold medicine. Coming from my time in America, it was heartbreaking to see how little we had in Romania, and how little I could do to help. I thought, "How can we preach salvation and teach disciples to grow, when we see the same people hungry and sick. Aren't we supposed to first give them a lifeboat? Let's feed and treat them, getting them to higher, healthier ground, so that they are well enough to hear the word and obey its truth.

Warned to Watch My Steps

I met with many leaders and pastors, many of whom told me to be careful as I was being closely followed. They warned me of so-called friends who were set up to track me down, reporting back to the secret service. I wasn't careless as I had lived in this dangerous country for most of my life, but the threat seemed to worsen. Although I didn't focus on my safety, there was a concern that if I took a trip with people I thought knew and could trust, they could turn out to be government agents tasked to create a fake incident, causing injuries or death.

One such person I was advised about was senior Pastor Vasile who lived in Suceava. He was a native of Arbore where I was born and knew me since I was a child. Some people suggested that because he maintained a good relationship with the police, that he was someone around whom I should be cautious. But he was in good standing with the police for noble reasons, as most church pastors were required to show up for police appointments. And many of these pastors were there defending the church's worshiping rights, and their building projects which were not easily approved. To become skeptical of these pastors, and cast a shadow on their motives, was to side with evil as these pastors were the men who stood up against tyranny, for the sake of the church. This was true especially of Pastor Vasile, who suffered persecution all the while advocating for fellow believers.

He warned me, saying, "John, please be very careful because your sermons in the churches are being listened to by the secret service department. And as your brother, I'm telling you: watch your steps! Watch out for those who call themselves "friends." Those who want to hang around you may be telling the secret service about your travel plans and schedule. Don't announce to people where you will be or what you will be doing."

Chapter Twelve

A Romanian Love Story

This next season of my life would truly be a time of fulfillment as God had a divine appointment waiting. When I had presented myself to the Romanian embassy in Washington, my main reason was to get a visa in order to go back to my country and marry my fiancée. And this happened exactly when my life and ministry were established in the Lord. If you recall, the Lord had told me that there were three things that needed to happen before I was ready for my wife. The first was for me to leave Romania for America. The second was to complete schooling at Christ For the Nations. And third was to re-enter the ministry field back in Romania with Mission Possible.

It is fascinating that the first organization I joined when returning to Romania was in fact Mission Possible, not Christ

For the Nations. The Lord reminded me that, like the name "Mission Possible," there would always be a mission for me, for with the Lord, *everything* mission was possible!

Was Marriage for Me?

I had never seen marriage as my biggest priority, nor was I excited about it. As such, I was a bit older when it became a real possibility. I was also more selective as to who I wanted as my life partner. I didn't want to choose the wrong person, as it could compromise my future life and ministry. By comparison, leaving Romania was easier than figuring out marriage! I would also become easily discouraged when meeting an attractive girl who, besides her appearance, had questionable character.

Let me illustrate this point. A couple of years before I escaped Romania, I loved this blonde girl named Rodica. I wanted her to be mine, even though I had not yet asked the Lord. While serving in Timisoara, actively training the underground groups, we would have openings on our mission teams for girls to join us. However, we would make sure not to pair women with men. Rodica was a spiritual sister, very beautiful, who would on occasion become part of my group. We already saw each other at various Bible study meetings. And we began to grow too close, too quickly. When we were together, we would talk a lot about marriage, family, and what continuing in missional work would look like. Although we never talked directly about marrying one another, nor was I ready to ask her hand in marriage, we talked seriously about the subject. And I intended to ask for her hand only when I was one hundred percent sure she was for me. After we knew for sure, we would have an in-depth conversation about life priorities, interests, and everything else. And only then would we get married, because once married, we would be married for life. So, this was no light commitment. Even the rest of the world seemed to follow in the Christian's footsteps of total commitment in marriage. So, it was in communist Romania, as the government saw the wisdom in doing their part to keep marriages intact.

I believe that Rodica was likely expecting me to ask her to marry me, but I was not certain and undecided about it. I discovered that her preferred place to live was back in the city of her birth, in the region of Moldova. This was one of the first indications that our future could be diverging in two directions. What was favorable about her was that she had a strong desire to release her husband freely into the ministry, while she would take care of the home. A woman who wanted to support her husband in his pursuit for the Lord's work looked like the *perfect* woman!

However, I had a growing uneasiness which began to saturate my soul to the point that it became uncomfortable. It was a mix of affection and fear. Somehow, I felt pressured to get on with my proposal of marriage, or just let her go. One night while praying in my room at my flat, I said to the Lord, "Here I am! I need to know once and for all about this relationship. I want to know so that tomorrow I can deliver her a 'yes' or a 'no.' If the answer is the former, then I will stand by it no matter what you may say later. If you don't want to answer me, and I miss the mark, it's on you. I need you to decide for I am terribly confused. If Rodica is not the right one, then take her out of my heart and mind; but if by tomorrow nothing has changed, then in the evening when we meet, I will ask her to marry me. Lord, the ball is now in your hands."

I'm not sure how long I was praying for it felt like forever. But I just loved spending sweet fellowship time in His presence. I don't even remember how or when I went to bed, just that I was praying one moment, and the sound of my alarm clock going off the next moment. I got out of bed to get ready for work, feeling so good that I had forgotten about last night's praying. The birds were singing joyfully outside the window on the trees. It seemed right to investigate why I felt so good, when suddenly my memory was restored and remembered the contents of my prayer time. The next thought was about Rodica. I searched my heart to see how I felt about her, and try as might, I couldn't find her anywhere! She was out of my mind as well, and instead of thinking about her romantically, I only thought of her as a sister. I was purely amazed how my heart and mind had changed. It reminded me that with God, *all* things are possible!

I started to pray again, asking the Lord to be clear with me about my future. "Maybe you are trying to tell me not to get married at all," I said, "If so, better tell me now so that I will keep a safe distance from every girl I like. Then, I will make my decision as well, since you gave me free will, right?" A few minutes later the Lord spoke clearly to me saying, "Your request has been granted. But remember, I have all the time in heaven and earth to fulfill my word to you. You will know when the time is right. I will pick up a flower from my own garden and give it to you – a proper helper to stand beside you for your lifetime and ministry. But it should not be your concern to seek her out. Instead, you will receive it as a gift from my hand. But first, you will pass through three seasons in your journey before you see the fulfillment of my word. I want

239

you to establish the work I've called you to do for me. Then, your helper will come alongside to share in your journey."

Confirming the Marriage

Viorica and I were not officially engaged when I called her my fiancée. We had not made anything public between us; however, we gave each other the simple promise that one day we would be betrothed. The last time I visited her town in Arbore, it was around one month before escaping Romania. There was a special moment between us when I took a big step to deepen our commitment toward a shared future. I asked her, "If the Lord's will for us is to marry, then will you follow me wherever God takes us – whether in Romania, Asia, Africa, or America? Will you be content to be poor or rich without becoming negative?" She vowed, "Yes, I will! And I will be happy anywhere in the world, as long as I can be with you."

Next, I told her, "Still, we need to pray so that our love is sealed for a future marriage date which only God knows. Because we don't know the life events that will need to come before our union." From that point in time we promised to stay connected, by phone or by letter, regardless of where we were. Although she might have understood I was planning on leaving the country, she didn't know any details about my plan. This was mainly because while in Timisoara, Ioan, Viorel, and I vowed that no one else should know about our covenant before God to escape.

This was a very simple, but sincere vow of engagement, which required a real walk of faith in order to finally arrive at a marriage ceremony. Humanly speaking, once I left the country, it would be a miracle for Viorica and I to be reunited. The only immediate solution was to be married before fleeing from Romania. But this would not be the wisest move, as we recognized a higher plan coming from God, which required us to put our trust in Him. This was a time where, Like Abraham, our path was going to require faith in Christ, leading us out of our native land and into the unknown.

Now, the first week after I arrived in Austria, I wrote Viorica and my parents a greeting card as I began fulfilling my promise to her – to keep in touch with each other. This was the beginning of a six-year correspondence, where I would write a letter and mail it with a separate post card; Viorica did the same. For our own security purposes, we would create a special notification on each piece of mail that a second letter had been sent. This way, if one letter was confiscated by the secret service, another would arrive. Sure enough, there were many letters held by the government during this time.

In the first year, after I arrived in America, I took a year off from writing Viorica and she did the same. We did this because I was traveling a lot, and my address would frequently change. All my extra time was spent learning English, and the first several months I carried my English book everywhere as though it were my Bible. I would take it into recreational parks & stores, reading it loudly. I also believed that taking some time off from writing my fiancée would grow us in faith and in endurance. Indeed, we were allowing God to weld us together in the Spirit, so that once we came together, we'd be welded for life. After one year, when I settled in one place, I wrote a letter and a post card from Waco, Texas. I was wondering how she was doing, and to see where her faith in our union stood, because the love and commitment in a long-distance relationship can evaporate if faith doesn't stand. But I knew in my heart she was a special girl who was strong in faith. She wrote back to me saying, "I am the same as always! I've never changed in what I believe about you, no matter the circumstances around us. I am still here, waiting for the Lord's miracle to bring us back together some day."

Viorica didn't doubt our relationship at all because the Lord had spoken to her. You see, she had a vision one morning while lying awake in bed. She saw me at the door of her room, standing there, just smiling at her. So surprised to see me there, she jumped out of bed to meet me at the door. She exclaimed, "How did you get here, John?" At that moment, I immediately disappeared from her sight. It was clear that she had received a vision from the Lord. Understandably, she was pained by the vision as I wasn't there but was reassured that I was the man she would marry.

Now, she didn't tell anyone about her convictions, but asked God to confirm the vision if the vision was real and meant we were to be married. And so, Viorica attended an underground prayer meeting in Casvana, where a prophet was visiting from another part of Romania. There were a lot of people jammed into a large living room. And during the prayer time, the prophet came up to her and said, "You, young lady. The Lord is confirming what you asked of Him. The vision you got in the morning while you lay awake in bed – it was from the Lord. And the man you have seen in your vision is the one whom I have destined for you. And surely, it will come to pass as you wait patiently in faith. But do not waver, even amid challenging circumstances. Don't give up! He will come to see you. And don't let your own house or anyone else discourage you." This was a defining moment for my wife, which strengthened her and prepared her for the ministry that awaited both of us in the future.

Receiving prophetic confirmation concerning the person you want to marry is crucial, as it creates an impenetrable wall of certainty. To just say, "We should get married, sweetheart. It's God's will for us. Just trust me!" is a subtle form of manipulation, especially when one or both of you haven't heard the confirming word of God. Viorica and I made sure to allow each other the freedom to choose another life partner if that's what we felt in our hearts. We wanted each other to be in the will of God. I'd say to her, "Please, my dear, I know you might be tired of waiting for me. It's like an endless horizon, isn't it? I just want you to be fulfilled and happy all your life – strong and faithful in the Lord. If we do not get the chance to be together in this lifetime, at least we will see each other again in heaven." What's amazing, is that freedom of choice creates real happiness for all people. Isn't it odd then, that we demand social and political freedom, but insist on keeping others in bondage to ourselves? This is why Viorica and I placed so much value on giving each other the ability to choose who we would spend our lives with.

Viorica's Unwavering Faith

I was a legal resident of America for about five years, and Viorica tried hard to apply for a Romanian passport to join me. If she got one, it would be easy for her to receive the American engagement visa, and then she could fly over to be with me. Every so often I encouraged her to work on it, without putting too much stress on her, as I knew this process could be extremely stressful. But she was very diligent in her persistence, just like the widow in Jesus' parable, continuously knocking at the judge's door until she got justice. Viorica would ride the bus about sixty miles, back and forth from Suceava to put pressure on the police station emigration department. And from the moment she applied for a passport, she suffered their mockery and persecution, as they did their best to discourage her. They'd say things like, "Oh, we know *him*! We've heard that he is traveling all over like a vagabond, living a hedonistic lifestyle with multiple women, lying and cheating to get by."

Six years after I left Romania, I returned to Timisoara. This was right after I received the Romanian visa and passport. I wrote Viorica just before, and said, "If the Romanian government won't allow you to come marry me here, I will come to you! You're about to be a married girl!" After arriving in Timisoara one late afternoon, I decided to first take another train to Rachita, which is where my parents had moved to, located on the west side of the country. Although I told them beforehand that I was arriving, they were shocked to see me again so quickly, and that I was able to re-enter the country. It was as though they were speaking to me after rising from the dead. I was reminded of the prophetic word received six years prior from the old woman in Radauti town. She spoke of me leaving the country and then returning to a happy reunion. "Hey mom and dad" I said, "just remember that we can never treat the Lord's word lightly, as He is well able to fulfill it every time!"

I came a long way from America and was planning to see Viorica in Suceava very soon. But instead, she wished to do something special for me, as I had traveled so far. She took a twelve-hour train ride from Suceava to Rachita to celebrate my return. And what a joyous time of thanksgiving it was to see one another, meeting each other on my parent's doorstep. In my parent's new home, she and I got to inaugurate a new way of life, as the years of separation between us began to melt away.

However, after Viorica and I arrived back in Timisoara, the local police of Suceava, Timisoara, and Rachita sounded their collective alert system. To them, a dangerous traitor had returned, and it was time to hunt him down. Although they knew I entered legally, they were afraid I might exit again illegally, but this time with Viorica. Here, again, I became a dangerous felon that needed to be watched closely. We were unaware that they were tracking us down, investigating each place we went, interrogating people we talked to, all in attempt to see where we would be going next. We found this out later, and that the Lord allowed this hunting game to continue yet protecting us each step of the way.

A couple days after I found this out, I went to Rachita's police station, and gave them this notice: "Hey guys! I am here to stay now. But you don't have to be intimidated by me. I'm a good guy. And from this point, I will do everything legally. My fiancée and I will be married according to your laws." I found out that according to Romanian law, any foreigner staying less than twenty-four hours in one place, was not required to announce his presence to the police. And since I had been back, I kept moving from one place to another, not knowing that the police couldn't pick me up because I was complying with that law. What a blessing to be led by God's wisdom even when you aren't aware of it!

Now, after Christmas, Viorica and I rode the train to Arbore, where she lived, which was also close to my birthplace.

It was a yearly routine that on the second day of the New Year, the church of Arbore had a special youth service where mostly young people were involved. A few times in the past I ministered in this service, and really wanted to make it back there. My presence in that service stirred up the towns around, and many people came out just to see me, as I was the main speaker. Everyone was witnessing the miracle of this fugitive man who returned safely to his people. They knew I came back as an American citizen, so they called me the "American man." They'd say, "The American man is back with us!"

They especially wanted to see the joy in my strong-headed fiancée, who believed against all odds that she would see me again and that we'd be married. Many of the regional pastors discouraged her over the years, saying, "This is an unreal expectation and may never come to pass. You should instead be free to find someone else to marry before it's too late, and before you find yourself to be too old." The fact is, she even received several proposals of marriage during our separation. However, she would disappoint them by her vivid faith that she would once again see the man she loved. She became the heroine of this story, who received her promise at long last. The only people who were not excited were the young men, disappointed by her refusal to marry them. But what is undeniable is that one person's unstoppable faith will build up, and infuse with joy, the hearts of everyone around.

A Painful Flashback

About three months before my trip back to Romania and the joyful reunion with beautiful Viorica, a painful experience occurred that affected all of us, especially my fiancée and her family. Their precious, forty-eight-year-old mother, Paraschiva, died of a rapidly developing cancer. I was already in America for several months before finding out about this tragedy. Viorica sent me an emergency letter telling me to pray for the healing of her mother, as she had just been diagnosed. From that moment I was interceding before God, praying fervently for the healing of Paraschiva. I remember well the late evening that I was praying at a CFNI upstairs classroom, and the Spirit of God spoke audibly to me saying, "Do not intercede for her anymore, as Paraschiva is already here with us in heaven, and her body has been buried." I was shocked and I was trembling inside. I wasn't sure if I had heard correctly. I started to pray again but found it difficult just to form words. I simply said, "Your will be done. Now, please comfort Viorica, her sisters and father." Feeling a bit angry, I left the room without talking to anyone. From that moment I was not able to pray healing anymore, only for Viorica and her family.

About a week after this experience, I received a letter from Viorica which I was afraid to open. The first thing I observed upon opening it were the tear spots that had been dropped onto those white pages. Then came the written words, announcing that her mom had died and was with the Lord. The date of death was about a week before the time I started praying for her. And while reading the letter, I knew the whole family was in morning. Viorica was the second oldest of eight sisters who were left without a mother. Because the oldest sibling was married, the duty fell on Viorica to act as a sibling mom. It was also necessary for Viorica to train the third oldest, Dina, in anticipation of our getting married and her no longer being at home.

What's significant looking back, is that Viorica and I shared a love story that was mixed with joy and pain. There were times when one of us seemed to me winning while the other was suffering loss. Often, the bad news that one of us experienced, would be followed closely by good news in the other's life. However, Viorica and her whole family was comforted by the hope that at last, we could see each other, and go through the sufferings and joys *together*.

The Legal Battle for Marriage Begins

For the next stage in my journey with Viorica, it is important to understand how the communist system works. There was no emigration office, just the governmental militia which acted as the foreign affairs department. The only emigration document needed was a Romanian passport, and no one could get one without being approved for a visit or to emigrate to another country. And if a citizen wanted to visit another country, when they came back, they were immediately required to return their passport to the governmental office. Compare this with America at the time. The American government was very accommodating to those wanting to come in or out of their country. Acquiring a visa both to visitors and those wanting to emigrate was almost guaranteed. In Romania, however, the government became the iron wall keeping people in, or allowing people to leave; citizens of Romania were at their mercy.

Viorica and I had our first appointment at the government office so that her marriage to me could be approved, after which time they would issue a passport. This would be an easy process anywhere else – *not* in this iron-walled society. Typically, this request would take up to a couple of years for approval, however, most of the time it would be rejected. We needed a miracle!

Once in the office, we stood side-by-side, standing as tall as possible (although I am a shorter man, I trusted that heaven would make me appear taller!) We had a strong resolve in that room, coming across as though we would not leave until they granted our request. I began, "Don't you see, we were made for each other!" I made the strongest case that I could, holding Viorica very close to me, showing them that there was no separation between us. They did their best to discourage us, warning and threatening us and trying to do whatever they could to discredit any idea that suggested we were good for one another. But to no avail! They had seen our unmovable faith in one another and allowed us to file for marriage.

We were warned that these documents might take a long time to be approved by the central government in Bucharest. Furthermore, since my two-month visa was about to expire, they told me I needed to leave the country before my expiration date, or else I would be arrested. But I was tough with them. I stood my ground, reminding them, "I will not leave until we have our marriage certificate in our hands. I don't care if you have to throw me out of the country." I also repeatedly asked them for a visa extension, but they denied my request. I did my best to assure them I would comply with their rules if they could just extend my visa another month. But they would continue to hedge, asking if the American Embassy in Bucharest knew about my marriage proposal. I affirmed it. I told them that the U.S. Embassy issued me a document for engagement, which proved that the Americans knew of it. The fact is that the communist mindset was threatened anytime their image could potentially be tarnished in front of the rest of the world.

By the end of the month, we received the official approval to get married. Spiritually speaking, we knew this approval would come, as God already approved of our union in heaven; the natural government had no choice! Now, the next step was to have all the documents ready for the legal marriage. This process, like most others in Romania, tended to be bogged down by bureaucracy. Even today, there are still some remnants of this bureaucratic dirt that needs to be washed away. But we had our official approval and we were determined to reach our promised land. We presented ourselves before the city hall mayor of Arbore. We had a very small and simple ceremony with only our closest relatives, as it was wise to not create a big event which could stir up descent around town, causing the secret service to investigate us. Besides, we wanted to celebrate the most joyous moments of our lives in as intimate a setting as possible. And we did not want to schedule our larger, openly religious ceremony until we could make certain that we got our marriage certificate to safeguard against any delays.

Now, my visa expiration was approaching, and the police ordered me to leave the country. This needed immediate attention, because being late even just a few hours would give them cause to arrest me. I was firm with them and said that there was no way I would leave the country until Viorica and I had our religious marriage ceremony as well. We didn't want to merely be recognized by the State in the civil ceremony; we recognized God as a higher authority, and so getting married in the Church and surrounded by brothers and sisters in Christ, was essential. And once again, the favor of God fell on us, as I got an extension for my visa for another month. Of course, Romanian officials ridiculed me, saying that I was disrespectful of their laws, and unruly to continue badgering them about wanting more time. But I said to myself, "If they decide to get rid of me, by killing me somehow – if God allows it – then it would be alright, as I was not fully married and wouldn't be leaving a wife on earth." However, I knew Viorica would miss me, and it would be too hard for the family to lose another person.

Set Up to be Killed

I was needed for a family event in Timisoara right after I had severely angered the secret service, asking for a visa extension. I had to go it alone as Viorica had a lot of work to do to finish up preparations to leave the country with me; besides this, she was helping her orphaned sisters, and keeping an appointment for her passport papers. Mistakenly, I told a passport police officer that I couldn't be available for her next appointment, as I had to go to Timisoara for an emergency family event. Then, he asked me when and what time I was leaving. Naively, I told him, "I'm probably going to take the late afternoon train tomorrow."

Now, everything went fine on this trip until I reached the city of Cluj. Here, all my compartment travelers got off the train, and from Cluj to Oradea only one man came on, occupying the empty compartment where I sat. Right before he came in, he started to talk to me, mostly provoking me and prying into what I believe. I realized his mission was to challenge and contradict who I was, where I was coming from, and what I believed. He looked like a man of average education, was witty, aggressive, and similar in age. He was strongly built, with big muscles, possibly a weightlifter. I could smell alcohol on his breath, and it was clear that something was not right with this person. Although I didn't reveal my American status, or the Christian confession I adhered to, he already knew about it.

I then told myself, "Ok, this man is a little drunk and is behaving strangely. But he sure needs Christ." So, I didn't talk about anything having to do with the western world and America. Instead, I said, "Man, countries are the same everywhere we go. And why? Because no country offers much more than the next. We know that the whole world is under the curse of original sin. And so, the happiness of men is lacking the same everywhere. But only a joyful heart is capable of experiencing a good life – even in Romania!" He then became interested in hearing more about God, especially because of how convinced I was of God's existence. He asked, "Does he really care for *everyone?*" And from that point, I told him the whole truth of the Gospel, that Jesus is real and can be known by each person. Furthermore, I said, "Jesus would have come for just one person, because he is the lover of sinners. And you know what else? Jesus is present – right here, right now! He knows the innermost parts of your being, what you are thinking, and what you desire. You see, He knew ahead of time that we would be in this compartment together. This is a divine appointment. He asks you to repent, which is to change your mind! He is ready to show you His forgiveness for all your sins."

By now, he was dumbfounded, looking amazed at what he had heard. It's like he never heard these words before, and I knew that it was the Spirit of God speaking through me to this man. At last, he started to groan a lot, and became afraid to look at me, but was looking out the window. With his eyes still averted, I couldn't help but see the irony; he was formerly a tiger of a man, but now he had become like a little lamb. He then told me, "I know why I'm here, and what I was supposed to do. But I will take a risk and *not* do it. Because I see the God you believe in is true. This is the first time that I have heard Him introduced the way you have here. In the past, I could only dream about whether God existed. And now, I will wish you the best. Thanks for caring enough to speak to me. And remember, please pray for me to your God that I may be forgiven of the gross sins I've committed in this life. And if possible, that He would change my heart, because I am afraid to meet this God you speak of." Then, he stood up quickly, picked up his little bag and left in a hurry.

I continued on the train to Oradea station and there was still about thirty minutes until this man was supposed to get off. As I was pondering why he left so suddenly, I heard the inner voice of the Spirit speaking to me, saying, "He ran out so fast because he didn't want to change his mind about his mission and hurt you in anyway." I became aware of how perilous this situation could have been, that I had been taken out of the jaws of some evil. I believed that this man was going to throw me out of the train window, as most of the train lights were off, and the people were sleeping in the surrounding compartments. I felt safe in the hands of the Lord. So, I just thanked God for His quick intervention. Then, I reminded myself that this kind of near-death situation has happened to many holy giants in Romania. Those who were killed were lied about by the government, which pronounced these deaths as suicides. This was a rescue story that makes me wonder about the many times God has done this in our lives, and yet we have not been aware of it! But I'm sure that we will be shown all the moments where we were snatched out of the jaws of death, once we arrive in heaven.

Our Joyous Marriage Celebration

At last, we were able to hold our marriage ceremony in Rachita, in the county of Timis, where my parents and two of my sisters lived. The church where this was set to take place was rather small, as it was held in an extension of a home that they remodeled and enlarged. But because it was in the country, and the pastor was friends with the town's mayor, getting approval for us to move the service outside was easy, and the front yard was much more spacious. We had relatives, pastors, and friends coming from Suceava as well as Timisoara and the surrounding areas. All included, we had a few hundred guests show up, with the ceremony spanning over four hours.

In the afternoon, we went to my parent's home where they had a large tent set up in their orchard for the marriage meal. Part of the evening was spent in an evangelistic fervor, as people were sharing the gospel with their neighbors, people with whom they were friends and those they didn't know. Many bold men and women took this evangelism into the surrounding areas as well, singing special songs and sharing evangelistic messages. We knew this would be a great opportunity to reach those people who we normally wouldn't have any contact with. Who wouldn't want to come to such a celebration? Furthermore, since Romania was experiencing a food shortage, this event would provide sustenance for many people. Most of all, this time was used to demonstrate the love and power of God's kingdom, as we had such a freedom in His presence to proclaim God's goodness amid an atheistic society. Many of our friends would remind us of this event for years to come.

Our Final Push to Leave Romania

Marrying Viorica was like the proverbial fairy tale. I felt like the prince who had to go through hell and high water to finally marry his princess. While still in Romania, we were working hard to get Viorica approved to join me in America. Unfortunately, this cast a shadow on the beginning of our marriage. For the last three months, we spent a good amount of time in Bucharest working to acquire emigration documents. Although I had my American passport, and Viorica had her Romanian identity card, we were immediately rejected at all the hotels, even the intercontinental ones. This was likely because I was still on a Romanian blacklist. And so, along with the stress induced from the passport process, we were forced to stay in the two-room apartments of some of our friends. Being crammed into small rooms with tiny beds is a good picture of what living in a communist country looks like.

My visa had been renewed for another month, but as I approached my fourth month, I was strictly warned by government officials, "Mr. Dolinschi, from now on, you will not receive any more visa extensions. Just prepare your luggage and be ready to leave at least one day before the visa's expiration. We've already been very generous with you. We've been lenient, giving you time until you got married. Now that your main goal has been reached, this is the time to leave. Your wife will leave soon after." But again, I told them, "You're right when you say, 'your time is coming.' But I will leave only when I am hand-in-hand with my dearest wife." They replied, "No way, this is just impossible. This process takes anywhere from six months to one year, to legally process all necessary documents so she can leave too." I responded, "In no way would I ever leave without her. You can't separate us either! That would be cruel and merciless."

They looked at me and then at each other, as though thinking, "This man is crazy! Must be why he keeps getting what he wants." I then told them, "I know president Ceausescu signed the Helsinki International Marriage Freedom act, stating that after a Romanian and a foreign spouse get a marriage certificate, the couple is free to go and choose between the foreigner's country or stay in Romania. But this international legislation doesn't mention anything about a certain separation time for a married couple. So, I am standing with our president who said that married couples can stay together and not be separated, no matter what the local laws say. So why not just give me that extension? Thank you!"

On the last day, before my visa expired, they gave me another month extension, without any issues. At that point, Viorica and I began working to get the passport approval we needed. This process took longer than we wanted, but stacks of official papers needed to be filed, like criminal records, duties to the State, bank records, and so on. On top of all that, a person had to deal with all of the bureaucracy involved in wanting to leave the country, which would typically take weeks until resolved. But when all was said and done, we only needed six months of preparation to be ready to fly out of Romania. The miracle in this process was that until communism was overthrown in December 1989, there wasn't one account of another couple who left the country six months after getting married. It may have happened, but we had not heard about it. All who heard our story thought of it as a miracle from God.

Once Viorica obtained her American visa along with her Romanian passport, she would be considered a legal resident of America as soon as she stepped onto U.S. soil. All of this was made possible by an unmovable faith, amid great opposition. She was not allowed to leave the country with me, as she needed to fly out of the Bucharest airport. On the other hand, I needed to leave the way I came in – by train. This is a good example of how a socialistic system controls each movement its citizens make.

I wanted to make sure I made it to Frankfurt airport before Viorica, so I could be there when she arrived. It was out of Frankfurt, Germany, that we would fly to America. Thankfully, my train ride and her plane ride dovetailed perfectly, as we met up in the terminal and made our way to the land of freedom. This concluded six long years of patiently waiting for one another. And we had compiled a large suitcase full of the love letters and post cards which we mailed weekly to one another over that time. Looking back, the number of pages written was staggering, and would easily eclipse the number of pages in this book.

Harassed One Final Time

Just before leaving Romania, I faced a final test. I was at the same customs service gate where I entered just six months prior, being held for twenty-four hours. Viorica was on her way to Bucharest to meet me in Frankfurt. But now, I naively thought I could get out of the country safely and without issue: not so!

Before getting to the border, I made sure to pick up all Romanian issued documents, in whatever home or office I had left them. I grabbed identity and professional cards, job training certificates, school diplomas, and my military bulletin record. I also packed valuable things of a personal nature, like my childhood pictures, part of Viorica's letters and post cards written over our six-year separation, as well as our wedding pictures and several underdeveloped photo films. We were blissfully forgetful that Romania was still gripped by the iron-clad communist system.

As I made it to the customs office, a man came out to check passports and luggage. When he got to my passport, he stepped back in shock, looking at the American passport with my name on it. He said, "Wow! You are that Dolinschi man. You've been in Romania for quite some time on this visit." I replied, "Yes, but it has been legal. Look at all of my extended visas please." He then checked through my passport, and said, "I see that. Six months in a row! How come? Are you a diplomatic person? It seems that you stayed for another reason. What might that be?" I answered, "Yes! I was married, and so they extended my time here so that it could be done officially, once and for all!"

He then sternly declared, "I need to check your luggage thoroughly, piece by piece. Wait here, as I need more help." He then went into the train hallway and called out for two other officers. I overheard him saying, "Guys! The American man is here. Come help." The three of them found my former documents, all those issued in Romania, after which the man in charge said, "He is not entitled to have these anymore. These belong to the State." He then faced me and said, "These items are only legal in Romania, and need to stay here." I asked, "Could I have the Romanian driver's license, as this was with me while in America, and it was my driving license for my first year there. It is an international card that I can use in the States, as well as in Europe." They looked at one another, and returned the card back to me, looking proud that a Romanian card was internationally recognized. After a while, however, they snuck the card back and hid it from me; I never saw it again.

They discovered my pictures, the photo films, the letters and post cards, and confiscated them. I asked them, "Why did you take my personal things from me? Why do you need them? They are just the love letters between me and my wife. Everything went through the governmental post office. Please, you can look at them, but give them back to me." But they said bluntly, "We don't have enough time to look at each of them before your train leaves. We can give you back the ones we have time enough to look at. Unless you want to leave on the next train. But you will need to buy another ticket as the one you have will not be valid." I reminded him about the twenty-four hours we had already spent here, and that it was enough time. So, I said "No. I must hurry so we can catch our plane to America."

Then, they affirmed, "We will send your belongings to your address either in Romania or America. But we need to check them and make sure they are safe to return to you." But we never got anything back from them. A year later I made an inquiry about them and received this reply: "We've got nothing here from the last year – all the materials were destroyed." Now, had I compromised with the Romanian government I would not have been treated like an enemy. If they couldn't kill me, then the next best thing would be to destroy my valuables.

Fortunately for me, they could never take the most valuable of God's gifts from me – my wife Viorica.

Chapter Thirteen

They Needed Spies

A question that has come up over the years is this: "John, after your return to Romania, did the secret service ever try to turn you into their informer?" The truth is, I'm not consciously aware that they did; however, their tactics were often subtle and hard to see. I do believe I escaped more forceful attempts of any secret service officer to convert me, simply because I was always trying to win them to Christ. For this reason, I'm sure many officers saw me as incorruptible, and probably stopped before they got started!

I had heard that other men were sought out by the police to be used as informers, and were later beaten and their families threatened, because they would not turn. However, if a man was more highly educated and in a position to influence many in the church, it is likely he was not physically harmed or threatened, but promoted within the church by the secret service, so that he could be a valuable asset to them. Anyone looking for more power, money, or influence, would compromise more willingly.

Thinking back, I may have been tested when I was inside the Suceava police office while our marriage approval was being processed. There was a new officer there named Pit, who used to be a sports teacher in Iaslovat, when I was in fifth grade. But after he had retired from teaching, I lost track of him. He went on to be trained and promoted as a police officer. I saw him after many years when working to get Viorica's passport. He came up to me and asked, "Were you one of my students at Iaslovat general school?" I thought that he might have known me or was assigned to me by the secret service.

There was an occasion where I was preaching in the Pentecostal church of Iaslovat. I found out that his uncle was a committee leader there and told me that Pit was his nephew. I felt free to share my faith with Pit as I knew of his Christian relatives. I recall Pit asking me if I had any aspirations to be promoted within the church. I told him that I wasn't interested in money or promotions, as I was doing it for the love of my Savior, and a passion to serve people. I said, "Sir, I believe firmly that God rewards the faithful and supports them with provision. He then asked me if I was interested in small jobs, to work with him here and there for extra money. I laughed and said, "Maybe I should convert you to my faith first, and then we can work together for the Lord. And then, I will pay you with whatever God gives to us! But honestly Pit, money isn't my motivator. If it was, I'd give up on this church stuff and create a profitable business in America. But I am content to do the will of the Lord, because there are so many needy people around us. And if God takes care of my basic needs, I am happy! Afterall, isn't this what the communists believe? That we are to spread our goods to those around us in need?"

This kind of bold language was normal for me to use when talking to communists. I would say, "Did you realize that the communistic system of social welfare was stolen out of the Bible? Except, you threw the rest of the Bible out the window! And did you realize that the early church was living in an equal society, spreading all their goods around so that nobody lacked? The problem with communism is that it has taken Jesus out of the equation. You see, this equality of life can only work if God is in the picture; otherwise, a man without having the necessary heart change will not be able to sacrifice for his peers. And no system on earth can affect any lasting change in a man's heart. Let's put Jesus back into the center of this communistic system, and practice sharing true love – then I will be fine with this social system."

On one occasion, Pit was hanging around another co-worker in the office. They knew that the previous Sunday I visited the Radauti church. In a friendly manner, he asked me,"Does anyone in Radauti want to leave Romania for

America?" I replied, "You know what I'm afraid of? That all of them may want to move to America. However, I do encourage them that it is better to stay here where God has planted you, and work to change the people's hearts in Romania. There's still a lot of work that needs to be done here, as there are many liars and thieves. Daily, I hear curses on the streets; we really do need to change this evil among us as it becomes a curse for the whole country. I believe that with God, change is possible!"

One time, I was asked about my father-in-law, if his family wanted to leave for America. I said, "If justice will not be done for my family by the State concerning their home, they will emigrate to America." You see, because they were Christians, they were unfairly targeted by the government concerning their large home which took most of their income to build. The country had an unjust law that created government control over free enterprise ventures, including building houses.

There was another instance where Pit wanted me to check up on some emigration papers for Viorica, to make sure they were filed with one of his secretaries. I noticed on his desk a few blank, white papers with names written on top of them. I observed on the first, the name of a man I knew from America. And on the second page, another person a I knew. I was asked by the secretary if I would write something about the people on the pages whom I knew. I wrote things like, "He is a really good Christian, a hard worker, makes good money, a family man, a decent preacher, accepted by the church."

The secretary looked at me and said, "You really didn't say much of anything here." I replied, "I wrote exactly what you asked of me. 'Write what you know about these people.' And even if I knew something that put this or that brother in a negative light, I wouldn't write it; for the scriptures teach us not to slander others. I will only declare good things about my brothers. Of course, God knows everything about us, even the questionable stuff! But He will forgive us and change our hearts as we repent for our sins."

The poor man turned toward me and said, "Please, don't preach to me here." Then Pit entered the room and saw that his colleague was unhappy. I, on the other hand, was very happy. He said to me, "John, you really should say more on these papers. Like, what are their politics?" I responded, "I am not a politician. I don't even know the meaning of the word. My hear doesn't hear politics. All I want is the truth of Jesus' Word. And no country is following Him as they should." I then heard Pit mumbling curses under his breath. I knew he was mad at me. Surprisingly, he turned toward me and said laughingly, "John, you are a really funny guy. Hard as granite."

He then turned to his secretary and instructed him to take the pages and work on them later. At first, I didn't understand what he meant. And then, I realized that they would probably alter some of my words and add to what I had written to say whatever they wanted to about these individuals.

Now, just a couple of Sundays before leaving for America, I preached back in Iaslovat church. This was my second home church after Arbore, as it was the closest to my little Bodnareni village. This was also a large group of believers consisting of a few hundred. This time, Pit's uncle sat with me on the front bench where I was seated, and softly asked me, "Did you finalize all of Viorica's passport documents?" He added, "And is she going to America the same time as you?" I replied, "Yes! At last, she has been approved. It was hard work but only by God's grace did we obtain the victory." He responded, "You know, I told me nephew Pit, 'If you are not going to fight hard to approve John and Viorica's paperwork, then you will not be welcomed here anymore. Also, you shouldn't expect any more beef or vegetables from our gardens to fill up your truck.'" He went on, "Brother John, I tell you that everyone in our family has pushed Pit hard, and I'm sure he has pushed others to help you. But I understand it wasn't easy for him. But you and Viorica are respected around here, and we love you very much. Even the unsaved from our family knows you and stood on your behalf. But we know that God engineers our life's events including who is placed around us so that His will is done."

After hearing Pit's uncle speak these things, something became clear to me. I understood why Pit was so desperate for me to write something negative about those people on those sheets of paper. He needed written proof in order to brand me as an informer. But he must have known I would not compromise my faith. And I don't believe he was trying to get me to turn on the church. He was most likely securing his job. And as stated earlier in this chapter, when others see us as people of no compromise, even our enemies will hesitate before trying to corrupt us.

This experience is not unique to me, as I heard from other pioneers of faith who told me the same thing. communists are very proud people who are not willing to mar their image in front of others. And so, when dealing with a strong man or woman of God, their best option is to get rid of that person rather than trying to convert them. For me, this incident with Pit was the last one where anyone tried to compromise my faith in Christ. Even after Viorica and I got married, and moved to America, we would visit Romania for a couple months each year, and not once were there any traps laid by the secret service. We were able to do medical outreaches as well as work with the underground churches, full of the favor which God gives to those who do His will.

Chapter Fourteen

Together in America

Our flight from Frankfurt landed in Los Angeles, California, where I left my car before leaving for Romania. We stayed a few days with Nicu and my sister Silvia, and then drove to Dallas, Texas. And for the first time, I was not a lone man driving by myself, but had my wife in the passenger seat next to me. She added a sense of responsibility to me which was a burden I was not used to. As a single man, whether I was rich or poor, living or dying, in safety or danger, it made little difference to me. Now, having a wife on this new journey was a major adjustment.

Viorica had an opportunity to see her new country from the west to the south, driving interstates five, ten, and twenty from Los Angeles to Dallas. She was amazed to see restaurants and department stores everywhere, with large signs that inspired a sense of wellbeing at every turn; however, she understood that we didn't come here for all the shopping or fashionable apparel; she was following her man regardless of whether we had riches or poverty. Her happiness was found in being around me. Instead of indulging in all the new foods offered in America, she didn't have a desire for it. Instead, she actually became skinnier after coming to the states. I felt bad that she wasn't excited and curious to taste the American way of life. I also became concerned about her losing so much weight. I thought maybe she was developing allergies to certain foods.

But she loved Christ For the Nations as much as me. We lived in a campus apartment and enjoyed the spirit, the big smiles, and the joy of life that was manifested all around the campus, as well as the freedom to speak out. Most of all, we loved the praise and worship time. Viorica called it "the city of the Lord." The president, who we affectionately called "Mom Lindsay," was very happy to meet Viorica and to see both of us married. She was especially glad because she knew I was getting older, already thirty-four. We invited her to eat dinner in our home on several occasions, and she was always happy to visit with us. She loved our fellowship as well as Viorica's special Romanian dishes.

At this time in our lives we attended the Romanian church of Dallas. This included a large group of families and singles who were awaiting my return from Romania so I could lead the church again. This was truly a wonderful time of ministry where we could experience the unity of Christ's Body. There were Baptists, Evangelicals, and Orthodox people who joined with our Pentecostal pastor and small congregation. It was amazing! I felt very happy to see all of them coming together as a family in Christ, without any quarrel about the other's confession of faith. This was my first experience shepherding a group of believers in this way. This was the most spiritual season for the church of Dallas, with love, joy, and peace being our church's emblem. The leading and teaching were done through the power of the Holy Spirit, and so that some of our members didn't have to drive too far, we moved the church location to different areas.

The best place for all of us to meet was on a street called Willow Creek, north of Dallas. My friend, Pastor Morris Sheats, lovingly allowed our church to use his facility for free. His church – Hillcrest, rebuilt and remodeled an old barn house on their newly acquired land, turning it into a gorgeous auditorium. The only other building besides their offices was a rented building close by. Sometimes they would use it for their youth ministry, but it was mostly used by the First Romanian church of Dallas. For us, this would become our church building for many years, and remained even after we went back to minister in Romania. I will be forever thankful to Pastor Morris, and the church staff, for allowing us to use this wonderful building in a central location for all our Romanian believers.

For her first year in America, Viorica was required to stay in the country for most of the time, as stated by citizenship laws. However, we later got an exemption from this rule, as we received a religious ministry status and were considered ambassadors in a foreign country. And since the time we left Romania in June of 1987, we have continued to do outreaches there, up until this day. But we were having the time of our lives in America, staying busier than ever before, pastoring a church while continuing to send medicine and supplement packages to Romania. And while building a ministry base in the U.S., we were raising money for our Romanian relief packages, creating contacts with different pharmaceutical hospitals. We even got to know a few doctors, who provided medicine for us free of cost. This is a testament to the favor and provision released by the Lord to those who take care of His family before anything else.

We also needed to trust God for our own money, as the small Romanian church didn't provide any funds for us.

So, we got jobs to support ourselves, and sometimes to take care of the ministry needs in Romania. We didn't want to burden anyone else with these needs, as we knew we had been called to serve others, and we didn't want to compromise the Gospel in any way. But the Lord's provision has a way of coming to those who trust solely in His desire to bless those who are blessing others.

Then There Were Three!

In June 1988, our daughter Alina was born while we were living in Dallas. We became a real family, as I've always believed that a family is not complete until there are at least three. Even as the scriptures declare, a three-cord strand is not easily broken. Three months after Alina was born, we took a family trip back to Romania. This was a little bit crazy, to travel with a three-month old on a plane, and even more challenging on those Romanian trains which were old and rickety. But we had that missionary strength going for us, which is a strength had by all those called to travel with the Gospel. We don't live life according to the rest of the world's normal trends and comforts. Alina was a well-behaved baby, and a good listener too. Even in her first couple of years, she would want to help us carry our things around, until her little legs failed to keep up with her desire.

At first, the Romanian Embassy asked me to clarify my citizenship so that I could visit the country. They did this because when I was a fugitive, my original citizenship as a Romanian would have been revoked. However, Viorica still had her Romanian passport, which was valid, making it easier for me to enter the country behind her, as well as to obtain a visa from the Romanian embassy in Vienna. But I do believe our own ignorance of the regime together with our walk of faith in God, as well as the customs' officers confusion played an important role in us reentering the country. In any event, it was the Lord who was leading this mission, not us; we were simply moving out of obedience.

On this first trip as a family, we visited Germany and Austria as well, which would become the staging ground for launching our ministry into Romania. Here we made plans for a permanent missionary base in Europe. At first, we wanted to rent a house and an office for our ministry headquarters, in Austria. The plan was to smuggle Bible materials into the underground church of Romania. But, the official front door of opportunity came by way of providing medicine and vitamins, including nutritional packs for the urgent medical needs of the Romanian people. These physical needs hit us in the heart like a bullet, leaving a deep reminder of our missional purpose. Our unique desire was to convert and rescue as many as possible. But our initial efforts seemed so small, like trying to water a desert with a cup of water.

Back in America, our financial support was small, but enough to establish simple living expenses. Some close friends and a couple of churches were helping us, especially those who knew about our heart and mission for Romania. Most of those who helped us were doing so because they heard God speak directly to them. We didn't even have to ask for money. Most of the money we received came from my job, moving furniture around the city. Whenever time permitted, I worked so that I could not be accused of being lazy. It is true that all missionaries learn this fundamental truth: God doesn't like to use a lazy worker!

In those days, we always had just enough to live, eat, and pay rent. Miraculously, we received extra money whenever we needed to travel here or there. And somehow, the little we had always multiplied, and we didn't lack anything. We were never late in paying any bills, and never borrowed money from anyone. We had no credit cards or bank loans. Instead, when we had a little extra, we lent the money to those who needed it. It was understood that extra money was not for us to hoard, but to fuel our mission.

In this time period, I was constantly ministering in our Romanian church and in the other churches where I was scheduled to go. We then used the rest of our time to work night shifts throughout the week. Sometimes I worked for twenty-four hours in a row. A couple of times, I worked Friday straight through till Sunday. Then, on Sunday morning and straight from my job, I went to our little Romanian church to lead the service and preach a sermon. This was not easy! But I made myself stand on my feet and with a sound mind, bring the right Word of God to the people hearing the message. His grace was more than sufficient, and I felt happy and fulfilled.

Establishing Missional Support in the U.S.

While in Europe, we couldn't publicly use the name of "Mission Possible," as it was an underground organization which received no mailing or money by this name. And so, because we were actively involved in taking medical aid into Romania, we needed another ministry name. We then got connected with Oasis International, based in San Bernardino, California. And later, under this ministry outreach, we sent medical packages and little containers to Romania. Mission Possible was also involved, both for storing medical supplies and Bibles which were then sent to Austria.

One missional base in America, which we considered a covering for our ministry, was called "Hope for the Hungry – WE GO" and was based in Belton, Texas. We did work with WE GO, an organization started in 1989 until Christ Commission for Romania was established in 1994. Over time, there was a need for us to have a strong missionary assistance in America, a staff who would be able to edit our letters, print and mail the newsletters, as well as fulfil any legal issues that could arise in our international endeavors. Although WE GO charged us ten percent of our gross monthly income, their professional services filled the need.

Should I Go, or Should I Stay?

We went on a couple of trips around America, ministering in places like San Francisco, Phoenix, and Chicago, speaking wherever there was an open door to share our vision, the works already in progress, and the church building being done in Romania. At the top of the list was presenting our vision of moving to Austria to make our home and missional base, so that we could launch into Romania. These efforts produced immediate support for our livelihood.

However, there was not enough money raised for the airfare tickets or for making a living outside of America. Initially, we received about four hundred dollars of regular support, along with one thousand dollars which we set aside for settling in Austria. We felt that we couldn't wait too long for everything to work out just as we wanted but began to pray until we felt a unity of heart in setting a date to move to Austria. And instead of waiting for all the funds, we knew we had to move by faith, not by sight.

In the Dallas area, I made a new friend in Pastor Hanks, who was part of the Assembly of God presbytery over the north Dallas district. He sympathized with my passion for the Lord. Eventually, he asked me to speak in his church. Again, and again, I was invited to share in the church he served. And it was a blessing to receive an honorarium of five hundred dollars each time. In the meantime, in order to become a recognized pastor in the Assembly of God network, I was invited by him to take a minister test. I passed it and became a recognized, ordained minister with AOG. Although this helped momentarily, later, Pastor Hanks wanted me to become their missionary to Romania within the organization. Their churches would support this effort, but we would have to submit to their missionary jurisdiction.

A conflict arose as there was only about three months left before the scheduled date for our departure to Austria. I told him, "In this short time frame, it may be impossible to go under the rules of the AOG. Unless of course a miracle occurs." He encouraged me not to give up hope, but instead join him to present my vision at their Fort Worth branch. "Let's give it a try, John" he said, "You never know. It may be that we can't work it out, but we can trust our living faith to work." I replied, "Yes, Pastor Hanks, thanks for your availability to care for us and Romania." However, in my heart, I knew I might not be accepted on my own terms. And my dear brother was a gentleman and did not try to correct me; however, I remained open to his counsel, even as the Bible instructs: "Honor your elders who are leading among you!"

We went to the meeting and had a good time. Those wonderful people gave us much of their precious time, but we ended up as I had suspected we would. They set up the rules ahead of time that required me to stay in the U.S. another two years before leaving. Also, we would need to set up a speaking itinerary around their churches all over America, staying on the road until raising at least twenty-five hundred dollars of monthly support. And whenever I was released to go to Austria, I would need to make around $2500 to $4000 a month in order to provide a decent living in Vienna, depending on how many were in our family and what we needed to accomplish in our ministry outreaches. They made it clear that I would not be able to leave the country unless I raised this support.

Now, I appreciated the way this organization took care of its own ministers and wanted to protect them from becoming unsuccessful in their missional work. However, my problem was that many of my Romanian brothers and sisters would continue to lay sick, and stay unsaved, dying before I would be able to help them. I also feared that Jesus would return before I reached my mission field; I would still be speaking my vision around America, struggling to make the amount we needed. At this point, it was clear that my belief system was very different than the ruling policy drawn up by these dear, caring brothers.

Finally, I decided to tell them that by the end of these three months, we were going to leave regardless if we received support. However, I conveyed my hope that we would obtain a sufficient amount of money for our living there. I emphasized that my decision was based out of faith in God, not in how much money I had. They began looking at each other, shaking their heads as though they had heard something strange. I'm sure some of them thought, "Poor man. He may not know what he is doing by exposing his family to the unknown hardships that await. But after learning this the hard way, he will make the trip back to America." I could almost hear them saying, "Doesn't he care for his family?"

On the return trip with Pastor Hanks, we were both quiet and a little bit sad. It was as though we were returning home from the battlefield, two wounded soldiers who fought on the frontline but didn't win the battle. But it didn't matter, as I had to follow my conviction that God, not human organizations, was the Commander and Chief who commissioned me; He would provide for my family and our mission.

Chapter Fifteen

The Austrian Stage

In the Spring of 1989, Viorica, my daughter Alina, our second and unborn child, and I, flew to Vienna, Austria. We were not sure how long our stay in this country would be, but we trusted the Lord to show us. First, we needed to buy a car for personal and ministry use. Second, we needed to find a home which would be our ministry base for Romania. After we bought a car, we planned to drive into Romania for ministry and to unload the medical supplies we carried on our flight from America.

I knew a wonderful man named Dumitru Unghianu and his family, who among others, was a church leader assisting the senior Pastor Moise Gaode in pastoring the Romanian church of God in Vienna. Over the past seven years, Dumitru had opened his large family home to the refugee's camp so that a Romanian church could form. Years prior, I served alongside him in our first church in Traiskirchen. The Ungheanu family opened their home to us for a temporary stay until we found the right place to go, as this time they were living in a Vienna apartment. We decided to stay with them for several days in their basement room, giving us as much privacy as possible. We then stayed for a couple of weeks with an international outreach operating out of Traiskirchen, as they had an empty, unused room with mattresses laid out for us.

Soon, we purchased our first missionary car in Europe – a two-door Volkswagen station wagon. Our wonderful brother Pesel, who was a missionary minded minister, lovingly assisted us in finding this car which was the best bet for the small amount of money we had to pay for it. He also spoke German very well, so he was able to make the best deal possible. We paid only $1800 for this ten-year-old car. Despite its age, it was well maintained by the former owner. However, there was some serious rust building up on the underside of the car, including beneath the doors. This required that I learned some basic mechanics. I got the necessary parts at a local automotive store, drove my car to a local brook-side road, and began working on the repairs. With Viorica as my helper, and our playful one-year-old Alina trying hard to fix the problem, we removed the failing parts, cleaned and sanded them, and sprayed and shined them. I then strengthened the pieces with wire and steel bars, cementing them together, and consolidating the grout with filling. At last, I coated it with the same color paint as the rest of the car. Afterwards, you could not tell that anything had been wrong with this car. I was proud of myself as this was the first time I had ever done anything like this.

This car was mission ready, as it never gave me any problems, even as I drove it over the broken roads of Romania, and all over Europe. After a couple of years, I sold it to a minister in Romania just before we flew to America on furlough. Many years after this transaction, the man who bought the car told me of how miraculous it was, because it never broke down and the engine behaved like a newer automobile. Perhaps this is because Christ For the Nations gave $1500 toward the purchase of this car, and there was an anointing on it from brother Pesel's passionate heart for God's missionaries.

In the summer of 1989, we drove our newly purchased car from Austria to Romania. I was joined there by Viorica and Alina. Our car was packed with valuable medicine received directly from hospital doctors in America. By the time we hit the Hungarian border on the way toward our destination, the customs officers were shocked to see that our car was weighted down by a great deal of medical supplies. The officers did not allow us to take our medicine out of the country but told us we could sell it in Hungary. So, we prayed and drove for about two hours till we hit the border check point for Romania. And by God's grace, when they inspected our medical supplies, they had no issues letting us pass. In part this was due to the crisis going on in Romania, as medicine was necessary for the survival of whole communities.

The border officers did search for Bibles, however, as these stood in opposition to much of the communist ideology. Out of about two dozen Bibles, we put a dozen close to the top of our luggage. I said, "These are gifts for our large family." I did this strategically as I knew if they confiscated the Bibles on top, we would still have several dozen hiding underneath. After a small debate with one of the guards, I gave him a couple of Bibles to read, stuffing them into his large pockets. He then waved us through into Romania.

Typically, the medical supplies were also very strategic for the border secret service. The reason is that our arrival into the country was more plausible with medicine as Romania was in grave need of it. We also had a few doctors from America and Romania who endorsed our medicine as being prescribed and distributed to the sick people by their personal doctors.

Though, the Christian doctors we worked with in Romania didn't prescribe the medicine unless it met the specific needs of each person. And, in a short time, we were fulfilling the vision to help our beloved country, both in meeting the natural needs through our supplies, as well as in supplying spiritual sustenance through the preaching of the gospel.

Our Austrian Home

After spending a couple of months in Romania, I left for Austria to prepare a home where my family could settle. Viorica stayed with her family in Romania until I secured a place for all of us. Now, Austria became like our third home, and was part of the destiny which God had for us, which we could be clearly seen over the course of our travels. I knew that it wouldn't be a good idea to look for a home in Vienna, but to settle in a town closer to the border of Hungary. Also, the average rental in Vienna was about $2000 per month, which was too high. So, one Sunday morning, I met my longtime friend, Joseph Samusi, and brother Nicu from Brasov. Being from Timisoara, I knew Joseph for quite a while, and got to minister with him on some outreaches. When he heard of our plans to marry in Rachita, he didn't hesitate to be present at this prophetic wedding. What I found out was that Joseph had recently defected from Romania, and that he and Nicu were staying in a refugee pension motel in the little town of Gussing, located by the border of Hungary. I was quite happy for the opportunity to see my brothers again.

By now, they had heard that I was on a missional endeavor to Romania, and that we needed to rent a home. They asked me if I was willing to stay with them in Gussing at their temporary housing. Their reason for asking was that a few days prior, a bank teller asked them if they knew a decent family who was willing to rent out her old home. Apparently, she had just built a new house on a different part of land that this older home resided upon. Immediately, I approved this venture. They didn't have a car, so they rode with me to the town of Gussing.

After driving a bit, we arrived into this midsized town, surrounded by beautiful hills. I then heard that this was a tourist destination with castles and monasteries, and furthermore, it looked to me like a luxurious and expensive city to live in; yet, it was only ten miles from the border of Hungary. I made sure not to tell Joseph or Nicu of my meager $400 of support, as I wasn't sure if our monthly rent would be $500 or more; I simply told them that we were standing in faith with the money we have and that coming up with rent will not be a problem.

The next morning, we all went to the bank, and upon entering, we saw a woman at the teller window who turned out to be the person that Joseph knew. Joseph then introduced me in the German language and told her that my family were Romanian missionaries coming from America to work in Romania. I then spoke a few words to her in English. For a little while after, she didn't say a word to us, but became quiet as though in a trance. She continued doing her job, signing and filing some papers on her desk. I thought, "She may not like me because I'm a missionary. She looks like she's about to turn our offer down! Maybe we should just say goodbye and leave." But suddenly, she lifted her head and said to me in English, "Mr. John. Will $200 a month work fine for you?" I couldn't answer quickly enough to say "yes!"

Before I could get out a sentence, Joseph interjected in a doubting tone, as though he misheard her, saying, "What? Did you mean *only* $200 a month?" I became afraid that he would go on to say something like, "You know this man is American, right? He can pay you more than that!" I didn't hesitate to snap at him in Romanian, "Shut up! Can't you just stay quiet?" I hoped she wouldn't change her mind after that.

I continued in English, thanking her and promising that we'd be excellent renters in her home, keeping it in the best of care. And sure enough, we got it! Up until this point, it was the best home we had ever lived in, with three large bedrooms, a massive kitchen, and a spacious bathroom. This home blessed Viorica's heart, as she became the queen of the castle.

Multiplication Miracles in Austria

God always does abundantly above what we ask or think, if we let Him do His work. The one common mistake with many believers is that they draw their own life's blueprints. And after they design their journey, they ask God to intervene and bless what they've created. They may call it "the will of God" but in fact, it is their religious activities that have replaced God's will. This is why I didn't continue with the Assembly of God missionary organization. If I had, many of the great works God has helped us build would not have happened. Sure, I may have received more money which could have benefited my family for a season; however, it might have also come with unforeseen agonies and ordeals. I know for sure that the ministry would not be where it is today had we went a different way.

We had a monthly support averaging $450 to $550 depending on the month. As far as expenses, there was enough for three meals a day. All utilities were paid on time – the electrical and gas bills. Sometimes, we were able to buy clothing at special prices. A few times, we purchased medicine that was desperately needed by someone in Romania. The pharmacist already new us and gave us what we needed without a prescription! Adding to the expense was the car gas needed for driving to and around the border, to the Gratz and Vienna churches, including trips to Romania. With the baby's delivery date nearing, we would do driving tours to Vienna and then back to the hospital for Viorica's pregnancy checkups. Sometimes, we made driving trips to pick up medical packages shipped from America to the main post office in Vienna customs service.

If you're wondering whether we had enough to cover these expenses, the answer is a resounding "No!" Moreover, I asked Viorica if she had saved money on her own, funds she would keep aside and put in the desk drawer. She said, "Not at all! I don't have any extra money, John. Otherwise, I would have used all of that up by now." I replied, "Viorica, you don't understand. I am counting on $130 instead of the $70, which I assumed was left over in our drawer, and I'm positive about it because I counted it well." As time went on, I decided to stop counting the money in the drawer. Whatever was there, was there. And although I was continually taking money for various needs, our supply never dipped below $100.

The same thing happened with our gas tank. We did a couple of trips to Vienna and back with the gauge staying at the "full" line. I told Viorica, "I think our car is giving up! The gas gauge must not be working as it says we're still full. But then, on a couple of occasions I used a dipstick to manually check the gas tank. To my surprise, the gauge was reading correctly – our tank was still full! Somehow our gas remained untapped even though we made trips all over Austria. It was as though our gas was multiplying the more we drove, the money was multiplying the more we spent, and our food was multiplying even though we were consuming it regularly.

Mystery Money Coming In

We were already experiencing the mighty providence of God, as we were living on the edge, without a worry about tomorrow. Our first concern was to continue the work of ministry assigned to us, knowing the Lord was our leader and provider. But at this point, some bad news came. We received a letter from brother Angelo Cosmides from San Francisco, telling us that his $200 monthly support would end the following month. "Brother John," he began, "for a period unknown to me, I may not be able to send the monthly support as my translation job came to an end. And right now, there's little hope to find a job like this one, as it paid a good salary." Now, about half of our support came from this brother, and the other half from Word of Grace church in Arizona. The money was sent to Hope for the Hungry, who then wrote us one check. We were also receiving smaller donations from different people at this time, so even with the potential loss of Angelo's donation, we still were being sent a total of $455. Honestly, I didn't care where the support came from; I knew the Lord would provide one way or another.

The next month, we received a check with $200. Happily, I called Viorica and said, "My love! Angelo changed his mind and continues the support for us." However, when I looked closer, I realized it wasn't Angelo's name on the check. It was a church I had never heard of called The Latter Rain church of Garland, Texas. All we could do was praise the Lord for this replacement miracle from an unknown giver. And this amount came in from the same person for months after. I wrote to the missional organization Hope for the Hungry to see if they knew about this church, and if they had a number which could be used to call them. They wrote back telling me that they didn't have anything but an address. I wrote to them and thanked them, asking why they decided to support us. To my surprise, I never received any replies, except for a check mailed monthly. I thought maybe God set up a fictitious church address in Texas, so that He could just get money to us from heaven!

We flew back to Dallas a year later, and about a week after we got there, decided to find the address in Garland. Along with my wife and two little kids, we stopped along the way for errands, finally reaching Garland by late evening. The month was December, and it was beginning to grow dark. At last, we found the address. However, a little confused, we found out that this address was a neighborhood family home, and not a church building. I told my wife and kids, "Let's knock on the door." I held the kids close, as I didn't know who lived inside, and didn't want to scare them, or God forbid, cause them to open the door with a gun in hand! We rang the doorbell and a man and his wife came to greet us. I began to excuse myself for interrupting their evening, when the man stopped me and said, "Are you Pastor John Dolinschi?" I said,

"I'm sorry, but how do you know us? I was inquiring as to who was supporting our mission financially."

The family then invited us inside the home, telling us their story. Before we left on the mission field, we visited their former home church, and I spoke there for about twenty minutes. After I spoke, there was a one-time offering. He went on to say, "At that time, we were part of that church's leadership, and only the pastor knew you. But you left a positive impression on my heart. Then, about a year after that, with the pastor's blessing, we rented a building and planted the Latter Rain church. Our heart was focused on reaching the nations as well. After only a couple of Sunday services in our new church, I made the announcement that from our very beginnings, we would support other nations too. And sure enough, other people agreed with this. But not yet knowing who we should support, or what country we should look for, my wife and I started to pray for God's guidance. While praying, in my vision I saw you, John, speaking about Romania. Then, I knew that I needed to support you, and that I needed to find you."

However, this brother forgot my name, and just knew that I was from Romania. So, he went to his former pastor and asked the contact name and address of the Romanian missionary who spoke to the church a couple of years ago. He then worked hard to locate me, first calling Oasis International, Mission Possible, and then Hope for the Hungry based in Texas. The miracle of this whole situation was that the month following Angelo's last check was when this couple sent their first $200. This was no coincidence! I also believe that God was allowing me to participate in His plan to support us. I recalled speaking the prophetic word to my friend, Pastor Hanks, that God would support us with $400 to $500 a month. And here the Lord was demonstrating how He works together with our faith, with the very words we speak.

When Nadine was Born,
Money Chased Me Down

On December 1989, we checked into the well-known Elizabeth Hospital in Vienna, as our next daughter, Nadine, was on her way. Viorica identified herself with a Romanian passport, while I showed them my American passport. Both Romanians and Americans would be charged either by their insurance or by paying cash for medical care. Viorica was considered a Romanian national by her doctor and was treated accordingly. However, I found out that she would not be getting higher medical care that Austrians typically received. I asked her doctor to apply this higher care to Viorica, prompting the doctor to turn to his assistant in a huff, as though he was upset that I knew about this service. He asked the nurse, "How does a Romanian know to ask about this level of care?" She replied, "Viorica's husband is an American citizen, and they have another child who was born in America. They all received the same level of treatment there." Then the doctor turned around without another word and proceeded to give my wife the very best course of treatment.

Now, we knew that the medical bills would be higher, about four to five thousand dollars. But I really didn't worry about it as I was just praying for divine intervention. Shortly after Nadine was born, I was coming down the stairway toward the main exit when I was stopped by a lady speaking German. I understood the language but was not able to communicate it too well. I asked her if she knew English as I could communicate better. She then said in English, "Are you in need of any financial assistance with the hospital expenses?" I replied, "Yes. We sure need a lot of it. Not too long ago, my daughter Nadine was delivered, and as you know, in Austria the delivery expense if very high." She then asked me to follow her into their Caritas office in the neighborhood close to the hospital building. I filled out an application for assistance and received an approval letter a couple of days later informing me that our bill was covered. We would just be responsible for some doctor visits later. I was thanking and praising the Lord at this money miracle. It literally tracked me down without me asking for it! Jesus really does know our needs without us saying a word.

Smuggling Supplies into Romania

Our mission to Romania included smuggling medical aid, Bibles, and other literature, which would be transported either by our family vehicle, or with the assistance of other people. Usually the packages were shipped to us from America, as well as from those in Austria and Germany who would donate supplies. We did this for the poor in Romania, including the fathers, mothers, and children, who were hopeless in finding cures for their diseases. This also helped to build their faith so that they could receive supernatural healing if they could not receive over-the-counter medicine. There were also shortages of bread and milk in the stores. The government would issue ration cards in different cities; however, many were not eligible for these special cards. One time, while traveling through Romania on a mission, we went hungry the entire way as we were not able to find rationed food.

Now, behind the scenes we were smuggling Bibles for the underground church. At the border, however, my name was on a blacklist which required the security guards to do a thorough check of my vehicle and person. Usually, they would call the head officer to check everything – the body, the luggage, and the car. We prayed during each border run that God would conceal our Bibles from their eyes. Sure enough we would repeatedly pass the border victoriously with the officers likely blinded to our Bibles, which were in many cases, right in front of their eyes.

By the Fall of 1989, we showed up to the border with a lot of Bibles, as well as medicine, vitamins, and nutritional supplements weighing down the car. As they checked my passport, they did the normal routine of guiding me to the checkup lane. A short time later the customs service chief came over and asked, "How many Bibles do you have there?" I said, "Just what you see in that corner. About a dozen Bibles to share with the poor and sick friends who need them and this medicine." He replied, "You don't have permission to have any Bibles with you except the one you own." I then said, "Well, you see, these Bibles are a kind of anesthesia for the poor souls

307

who need some comfort." Despite my words, this man was determined to do a thorough check of the car, unloading it piece by piece.

Now, Viorica started to protest, as our car was getting colder the longer the trunk stayed open. She began to complain about the weather and that our baby was getting cold. He then sent her inside the public waiting room where it was even colder than outside. She said, "Don't you have any place that's warm?" By now, all our clothes were messed up as they were being tossed around out of our suitcases. This really angered her. The man ignored her and continued digging down into our stuff. All the while I was praying as he was coming close to uncovering the real Bible hideaway.

While praying in the Spirit, I did something that shocked me. I caught him by his neck, pulled him close to me and told him, "Excuse me sir. I'm trying to be nice and friendly with you. I really don't mean you any harm. But if you continue freezing us out and messing all our stuff up – if it takes another hour for us to pack this stuff back in place – I will appeal to my friend who holds a higher position in this country than you. I know you don't know him, but he is able to create a lot of trouble for you; yes, even fire you! So please, while it's not too late, let us go." I was amazed at what I just did, as though it were someone else doing it! Although he slowed his pace, he continued to dig. And so, I said, "Sir, may I use your office phone as I need to make an urgent call." I then prayed immediately, "Lord, if he allows me to call, give me the right number to dial. And I hope you answer it!" But just then, he stopped, stood up and shouted at me, "Load it back immediately, and get out of here right away!" In a frenzied hurry, he went back inside the customs building.

Two soldiers who were standing close by, came to me and asked, "Who are you, sir?" I responded, "Why are you asking?" Then they said, "We had seen how tough you were with our captain." I told them, "You know what, I'm just a normal person like you are. But I know someone greater than all of us put together. I really wish you knew Him as well. He has authority over this country. And once you know Him, you enjoy His safety and happiness." I then entered the car and waved them goodbye. As I drove away, I felt the elevated authority that I had been operating in lift off me. I could feel how powerful this was, and that it would not have been tenable to continue in such a high degree of boldness much longer.

Afterwards, turning to my wife I said, "This may be the last time we are able to enter the country. If that man checks and finds out that I don't have a higher physical authority, we may be blacklisted for good." What we didn't know at the time, was that the Communist Party was about to be overthrown in

Romania, and after two months, we would be able to enter our beloved country without a care in the world. What a miraculous God we serve!

The Romanian Revolt

After returning to our Austrian home base in the middle of December 1989, we found out that Romania was in the midst of an all-out revolution against the communist regime. For all of us who just fled Romania and were stationed in Austria, it was surreal to watch a place like Timisoara in an uproar. There were tens of thousands of people in the public square of Timisoara and all over the streets and markets, shouting freedom slogans and "death to communism and its dictator Ceausescu!"

The time had come for a reckoning in this society, where the people had their fill of living in the dreadful, deplorable darkness of communist Romanian life, the black nights without electricity, the food shortages, the lack of medicine, and the lack of any real hope for the future. Here, after five years the Lord was bringing to pass the prophetic word by Pastor Chuck Smith while ministering at CFNI.

It was amazing to see thousands of people with their kids in their hands, risking their lives, standing against the men with machine guns. It reminded me of all the brave people who escaped over the dangerous border line, a spot where traitors were shot and killed. The Serbian border had been spotted with actual blood, where thousands of people were killed and thrown into unmarked graves. Many escaped over time, but many more were killed.

Two of my good friends were killed trying to escape several years back, and their bodies could not be located; their corpses never made it back home for a decent burial. All this prompted me to remember what I told Viorica as we passed the border check and entered Romania a couple months prior. I realized that God overrode my dire prediction that we might not be allowed back; a lifetime of harassment was now being redeemed.

The Overthrow & The Aftermath

On December 25th, a new government was created with mostly the second-ranked communists who openly rejected the communistic system, specifically the Ceausescu regime. These new officials executed Nicolae Ceausescu and his wife Elena on Christmas day. Then, the radio and TV announced, "The false god of Romania has died, and the real Jesus takes over Romania now. We are a Christian nation from now on! We celebrate the birth of Christ on this Christmas day, forever." However, the new political group who grabbed power, created a confusion and rivalry between the police and the army. What's more, the Ceausescu secret service were named 'terrorists,' although they didn't really exist or fight after the fall. And because of this confusion, it created a small war that lasted for about two more weeks and produced many innocent deaths.

We continued to stay in Austria, where we had a lot more to do with all the severe needs in Romania. Even though the old system was dethroned, the new power was not equipped to handle the physical needs of the people. We made driving trips to Romania as much as possible, and the border patrol let us pass without much of an inspection. They even thanked us for helping. This time was truly good, as most of the church and aid organizations from Austria were given a green light to help with the needs of Romania.

Despite the newfound freedoms, it took a couple of years before the country recovered. All the grocery store shelves were nearly empty, with no meat, and little break or milk. So early in the morning, people would wake up early, and go to the store two hours before the stores opened, forming a line to get food for their families. Then, after hours of waiting, each person could only get a limited supply of about two or three liters of milk. And when provisions ran out, many others were left without any supplies. I returned home several times with empty hands, without even a bottle of milk or a loaf of bread.

The milk shortage lasted till the year 1993, when Nathan, our third child was born. It was so painful to see him unable to have milk to drink because there was no milk to fill the bottles. As a baby, he suffered the most in those crisis times for lack of food. It reminded me of when I was born, there was milk but no sugar available. However, this time, the choice to suffer was voluntary, as we did not want to return to the abundance of America because of the thriving work of ministry which was growing all over Romania.

The Shipping Container Ministry

About a year before the Fall of Communism in 1988, a container was shipped to Timisoara containing a few hundred pounds of medical supplies. We arranged this shipment, addressed to the renowned doctor Voicu Tudorache, who was working at the regional hospital there, and to the Philadelphia Church Pastor, Leontiuc Constantin, who was a church leader in that district. Mission Possible helped us with this shipment, though most of the supplies came from the Dallas area pharmacies. But once it got to Timisoara customs services, it was stored and held there as opposed to being delivered to the address we listed. During the last year of the rule of communism while we were arranging medical shipments from out of country, I visited the state warehouse as the expeditor for some supplies. The officer allowed me to see the shipping containers which were still wrapped in plastic. Overall, they were in good shape; however, some had holes in the corners where items had been stolen. It is likely that the secret service confiscated some of the supplies to see what was inside. Also, the State wanted control over where these supplies went. The officer tried to get me to approve of transferring these containers to the State, where these items would be distributed as the government saw fit. I refused, however. And the supplies I ordered from the U.S. ultimately made it to the Philadelphia church unhindered.

Over the next fifteen years, I would ship a few dozen, forty-foot containers to Romania, full of furniture for the Bible schools, camping tents for auditorium housing, as well as food, clothing, shoes, medicine, vitamins, and church materials, like electrical equipment and painting supplies. And, I made some beloved allies in this container ministry. Christ For the Nations, Life Outreach International, and other Dallas area churches and individuals supported us, along with people all over America. Bob Brown was one such soul, who for a long time, assisted with Christ Commission for Romania. At one point, he provided a warehouse where we deposited the container supplies. And at times, he unloaded the shipped materials by himself, as I was living one hundred miles away from Van, Texas, where he lived.

Medical Teams Ministering in Romania

We had a few medical teams over the years, but the one that made the biggest impact was headed up in 1994 by Dr.

Peter Schlair and Dr. Gordon Whitney. They did about a thousand medical checkups including consulting with the sick to give diagnoses. Their team also carried dozens of medical suitcases filled with medicine into Romania. They had a couple of assistants, nurses, and pharmacists with them. In this medical team, there were about twenty-five people ready to serve the needs of Romania, which made a big difference.

This was especially appreciated in Timisoara, where people in many neighborhoods would fill up the patient lists, regardless of their religion. And while people waited in line to talk with a doctor, we made sure to share the gospel with them, offering them Bibles as well. I recall two weeks of us having the time of our lives serving people, ministering to their souls, and witnessing the grace of God at work. One couple worth mentioning was Lowell and Sally Senitz, who were a part of this great team. They served passionately as leaders ministering to the people. After this time, this husband and wife duo served Christ Commission for Romania for about two decades, and were a continual blessing to us, without reproach.

Chapter Sixteen

Christ Commission for Romania

Before Christ Commission for Romania was founded, and before I originally left Romania for America, the Lord designed my life like a map. Christ for the Nations Bible school was part of the journey. United States citizenship was another part. Another piece was gaining a worldwide understanding of Christ's church, so that I could be trained to accept different cultures without compromising the Word of God. And let's not forget all the connections I made in the States, as these were instrumental in numerous future opportunities. This seems to be the way Christ trains us, in His diverse school that takes us, in many cases, all around the world, in order to learn how to be the most effective minister possible.

After I came back to the States a married person, and while the communists were still running Romania, I continued to work with Mission Possible, the ministry which enabled me to smuggle Bibles into the country. However, the ministry my wife and I were developing was multidimensional. Besides smuggling biblical literature, we were working with doctors and pharmacies in order to provide medical supplies for Romania. Soon we were able to move our focus and energies away from Mission Possible's vision, which limited us and didn't allow us to use their address for our shipping containers and packages. Yet, we experienced some notable miracles while working with Mission Possible. I recall not having a typewriter but writing everything by hand. I began writing our ministry vision to churches, mostly to the ones I didn't know. I would just comb through the phone book and find addresses to churches whose people I had never met. On one occasion, I felt impressed to write a Presbyterian church in Houston. After a couple of weeks, a check for $500 showed up at Mission Possible.

Dr. Mann asked me how in the world I got to know this church. I told him, "I don't know them at all! I was praying and felt like I needed to write the pastor a handwritten letter." He just looked surprised and said, "Man, man, man. Truly you are called out, born to be a missionary."

Then he shared that this was their first time receiving any support from a fundamentalist church. He then said, "John, be sure to keep the missionary fires burning. You are truly called to go and do great exploits for the Lord. From my

318

experience, anyone who does what you do, and gets the results you get, is a success at missional work." This meant so much to me, coming from a man I admired like a father. He was greatly missed after I left the organization.

I also wrote to a Spanish church in Dallas. The pastor's name was Armando Maldonado. The address was in the Mexican quarter of south Dallas. He also sent $500 to Mission Possible, writing a note back to me wanting to meet me. He was truly a passionate man of God, working day and night for Mexico's poor, imprisoned, and homeless around Dallas and Mexico. He would write handwritten letters to the prisoners who would turn their lives over to Christ after receiving his ministry to them.

The church was very small, with just a few families; but all of them were crazy for Jesus! I spoke many times in this church, and each time, I walked away with a financial blessing in my hand. We visited his family in their home, and he and his wife Marta visited us at our CFNI campus apartment. They always came with fried chicken and other meals from restaurants that opened late, who would give to those in need.

One time, I saw that his roof was leaking, and asked him why he hadn't fixed it. He said, "No money for it brother John." But Jesus knew better. And sure enough, he got the money to fix it. A couple of weeks later he told me the story.

He said, "Brother John, one morning, a man knocked at my door and asked me if I wanted to let him put a new roof on my house. I said, 'You are a roofer, then?' and he replied, 'Yes. I'm a roofer and a home builder.' I thanked him for stopping by but apologized as I didn't have the money at that time. I asked him for his phone number so I could call him when I was in a better financial condition. He then said, 'Sir, did I ask you for money or anything at all for it? I just came here to help you and I will do it for free.' So, I asked him, 'Who told you we were in such dire need for a roof repair?' He replied, 'No one but God. We are working on a house down the street from here. I would drive by your house and hear a strong voice in my ear that instructed me to stop, look at this house, and put a new roof on it for free. It took me a week of hearing this before I finally decided to knock on your door!'" After hearing this account from my dear brother Armando, I just rejoiced. It is this kind of simple obedience to the Lord that creates wonderful miracles in our lives.

Oasis International in San Bernardino

The Lord designed a little Oasis, a fertile spot in Romania's desert where spiritual water could be found for the entire country. Steve Mason and his brother founded a ministry called Oasis International. I was introduced to these precious people by Reverend Larry from Minnesota. Brother Larry heard of the Dolinschi vision and ministry to Romania, called me and took a flight down just to meet Viorica and me. Larry was a passionate, dedicated man of God who would travel from place to place to encourage and bring a prophetic word to those whom God was using. He stayed with us for a few days and fathered us during that time. He prayed prophetically over us to "go ahead!" This sacrificial man is a model for us today, one who would build strength in people no matter where he went, or the number of people present. He loved the people of Romania, and later did work with evangelists and churches in the Suceava area, until his departure to be with the Lord.

Now, The Oasis Ministry was rather small, but a bold outreach, which did missionary work in the communist and Muslim countries. For a time, while in Austria, Mission Possible was the actor behind the scenes, making our ministry possible. But it was Oasis which became the group that allowed us to receive letters and packages, backing us up with the necessary logistics to run our operation, and being a powerful traveling companion with us in our kingdom work.

Hope for the Hungry & We Go

There was another ministry of note in our journey called We Go Ministries, which was a missionary base that managed the financial and logistical aspects of missionaries who registered with them. Then there was Hope for the Hungry which was an international orphanage ministry, that also aided the poverty-stricken regions of the world. Starting in 1990, we looked for a ministry that might offer dual assistance, managing our personal finances, but also helping us with some of the physical needs in Romania. Hope for the Hungry was a blessing in the marketing of our newsletters and creating the right look for our message. They also raised $5000 in donations for the orphans and church building of Rachita, in Timis County, Romania. Although the fundraising aspect of our ministry was suffering as it had been in the early years of our own Bible school, I was committed to spending much time

322

in Romania, while only spending a couple of months in the U.S.; however, I continued to communicate our needs to our supporters through newsletters.

At one point the fundraising part of our ministry ran into a problem, as we would not publicly use the name "We Go" for donations; we would continue to use "Mission to Romania" or "Christ for Romania" instead. So, when asking people to write checks to "We Go," there was some confusion. We Go and Hope for the Hungry had hundreds of missionaries besides me, so not all our supporters felt confident that their donations were going to the right people. This created some hesitancy among them. Beside this, we wanted to stay legal in how we received money and qualify for the tax exemption on our donations. Having a personal treasurer would be a benefit as well. These needs taken together became the catalyst to launch Christ Commission for Romania.

Christ Commission Begins

In the year 1995, we began the operation of Christ Commission for Romania. The first steppingstone was to acquire the necessary legal paperwork, headed up by Rusty and

Linda Bowles from Garland, Texas. This was the dynamic couple who Viorica and I met the night we visited their home in an attempt to discover who had been mysteriously supporting us. Rusty's occupation was in the field of electronics. He was a dedicated family man, a faithful minister in the church, as well as a lover of missions. A couple of years later, Lowell and Sally Senitz joined the team as well. Their hearts were fused with ours to reach Romania for Christ and our new organization would be birthed in their home.

I traveled to speak in churches trying to raise funds needed for Romania, presenting the ministries that were most needy as I was the sole fundraiser for the operation. All of our offerings ended up at the Senitz', and then deposited into the bank. Viorica stood close beside me, as the board elected her to serve as vice president of CCFR. However, she mainly cared for our family, running an orderly home while I was running for Christ. Often, she would do chores a man should have been doing, just so that I would not miss any opportunity in ministry. She would also do most of the writing and making of phone calls. She truly sacrificed a lot for our mission.

Lowell and Sally volunteered all their free time for this ministry, and Sally treated this as though it were her first job. I remember a couple of times when they resisted receiving a bonus, because they were focused solely on heaven's reward.

324

And from the very start of CCFR, they were strongly qualified as office managers doing whatever I asked them to do, like making special calls, mailing personal newsletters, or other special tasks regarding our graceful sponsors. The Senitz' are a great family who will be rewarded in eternity. I'm also sure that Lowell's pure, Jewish heritage had something to do with the great favor which he received in everything he did.

The next great team that committed their lives to us and Romania, were Bob and Millynne Brown. They willingly replaced Lowell and Sally, when the Senitz' decided to start Safe House International, a ministry that raises up, educates, and trains girls rescued from the evils of sex trafficking. I met Bob when he was working for Last Days Ministries in Lindale, Texas, and immediately after our meeting, we hit it off. He wanted to help with a printing press plant in Timisoara. The first thing Bob asked me was if it were possible to find a native from Romania to be sent to Lindale, Texas, to be trained as a printer back in Romania. I didn't hesitate to send a young lady who felt called to go and to be trained as a missionary. After a while, Bob acquired a warehouse in Mineola for us to use at no cost, and in just a couple of years, Bob and Millynne were running our CCFR office out of their home in Van, Texas.

Provision for the Vision

Our income was never derived from a fixed salary. The Lord provided for us each month through our supporters. It may be that some ministries give themselves a fixed salary, but I just believed differently with what God had called us to do. At times, large ministries like Christ for the Nations Institute and Life Outreach International offered me ministry positions that I might consider accepting. They represented the possibility of my moving to a predictable and generous monthly salary. But as always, I dealt with each proposal in the same manner as I did with my very first decision with the Assembly of God organization: I went the way of trusting the Lord to be my creative provider versus an organization.

I would always advise our donors to give according to what was in their hearts. And when the money came in to the CCFR fund, we didn't use it for our personal finances. If there was ever more than enough in the fund, we would wire it to meet the needs in Romania. A couple of years ago, Bob proposed that we should take a fifth out, or a seventh, or a tenth from the donations of the general fund, as it was the first to be drained. A year later, I decided to take a percentage from those donors, but only those who personally approved it beforehand.

Since that time, we have not taken anything from anyone, unless they designate that it should go to the general ministry fund.

Another thing I did not do was to go around to raise personal funds for myself or the needs of my family. Whether it was airfare tickets, hospital bills, car expenses, or other emergency needs, we trusted the Lord to lead people to bless us. He is always faithful to the obedient. Regardless of our personal support, we paid all our expenses. And only occasionally was the financial burden heavy.

Some pastors made a point to ask me, "How come you didn't make any mention of your financial needs in your sermon?" Usually, I would reply, "We are living by providential faith, as there are too many projects on the mission field for us to get distracted by our own needs." However, on occasion we would have a pastor approach my wife after a meeting, telling her that he was going to sow money into our personal lives, and that she was not to let me use it for something else!

Actively Running

There were four major steps I took before the establishing of Christ Commission for Romania. The first step was Mission Possible, which helped launch me out while still a student at Christ for the Nations Institute. The second step was to establish a Christ's Oasis Land in Austria, for the purpose of reaching Romania. The third step was to go and feed the spiritual and natural hunger of the Romanian people. Finally, the fourth step was to build Christ Commission for Romania, which would ultimately spread the gospel all over Romania, thus fulfilling the prophetic words I received years ago.

Today, Christ Commission for Romania (CCFR) has been in active operation since its establishment in 1995. Our present heroes are Bob and Millynn Brown, who picked up the baton from Lowell and Sally Senitz. Bob, an expert designer and printer, has since taken over the marketing of the ministry with a fire in his bones. Our newsletter and ministry materials are the best in the country. I consider it a great privilege and a true blessing to have Bob's big heart and skillset to present the name of the Lord in our country. Bob is a Colorado native, and while young, moved to Texas to be trained as a missionary in

Youth with a Mission. I had the privilege of meeting him in Lindale, Texas. He was an internationally known printer specialist, planting printing presses around the world. And right after we met, the next printing press was planted in Timisoara, Romania. This was a turning point for him, as he fell in love with Romania and our ministry. And from there, his heart was to join with us and help keep the fires of our work burning. Soon after, he and his wife used their home in Texas as Romania's satellite office. Over the years, the favor on Bob's life has been seen in many ways, including a warehouse that was given to us for free, which would be used to house supplies for the needs in Romania.

CCFR supported most of the administration funds for all the Bible schools we started. Many believed that our support came from Christ for the Nations Institute; even some of our staff treated our financial situation this way; as though, we were only lucky because CFNI poured money into Romania. Some falsified information about how we were supported just to make themselves look good, and to manipulate the ministry's board. But our schools – like the one in Cluj, were fully supported by CCFR, until the moment I resigned the presidency of our schools. We had allocated thousands per month to the needs of the staff, and even more money to take care of utilities, rent, outreaches, and whatever other projects we had going. Our self-sufficiency was a testimony to the schools and ministries standing together in building our beloved organization.

Mistreatment Within Your Own House

To this day, there are those who still believe Christ Commission for Romania is owned by Christ for the Nations, and John Dolinschi was just an appointee, hired to direct it, while receiving a huge salary from this American organization. I understood this to be propagated by Romanian church leaders who, behind the scenes, have had a controlling motivation to benefit themselves. You see, many were and still are intimidated by the quick expansion of CCFR ministries. However, I didn't defend against these allegations, as they must be spiritually opposed, not physically. I would just speak the truth when asked about our organization, hoping this profit-driven mentality would be rooted out of the church. For as much as I tried to tell certain people the truth, they didn't understand, or they couldn't believe anyone would sacrifice so much for others – as we had. Furthermore, I never pointed the finger at myself to take any credit, because all credit went to Christ.

There have also been others within Pentecostal leadership in Romania, who've seen it as my mission to transform Romania into the likeness of the distorted, liberal church of America. This is a lying spirit that cannot discern truth from a lie, and lives in a darkness. These people don't need my convincing words, but to be delivered from a spirit that is controlling their minds. Unfortunately, a couple of leaders with our organization, who knew the truth of our identity, deliberately distorted our mission for their own selfish interests. They too wanted profit for their self-important personalities. They commended themselves as being "God's chosen vessels" who could do no wrong, regardless of their motives.

At one time, one of our leaders in the Timisoara ministries wrongly pointed out, "John, why are you correcting us, reminding us that CCFR is funding itself? Should we build a statue of you to worship or something?" Ironically, he ended up building a statue there, putting my name next to his on the name plate. And of course, I took my name off it. I do believe it is important to try and wake up these petty, ignorant hearts, as well as those Christians who are focused on building their own image first, and lastly the image of Christ. God still loves them, and they are worth our attention!

Chapter Seventeen

The Next Generation of Leaders

By the Spring of 1990, we were in Romania more than our missions base in Austria, and at this time, we made the move from the Austrian city of Gussing, to our Romanian home in Timisoara. It was here that I began to explore what it would look like to build our first Bible School. And this would be the dawn of God's prophetic word, which He had spoken five years prior about an exploding Bible learning center in Romania.

Right after the Fall of Communism, while still living in Austria, I contacted sister Freda Lindsay – the president of Christ for the Nations. I wrote this spiritual mother a passionate letter. I explained to her why we had great momentum to start a Bible school in Romania. I asked her if CFNI could assist us in fulfilling this prophetic dream, and if we could send a few young Romanians to get trained at CFNI, to prepare them as future teachers in Romania. Certainly, mom Lindsay was the greatest visionary woman I had ever met. And soon, I received an approval letter from her, saying, "John – the violent man for God – I was just here in my office with our CFNI board and they all agreed with you and me to go ahead and launch a Bible school in Romania.

She then encouraged me to pray while picking a few passionate young men, who were humble, submissive to God, honoring their leaders, and who were ready to submit to my leadership. She said, "They must prove loyal to the truth of God's word. Also, they needed to know as much English as possible, as they should be able to understand our Bible school teachers as well. Later on these men will become your Bible school staff, and a reliable help for you. Be sure to make the best selections possible. Until then, I will be praying for you and your team. My recommendation is that you recruit them as soon as possible and get them enrolled for the summer semester. Make sure that after they graduate, they have a big heart for the souls of Romania, as you do."

Now, this task was one of the most major challenges at that time. I had only a short time to accomplish it – a couple months to find the right men and send them out before the summer semester started in Dallas. I was focused on finding men in the full gospel churches of Timisoara, besides keeping my normal schedule of serving the people's needs around the churches. The challenge was trying to find those who spoke some English and were men who had proven themselves faithful. It was not wise to publicly announce what I was doing, as many wanted to get far away from Romania for fear that the dictatorial regime would be reinstituted. I didn't want hundreds of candidates knocking on my door.

I first selected two men who I knew personally to be passionate for the Lord, willing to sacrifice, flexible and linguistically inclined, smart enough to learn English. Later, I took a further step in relating my covert search to my friend, Pastor Valer Brancovan, who at the time was the pastor of Elim Church in Timisoara. He was the best English speaker in Timisoara, and a longtime translator for the churches around our area. He was very excited to hear of this opportunity. He immediately presented a few names to me, highlighting their education and learning abilities, as they were Bible students in his former underground Bible studies.

Valer recommended these men to me, although I did not know them as they were about ten years younger than me. Their names were Nicu Gramesc, Nelu Filip, and Aurel Avram. I decided to take his advice and interview the men. They looked smart, teachable, showing an obedience to God's word, and promised their loyalty to this new vision in Timisoara. Along with these three, were four other men I selected, whose names were: Daniel Junc, Traian Lazea, Avram Trip, and Valer Uta. These were the seven Romanian students which were selected, who would become the second generation of Romanian graduates at CFNI, after my graduation.

Later during the second and third semesters, I interviewed and accepted more men, including Petrica Bala, Ioan Mircea, and Rodica Mitulescu. At the time, Ioan was living in Austria. I knew him since we were very young and understood him to be a godly man. He was an educated person who loved learning and the academic environment.

After the first seven were accepted to study at CFNI, I followed up with a letter to mom Lindsay, telling her about the group who would be attending. I wrote, "There are two in this group who speak better English – Daniel Junc and Nelu Filip. But all of them are highly educated, teachable, and ready to pick up the English language. It would be great to invest extra time with them, especially an English intensive class so they can get the most out of their training."

In the next letter, I had a daring request, that CFNI would unburden me by funding these men's flight to Dallas, as they didn't have any money to buy their own tickets. I said, "They are poor Romanians who have just been delivered from the yoke of communism. And while I am in Romania, I'm not going to be able to raise all that money for them." And what a blessing Freda Lindsay was to me! She wrote back saying, "Yes, brother John, I understand. And the traveling funds had been approved. Now, how should I send this flight fund to you?"

There was still a problem for these men, however, as they had not yet gotten their visas. They went to the American Embassy in Bucharest at different times, splitting up into two groups. The first group received visas, whereas the second was denied, even though both groups presented a strong recommendation letter from CFNI. So, we set up another American Embassy appointment; this time, I joined with them. I was interviewed first by the American chief counselor. I said to him, "This is the time to help breathe fresh new life into Romania. Let's jump-start this deplorable country and do what will make for lasting change in the culture and people."

Then, he asked me, "John, how can you be so sure that after graduation, all your guys will return to help you here in

Romania?" My answer was, "I'm one hundred percent certain they will return, without doubt! I promise you. The ones who go to America will be the same who return. And I promise not to return here until each one has returned to where they are from, even if I must bring them back, hand-in-hand with myself. You see, I need these teachers as the earth needs salt. And if possible, I will sign a document under the USA flag as an oath – I will be solely responsible for them!"

The man laughed and said, "Alright, we'll let them go!" He had taken me at my word and quickly stamped visas on each passport. And for good measure, we all signed a return agreement, as a witness before God and men, that I have filed to this day. I told them, "Hey guys, this is about the same as when you vowed your lives to Christ. And if you stay behind, you'll be losing the rewards of heaven." Indeed, everything worked out. They were good boys, each one of them returning to Romania without looking back at the good life in America.

CFNI Teams Up with CCFR

During this time, we made shifts in our itinerary. For about one year, my family and I traveled Between Romania and America. While in the States, we raised funds, presented the vision, and made new contacts. Sister Lindsay told me from the very beginning that they were financial partners with me, and that CFNI was not interested in controlling any aspect of our ministry. The Bible school in Romania would be autonomous, able to make its own decisions. We just needed to stay independent of any religious denominations in Romania, being in a mutually beneficial relationship with CFNI. Moreover, they agreed to help Romania because they knew me for a long time, trusted me and my character which had been proven over the course of many years by CFNI leaders. But most of all, they appreciated the vision and passion with which I stood firmly in raising strong equipping centers for the future of missional work in our beloved country, and throughout the rest of the world. I was responsible for raising my own money; however, they would help if funds were needed to build a building, or for a special project that I couldn't do by myself.

From here on, my main ministry time in Romania was spent breaking ground for the Bible school. It was a special work, not just from the standpoint that there hadn't been an officially recognized Bible college in Romania, but that there had only elapsed a few months since the communistic regime had ended. And, because of the political games of the day, there was reasonable concern that this regime might return. So, it was part of this special work that I dismantle old belief patterns in the pastors and leaders in Romania, introducing the need for Bible training ministry.

I tried hard to instill a unified vision amongst leaders for training all believers wishing to know the Word of God. And it was here that I hit the controlling communist mindset, dug deep into the society and church. This mentality looked like institutional leadership becoming the rule of law over the people, as opposed to a national constitution. This type of leadership leads to tyranny, as a few at the top of the ladder make decisions for the mass of society. Religious leaders bought into this evil as well.

Now, I was among the "second-level" leaders, as I was not a pastor of a church. It was the denominational leader who decided what the city churches should do. And the general attitude of leaders was that the church was not prepared for an independent Bible school or ministry. And even worse, if a new training school were to arise under the leadership of just one church, then that entity would be limited to just that single church group and could not do anything in the region unless the leadership approved it. Then, other city churches would likely advise their people not to attend this "unapproved" school. This is the essence of control! Thankfully, much of this has changed over the years; however, this controlling spirit still exists, especially where fathers from the old order transmitted their ministries to their sons.

Let's remember, these people grew up under a cruel dictatorship, regularly controlled by evil authorities. They became convinced that staying under this type of ruling authority, mixed with some Biblical truths, was a good religious system. Consequently, many believed that this is actually what the Bible taught. After all, we need to submit to all authorities set over us by God, right? And this is where confusion crept in – they combined the truth of God's word with distorted governmental authority. This becomes hard to discern unless the Holy Spirit opens one's eyes. It was a well-known fact that communists had religious departments where those well-educated in the Bible were taught how to mix up the communist manifesto with Biblical truths. These were not actual believers, but rather assignees by the Minister of Culture who created recognized, "legal denominations", which became a religious cult. And these evil men delegated authority to pastors to keep the congregation under their control. The pastor was the one responsible should anything in his services displease the government. So, to speak new things in uncertain times, as I was doing, was not accepted or advisable for those steeped in our former way of living and thinking.

This was understandable, as the country was just freed from a dominant atheistic yoke. It was not an easy job to convince the denominational church leaders of any other way. Their first questions to me were: "Who will be controlling this school?" They would then say, "Won't you be imprudent if you are not under my church, which is revered in this city?" Also, "If you don't submit to me, then I may not agree with your school, and may not let my church members enroll in it." Moreover, many church pastors were not in good standing with other city churches, even though part of the same denominations. The communists truly succeeded in sowing discord amongst the churches and their leadership teams.

Our Ministry Name is Born

In order to keep our newfound school on neutral grounds, I decided to declare this city Bible school as belonging to Christ Jesus. And Christ opens wide His arms to all those who are hungry and needing to be fed by Him. Now was the time to let the hungry eat the Bread of Christ, regardless of the church or denomination in which they were a part. Regardless if students were Pentecostal, Baptist, Evangelical, Orthodox or Catholic, all were welcome. Moreover, we opened wide the doors for atheists and other religions who were hungry to hear the Word of God, as we had been assured that God's Word would conquer the hearts of *all* registered students.

Christ for the Nations didn't give us any mandate to call the new school by their name. They understood that from an American perspective, they lived in a system that allowed freedom of choice unlike their Romanian brothers who lived under constant control – whether it be what we do or say. And so, I was free to name this school in such a way that it would sound the best for our Romanian religious culture. I called it *Christ for Romania Bible School.*

At this time in Romania, women were not accepted to become students at Bible schools, as they were never accepted as fully qualified ministers. But God called us to create a school environment without prejudice or bias against anyone. This unique project would pave the way for a school that would accept people from all over the denominational spectrum, regardless if they were men or women. Now, the existing church in Timisoara understood that those who graduated from a Bible school would become clergy in some capacity, otherwise there would be no need for this type of specialized schooling.

However, a potential conflict could occur, as graduates might come forth demanding positions in the church. The fear was that Christ for Romania Bible School students would create similar problems for churches, pushing away unschooled pastors, seeking to replacing leadership. But I assured all pastoral leaders that our graduates would not challenge them, because they would not only be trained in Bible knowledge, but in service to the needs of existing churches. We wouldn't train students for positional offices unless they would pioneer new ministries or would be invited to fill up some needful posts that were lacking.

In the year 1991, the first generation of graduates returned from CFNI to Timisoara. And as promised, no one was left behind. By now, the foundations for the school were laid. And most of the city pastors accepted this school's presence in Timisoara. However, when our graduates returned from Dallas, they were greeted by some of the old-order mentality Christians in Timisoara's church leadership. Sadly, a few of the returning men strongly doubted that this religiously controlled city was prepared for such a school as described in our charter. Indeed, they were still intimidated by their former pastors and leaders. The fear emerging was that we would not have enough people enrolled and that we would become the black sheep of the church community. In contrast, the graduates who knew me for a long time stood even more committed by my side, regardless of the outcome.

In any event, I would go ahead with the school no matter the opposition we faced. And it became clear that I would need a ministry team that would be dedicated to this work with me. Furthermore, I considered this team of CFNI graduates to be mature men, and I didn't have the will to lose any of these trained leaders – they would help me carry the burden for Romania. I also knew that besides a disciple maker, I was always a team builder and needed an army to fight alongside me. However, sometimes this strength became my weakest attribute, as I would ignore some of these men who would play games behind my back, trying to build their own names and reputations.

346

Chapter Eighteen

Tale of Three Bible Schools

In my late teens, I moved from Suceava to Timisoara, where I lived for a long time. And while living there, I made at least a couple of visits each year to see my family and to speak in churches. And all the while I built an outstanding relationship with pastors, leaders, and Christ's brotherhood in general. During the first years after returning from America, and while living in Austria, I included Suceava in my ministry itinerary for Timisoara. I did this because of the need there, as the Suceava region was living in dire poverty being located on the northeast border of Romania, just south of Ukraine.

I told my team, "If you're not ready for a Timisoara Bible school, then understand this: we're not going to sit around and wait for it to happen. No! Let's get our hands ready to start a training center in Suceava." They all agreed, considering that if anything went wrong in Suceava, we'd only be risking a little bit of our reputation in Timisoara. I did not mind the risk, as I felt empowered by the Lord that I must fulfill what I was commissioned to do.

I already felt comfortable that Suceava, spiritually speaking, was ready to accept a Bible school. It was the center of the Pentecostal cradle in Romania, and so pastors would be more open to educating their people spiritually. Suceava is not a large city, but is a denser metropolitan area, home to more Christians than anywhere else in Romania. And here, there were a lot of hungry believers ready to trade dead religion for true change that only comes through God's word. I also knew that there were many among the believers who were ready to begin sharing their faith with those around them.

I then drove to Suceava to prepare the groundwork for the first Christ for Romania Bible school. I spoke directly to each pastor, meeting the Pentecostal branch leader too. Indeed, I found more open hearts here than in Timisoara. The Christians in Suceava were more legalistic in their Christianity but were craving to see movement and change in the church. There was not as much of the polarized competitiveness amongst leadership, as it was among the pastors back home.

As for me, I was coming with a humility and an understanding that we were not replacing existing pastors. It was not about us growing prideful reputations at the expense of others; we came with humble and liberal hearts, people who would gladly wash the feet of the saints. Over time, it became clear that God was indeed expanding our ministry to this region, which was full of faith, unlike Timisoara which was embattled in doubt. Suceava was full of younger, hungrier souls who were often overlooked by their churches. Eventually there would be many spiritual giants raised in this place who would minister around the world.

The Speedy Miracle of a Building in Suceava

While working with pastors and the younger generation in Suceava, I looked around to see if we might find a reasonably priced home for sale. The objective was to remodel it into a Bible school. I asked my friend, Pastor Sofronie, if he might know a spacious home for sale. He told me about the Gheorghe family in the church who were emigrating to America and looking to sell their home. Brother

Gheorghe Iacoban was very happy to hear that his home would be transformed into a center for God's word; besides, his home had already been used as an underground prayer center. We did a quick purchase of his home for $20,000.

I then called CFNI and told them to plan a Bible school in Suceava, instead of Timisoara, as Suceava is a Christian center in Romania as well. I told them, "A great door had just opened to us, with many hungry youths waiting to enroll. Here in Suceava, Viorica and I found a spacious home for a reasonably low price." Amazingly, Mom Lindsay and CFNI leadership trusted me immediately with this project and decided to fund the purchase of it. And so, we purchased the home in a short period of time so that we could begin our Fall semester on time. This was the one time that CFNI gave me a major funding without asking any further questions.

We bought this wonderful property and went to work remodeling it, knocking a wall down to create a large classroom. One of the bedrooms became the school office, and another became the living quarters for itinerary teachers. We also had a large outside kitchen and family room to cook and eat meals.

The only challenge was for the teachers from Timisoara, as they would have to create a traveling itinerary to Suceava. Two teachers were scheduled to teach their courses in Suceava, and when they were finished, the next two teachers would come to begin teaching their classes. Besides our CFNI graduates, we added to our teaching staff Brother Nicu Iliese. He was a fine Bible-trained minister with a great sense of humor, who added passion to his ministry. He represented a big step forward in our colorful teaching program.

The First Bible School in Suceava

We made it just in time to start our first school year during the Fall of 1991. We had a great start with about 120 registered students. There was no more room nor seats as people were packed in all over the classroom. It was so crowded that if there were an emergency, we didn't know how anyone would get through the doors! We also had a dedication service in which about half the city pastors showed up and expressed appreciation for what the Lord was doing through our ministry for their young people. These early years were like the honeymoon period between students and staff, as well as with the city pastors. And Timisoara teachers became sought after speakers in the churches of Suceava, as a result of their involvement in the school.

I could affirm that this was the most glorious season for all of us, with this first experience of a Bible school in Romania, as there were no other publicly recognized schools around the country. Christ for Romania was also a pioneer in becoming a legal organization which trained Christian leaders, regardless of their denomination, religion, age, or gender.

What was special about this school was that besides teaching theology, we implemented outreaches which touched all levels of society. Our motto became, "What we learn today, let's practice right away." All students were required to do practical missions work beyond their school desk, whether in politics, orphanages, homeless shelters, cultural and governmental buildings, even building homes for poor families.

Christ Commission for Romania's schools created hundreds of church and ministry leaders all over Romania, and eventually over five different continents. And the new breed of pastor didn't force out existing pastors, like many of denominational seminary graduates did, who grabbed positions based solely on their age, or because they had diplomas. This created a new ministerial culture and leadership vision, out from which church planting was pioneered all over Romania, and around the world.

In the year 1993, our teacher and missional secretaries of Timisoara, Nicu and Estera Gramesc, moved to Suceava. While here, Nicu began to explore how to make inroads into the surrounding counties, including Botosani and Iasi. To this day, he is still the director of Suceava's Bible school mission center, and pastors a church planted he and his team planted. In the year of 1997 a new property was bought near downtown Suceava. Brother Nicu managed the construction and building of this project, and I supplied the funds. He built a gorgeous building with a lot of space to house the Bible School and the mission center of Romania.

Breaking Ground in Timisoara

By the first year, our staff was convinced that if a Bible school was possible in the religious cradle of Suceava, then why not open one in Timisoara? Sometimes, leaders just needed time to grow through hard work, like traveling long distances from west to east to teach classes. Throughout the process, their faith and courage to take risks was being built up. At last, the second part of the plan could be enacted – start a second Bible school to be located in Timisoara. And I was ready to help with this God-vision.

CFNI and mom Lindsay agreed that we should have a second school built in the west side of Romania. This was groundbreaking for CFNI, as this was the first time they assisted the start of two schools in the same country. Romania had already become a special mission field for them. In the Spring of 1992, Viorica and I returned to America to raise funds, just as we had been doing since 1988. We had a great time presenting our mission project.

On one occasion, just after we had returned to Dallas from raising awareness and money for the school, mom Lindsay had also arrived back into the States, as she had just led a team of CFNI supporters to the mission field. This was a long, strenuous summer trip, as they visited many CFNI fellowship ministries in Latin America, Africa and Russia. And upon returning to her campus apartment, she heard that Viorica and I were back on campus as well. Almost immediately, she called with an urgent message for me.

She said, "John, welcome to campus. We just returned from a long trip and I'm really tired, but I have some time for you. Are you free to see me at my apartment?" I agreed, "Yes, mom. I would be very happy to see you. I will be there." Then she continued, "John, it's not just to see me, but I want you to meet with a family – friends of our ministry – Stanley and Helen Walters from Washington State. And you know what? They were on this mission trip with us, and we got wonderful projects that were presented to our American team. But this couple was amazingly unmoved to pledge anything to these valuable opportunities. So, I'm happy you are here, because I felt in my spirit, that you are to present the Timisoara building project to them. But we need to do it very quickly as by tomorrow, early morning, they will fly back home to Seattle. And who knows, maybe the Lord will move last minute on their hearts to pledge to this Timisoara Bible school project."

I then made my way directly over to her apartment, where the three of them greeted me at the door. The Walters were a sweet, precious old couple. I presented to them the spiritual hunger of the Romanian people, along with the emptiness in their souls after communism had left its darkening influence throughout the country. I said, "We are meeting this great need through Romania for Christ. We are filling the void of untrained church leaders, as well as creating the momentum to educate many who will become leaders."

Finally, I presented the house property we had in Timisoara which we wanted to buy. After about twenty-five minutes, they asked me for the property's price. I said, "This is a big house, ready to room at least one hundred students. But it still costs a lot of money. It will take $70,000. It also needs interior design work and some remodeling done to create a large classroom. The goal is to have it ready by this September, so we can start classes." Their reply was direct. "Dear John, you've got the $70,000. Please go and buy the property so you can start this wonderful Bible school."

And then Stanley continued, "I believe Helen will agree with me too, we foresee that Romania will be a blessing on the earth – a revival center for the entire European continent, stretching into the far east." Well, I praised the Lord right there for that prophetic word, as well as for how easy it was to raise these funds for the kingdom! We prayed, and then I thanked them and God who moved their hearts for us. After blessing one another, we left rejoicing. Mom Lindsay rested happily that night, and the Walters felt their mission trip had been accomplished without even visiting Romania. On the next day, mom Lindsay told me, "John, this was a big miracle for me as well. I don't remember the Walters picking up a project so quickly and enthusiastically like they did last night. I felt frustrated with the fact that they were closed to other country projects; but I'm so happy that our trip ultimately became successful. It would have been very hard to see them leave for home without making their pledge. But John, you just saved my trip. I feel my mission has been accomplished." If she was so excited, you can only imagine how excited I was to take this blessing back with me to Timisoara, even as I had done in Suceava the previous year.

Romania's Second Bible School Begins

By September 15, 1992, the house church in Timisoara was ready to receive the first harvest of students. We had a rather high registration in this first year, with 130 students registered. The two classrooms were linked together, and the large classroom hall was filled. There were no extra seats left over, just a wall-to-wall crowd of desks and students. And to our delight, the city pastors were not opposed to this school as much as had been predicted a year ago, and over time, the Timisoara school grew the registry from 150 to 200 students.

Over the years, thousands of ministers have graduated from this school, ready to do the work of Christ. Our graduates are missionaries in about a dozen countries, pastoring churches and leading ministries all over the world. Though most of them are in Romania, there are many scattered around Europe, America, Africa, Asia, and Australia. The Bible school missions outreaches were doing the same thing that Suceava did; students were required to be part of outreach teams around the city, reaching all the way to the southern Oltenia region.

Breaking Ground in Cluj

The vision for a Cluj Bible school came several years after the first two schools were founded. Cluj city is about halfway between Timisoara and Suceava, set in a beautiful plateau of the Carpathian mountain range. This is the largest city of the Transylvanian region. On our regular trips between Timisoara to Suceava, we would often stop in Cluj to do shopping or eat a good meal, sometimes visiting friends living in the city. Personally, my love for Cluj was mixed with grief as there were a lot of evangelical churches centered there. There were many believers, but no Bible schools or theological learning centers. This was considered the second largest religious cradle of Romania.

Many times, I stopped on the beautiful heights of the Felnac hills as Cluj lay in its northern valley. From this point, you could get a gorgeous view of the whole city. And while there, I would usually pray for a Bible school in Cluj, which would be a Christian missionary center for Transylvanian towns and villages which have no evangelical churches. Then, at times I passed with other pastors and missionaries from America, and we did the same thing, chatting together about a Bible school plant in Cluj. The vice president of Christ for the Nations, Randy Bozarth, was one such man who joined up with me to pray for this project. On one occasion, I passed through this region from Suceava, to get to Timisoara, with Stanley and Helen Walters. I purposely kept my visionary love for Cluj a secret. But once we reached the hill and parked to look over the city, Stanly and Helen asked me if there was any vision to build a Bible school in Cluj. I told them, "I have a vision and a prayer in my heart for school here. But it might be too much for CFNI to hear it."

I continued, "You see, there was a time when I mentioned it to mom Lindsay, and she bluntly corrected me, telling me that my vision was too lofty and too hasty. After all, we had two schools in Romania already, and at this time, CFNI had their hands full with the World Center project. So, for a few years I didn't expect any Romanian building assistance from them. And you know what? Mom Lindsay advised me to refrain from presenting the vision to you too. But now that you are asking me, so I simply want to share what is in my heart and in my hands. We're planning to start something in Cluj in a rental building, and mom Lindsay agreed with the project, but she wouldn't give support from their organization or from sponsors. Instead, vice-president Randy Bozarth supported our idea and told us to go ahead with a Bible school in Cluj, since it was in his heart too. The same was true for other CFNI staff, along with Dennis Lindsay who also approved of this school getting started."

Stanley and Helen were grieved and a little offended when they realized Randy and I didn't tell them about it. They said, "No one controls our money and where it should go, and our hearts have been for Cluj for quite a long time now. We really would love to help with a Bible school here. But it will be here or we'll put our money on other projects." By now, I almost regretted telling them as I was a little alarmed that my good relations with mom may have to suffer if the Walters' hearts and money gravitate toward Cluj instead of the World Center building. And I earnestly tried to calm them down, saying, "Let's take it step-by-step, as I don't want to move forward too hastily. First, we'll rent here and there, and then we'll build a beautiful building for this school. Let's introduce this wonderful plan at the right time. Let's first wait until we have a Bible school class started in Cluj."

Finally, they said, "Fine. First you go rent a building and start a Bible school class and then we'll commit to purchasing a house or property for this school." Stanley concluded, "If Freda Lindsay is not willing to go with it, then we'll be sending this fund direct to Christ Commission for Romania, not through CFNI." This scared me a little too, when I heard this statement; but I knew for sure that mom would agree to this project in the end.

Cluj Becomes the Third

Now, the preparation had already been done to begin a school in Cluj. I had a few close friends here, too. Ezechel Suciu was one of the most influential church leaders there and pastors were used to taking advice and guidance from him over the years. The first time I met him on CFNI campus in Dallas, was in 1988. Before communism fell, we hosted him in our little CFNI apartment, and often visited his family while passing through Cluj. I also knew other leaders, like the great

Bible teacher Zaharia, Romeo, Ghita, and Nelu Pop. Together, we started a couple of special meetings regarding the CFR school, and included other Cluj Pentecostal pastors who joined brother Ezechiel – our moderator and advocate.

Then, Pastor Ezechiel recommended Pastor Aurel Pasca, a bold and risk-taking teacher in Cluj. He was stubborn and motivated to implement the truth quickly, standing against the controlling ways of the denominational elites. He was a wonderfully sincere brother in the Lord. From the very beginning, our spirits were built up and a strong relationship formed. He confirmed to me that he would stand against the main legalistic current, bent on keeping things the same. Most of the pastors were not open to a real Bible school, unless they could control every movement of the organization. Sometimes I would have to tell brother Aurel to speak less, as he could accomplish more if he was just present and not always trying to beat the religious system down. Because he was a humble man, he submitted to my leadership.

And from there, brother Aurel went on a search to rent a building, finding one at the State Railway Club. At that time in our history, there was not much else available, but this building was a rather spacious place. Aurel, who also got his theological bachelor's degree from Oradea Baptist seminary, became the first director of Cluj Bible school. From my point of view, we could call him the founder of this school, as he pioneered the hard beginnings, breaking ground. Since the beginning, he was positioned as school director, while administrating the first year of student enrolling, scheduling the school curriculum, as well as the teacher's schedule and teaching a class.

The school started with a class of 80 students, most of them locally raised, and only a few from other parts of the country. My heart's desire was fulfilled once we got a blessed start to our third Bible school in Romania. Though some local pastors were reserved about it, no one really hindered their church members from attending.

In the meantime, while in Dallas, I made an appointment with Cornel Bistrian, a young Romanian man who just graduated from CFNI. He was looking to find some mission field where he could dedicate his life. I asked him if he would be willing to consider the Bible school in Cluj as his mission field. Cornel agreed but asked me to give him a little time to pray and decide. He got back to me and agreed to go to help Cluj with praise and worship, leading it the worship team as well as training and teaching Bible classes. Here I know that Cluj badly needed a worship leader to lead the students into the presence of God. An uplifting, godly worship time was essential to building the spiritual backbone in this city. I also thought he would be a blessing in assisting Aurel as well as our pastor and teacher, Ionel Burzo, who got involved from the very beginning.

In the meantime, Pastor Ionel Burzo, who was also an assistant pastor of a large Cluj church, was filling up the teaching and secretary positions at our school. After a while, however, he took a year off and went to study at CFNI in Dallas. Now, in need of more staff members and well-trained leaders, many of our first-year teachers from Timisoara and Suceava came to help.

Less than one year after housing the Bible school in a rented building, I made inroads with mom Lindsay, who was at the time the chairwoman and co-founder of CFNI. She agreed to purchase a spacious house that was for sale close to the downtown area. We were backed by Dr. Randy Bozarth who was the CFNI vice president, as well as Dennis Lindsay, the president, as well as other CFNI staff who believed in the good work we did for Romania. Indeed, most of these people passed through Cluj city at least once, each person having developed a love for the place. She asked me and Randy if the Walters would have the $70,000 necessary to make this purchase. I told her that I was certain they did. She then asked us to follow up with them. I was, of course, keeping in close contact with the Walters, even staying some nights in their home, as they had already insisted upon being kept in the loop on this project. I also visited and stayed a few nights in their home. They were simply waiting for the green light to wire their funds to CFNI. And in just a couple of days after giving them the green light, the money poured into the CFNI account at the Main Bank. In about two weeks, I dared to carry all that money to Cluj, and straight away made the purchase.

Like the other homes, this one was remodeled and made ready for the new school year beginning in the Fall of 2001. In time, we gained the trust of Cluj believers, who became seriously involved in this educational base. The young people loved it, but some pastors were still reserved as they had been afraid and intimidated by the school's progress. Others, however, loved it and wanted to stay close in order to grow spiritually and administratively.

Cluj Outgrows Its Location

Another miracle occurred less than two years after we purchased the property in Cluj. The schoolhouse became too small for the overflow of students registering for classes. We had great success because young people were craving practical Bible courses where the head and heart were involved, including the robust outreaches around the city. Activating believers plays an important role in setting them up to fulfill their individual and corporate calling. Unfortunately, the local churches didn't create any programs for their young people; much youthful energy was wasted. And so, the school became an attractive jewel, with plenty of opportunities as well as top-notch teaching from our seasoned Suceava and Timisoara staff. We also had the well-known, national teacher Iuliu Centea ministering his gift. In the curriculum were life courses including how to succeed in management. As a result, we became known as a premier youth ministry center in Cluj, and a missionary center for the whole region. Truly, this was what lacked in the lives of thousands of Christians in the city, who were living idly from one church service to the next. From the very beginning our vision was to see thousands of young people from Cluj and its enlarged metropolitan area form a dynamic youth center that pumped life back into Romania, and the school became a key strategic center for that purpose.

Randy Bozarth came a couple of times to visit us, witnessing the overflowing classroom. And in the Spring of 2001, mom Lindsay came to visit Timisoara and Cluj with a CFNI team. The Walters were part of this team, and they were very impressed with this mighty and dynamic school. And by now, all of us knew this was the right time to begin the school's expansion. However, mom Lindsay was still in opposition for immediate funding for a new building, as in that moment her focus was to finish the CFNI World Center in Dallas. But she clearly knew what the Walter's heart was, and where our heart is, our money soon follows. So, the Walters were prepared to give one hundred thousand dollars to build a new structure beside the old house.

At this point, mom Lindsay restricted me from making any calls to the Walters concerning funding any further. She asked me to do it for the good of my relationship with her. But I told her, "Mom, usually they are the ones calling me, asking how the Bible school students are doing, especially how it is faring in Cluj. And I don't know how to do things differently with this precious family, except by simply answering their sincere questions. I'm not sure where my fault lies, as once they developed a love for Romania, their zeal to help has come from God. Frankly, the Walters told me, 'John, if Freda doesn't agree to OK our donation, then we're going to give it directly through Christ Commission for Romania.'" This situation truly put me between a rock and a hard place, as my heart has only pursued peace. I wanted God's will alone to be done.

Finally, the Walters made the call to mom Lindsay telling her that they were going to send a check for $100,000 through CFNI that would be designated for Cluj. And after a while, they would send a check to the World Center in Dallas. The truth is, I've always respected Freda Lindsay because she was a mighty woman of God, a real mom to me, and I didn't want to lose that close connection with her heart and mind. She was a sweet spirited woman, but sometimes harsh in the management of ministry. It's possible that she may have felt insecure because of my crazy vision for Romania, afraid I would want to build a school in all the large cities of country. She asked me about this once, to which I said, "I'm not planning for it, unless the right time comes, and God leads me to do so." But if God's will is to build ministries in Bucharest, Brasov, Iasi, or Chisinau, who are we to say 'no'?

Leadership Changes in Cluj

After a while, I became downcast when I heard from Cornel and Aurel that leadership disagreements began to occur, as some leaders started opposing one another as to how the ministry should be done. I tried my very best to mediate between them, but it was hard to do while I still lived in America. Then, Aurel felt it would be better for him to leave the school until the disagreement was settled, and the leadership of the school looked closer to the vision originally cast. At this time, Cornel received a green light to implement what he saw in the school's leadership and ministry schedules. While I was at CFNI, Randy Bozarth and CFNI staff decided that Cornel should be the stand-in director until Ionel graduated. Ionel was a pastor from Cluj, who lived for a long time in the city, and was the most reliable to relate to Cluj leaders and students. He was the best candidate to become the long-term director, and he would truly be able to enhance the good image of CFR Bible school.

Now, by this time, Ionel Burzo graduated and returned from CFNI to fill the director position at the Bible school, along with teaching and managing the finances. But after a while, our man Ionel had accepted a pastoral position in a Romanian church in Denver, Colorado, and he would be moving to America. This was also the time that the money which was invested into the building was all but drained. So, the precious Walters family made their last pledge, sending another $100,000 for us to complete the building project. Brother Cornel Bistrian was left to finalize the construction.

This gorgeous and spacious building still stands and is used today.

Cornel was a faithful disciple, trained up in the Thompson Discipleship School. His spiritual father Carol Thompson convinced mom Lindsay that he was the best fit for ministry director in Cluj. Now, I didn't protest, as I didn't want to create any dissentions in the CFNI leadership – Cornel was sent by me to minister in Cluj, not by Carol Thompson or mom Lindsay. Today, he remains the director of this school and is doing quite well, running a few dozen students each semester.

I had hoped that the student class would be comprised mostly of the young people of Cluj City, or at least with the regional students from Transylvania, according to the initial vision. But many come from Moldova, Walachia, and only a few from Transylvania. This might have been caused by a lack of relationship building with the area church pastors. However, this could also occur due to exporting leaders from outside the school's immediate region, and not training and releasing enough local leaders into the local area. Hopefully time can change this, as we get back to the youth of the city.

The High Price of Starting a School

Beside many sleepless nights working, setting up leadership teams, and building the schools foundations, we had the hardship of not having any money to cover administration fees, salaries, or utility costs. These we had to raise ourselves, sometimes sharing money from our own family funds. In the past with the Timisoara and Suceava schools, CFNI helped us here and there with special management funds. During the first years of these two Bible schools, each CFNI graduate on our staff were sponsored by CFNI with $100 a month each. But I usually needed to add another $100 to make a living salary for our CFR staff. In contrast, we didn't get any funding for our Cluj school. But I understood that our first few years with CFNI was a honeymoon period; later, we would need to support the entire workload.

Cornel would need to walk by faith and support the entire Bible school with all its expenses. But not only him, the other presidents as well, of both Suceava and Timisoara. These schools were required to walk by faith as well, like a mother eagle who must hunt daily to feed the next generation. As this was our ministry beginnings, so too are all pioneering, apostolic ministries who are called to develop sons and daughters in the way of ministry until the next generation can pick up the baton and do the same thing.

Schools Spread Throughout Romania

The following schools which branched off the first three, made a real impact in other regions as active CFR extensions: Botosani, Iasi, Mediasi, Petrosani, Motru, Urziceni, all started by the CFR staff and teachers from Suceava and Timisoara. Later, all these became self-operating, raising up their own local teachers. CFR Motru was started by my spiritual son, Pastor Milo Novacovici. CFR Urziceni was started by another spiritual son, Costel Gramada. Both of these schools are still active, training new leaders to reach their world with the gospel of Christ. Petrosani Bible school was one of the most outstanding of them all, and hopefully will continue to stand strong under Pastor Petrica Coman, a great man of God. From here, many leaders were raised up and sent all over the world.

Now, many other inspired CFR Bible classes and small schools are in operation all over the country, which were initiated by our Romanian Bible school graduates. The ball is rolling, so we give our blessing and then just get out of the way – Jesus is in charge! Although these extension schools were the responsibility of Christ for Romania and expenses were covered by Christ Commission for Romania, as well as our US supporters and pastors, they later became self-sustained by their local ministries and churches.

For each of the three original parent Bible schools, we encouraged the presidents and directors to keep the connections active with their supporters, pastors, and others who pledged money in the past. We told them to keep communicating progress, testimonies, and needs. Here, they became fully responsible to lead, teach, and provide for the needs of their local ministries. And the Lord will bless them mightily if they keep the initial Bible school vision aflame, as He had given us the mandate to disciple and train leaders for the ministry.

Chapter Nineteen

The Romanian Camp Revolution

Over the warm season in the year 1993, we arranged to have a very powerful evangelism tent outreach with the late Indiana evangelist, Reverend Walter Kronberg. It started in Timisoara, Deva, and Suceava with a two-thousand seat tent. Brother Kronberg was the chosen preacher each evening, who would take about two to three weeks preaching and teaching, and then our CFR staff would teach the new-believer classes in the daytime. These were attended by more than two thousand people each evening, the tent filled to capacity. There were a lot of people standing inside isles and outside the tent skirts. People were truly hungry to hear the word of God.

Surrounding these meetings was the tangible presence of God with signs, wonders, and healings accompanying His Word. Hundreds of people responded to the alter calls, giving their lives to Christ. Many others testified of being healed of diseases and infirmities which they had for years, some of whom carried them their entire lives. This was timely evangelism, a true soul-saving revival that brought many into the Body of Christ. We witnessed people coming out of wheelchairs, leaving behind their walking sticks and crutches, and those leaving behind their glasses on the benches where they stood.

There were some from our leadership staff who at first didn't fully agree with the tent evangelism in Romania and were a little uncomfortable with brother Kronberg's ministry. But by the end, everyone was convicted that they were letting their lack of trust in God influence their minds. Many today still believe that they need their eyes to see something in the natural in order that they might believe; this is not a true faith, but a weak substitute.

The Rise of Youth Camps

Brother Kronberg decided not to take the tent out of Romania but donated it for our use, and the following year, he evangelized under another tent he purchased especially for the Republic of Moldova. He returned several times to Romania, but never used the tent for city evangelism. After a couple of years, he used it to plant the Exodus Church on the west section of Timisoara.

At this time, we began praying and receiving a vision for the further use of the tent, which resulted in our starting Christ for Romania youth camps. And by God's divine purpose and grace, the first camp was dedicated in the Summer of 1994. However, there was severe opposition from the inside, once again. Complaints were generated from the same leaders who always seemed to oppose new beginnings. These leaders felt motivated to tell me that it was the wrong time to launch a new ministry, regardless of whether it would be good for Romania. They would say, "Don't you see that our older believers and church leaders are not prepared to take another blow in the face? They will turn around and destroy us. The wiser way is to let others take the first step, and then see if it is accepted by the mainstream church. If not, let the others take the blame, in which case we will say please, don't involve us in this kind of trouble again."

This wasn't completely off base, as in those early years, we typically faced hard times after starting a new project. Romania was truly still struggling with the old ways of thinking and living; and so, anything new came at a price for those pioneering it.

Also, at that time, any type of youth gathering was not positively accepted, mostly being rejected by the contemporary church leaders. And new gospel movements were restricted to the inside of churches, under the watchful eye of the elders. But a tent meeting was beyond their imagination – that hundreds of young believers could gather for a full week to praise the Lord under one big tent without being closely supervised by the older saints. A large youth gathering might be tolerated if it was under the watch of the older generation and led only by a few older men. This would be to make sure these young people were kept safe from doing something sinful under the tent.

Really, in many churches, the young people were not trusted in the prayer or Bible study gatherings without being well-guarded by the older people assigned to watch them. And indeed, you wouldn't find any of these older people spending seven days and nights in a camp meeting, sleeping in tents, eating meals from their own bags or makeshift picnic grills. Beside this, camping was considered a worldly idea, and was used only in the "fun" days of old, but not for the use of a humble church group. Most of these fears caused more and more tight control, which was disguised as concern for the safety of the flock.

But here was a fresh start and I found myself in a place where I could not move backward. By prayer and faith, I took the step forward. I became so convinced, to the point that I was willing to work with those who were loudly declaring: "This is not the time to start youth camps! You're leading us into a dangerous pit. Just wait for maybe a couple of years until the churches open their own camps. Then, they will get used to the new moves of God, and we'll then do it too." But I kept telling them, "Pray yourself! And then you will know the Lord's mind, if in fact He wants us to start these camps right here and right now. Let's take a risk and move all fears aside."

After a time of quarreling, everyone agreed with my objective, that we should at least have a meeting place for students to get to know one another at both schools – Suceava and Timisoara. I suggested we name it "The Meeting Tabernacle Place." And for over fifteen years, this title stood, until the leadership at the Bible school in Timisoara decided to terminate their involvement. A couple of weeks after the summer break in early July, our youth camp meeting was scheduled, so we decided to hold this camp in the secluded location of Padis, in the Transylvania mountains.

Youth Camp Provision

Another bump in the road came as we began a building project in Timisoara for the Bible school there. We were in the process of building a large chapel auditorium and upstairs office. While we used whatever money was in the account for this chapel, we found out that our camp expenses bill was lacking. We didn't have the $1500 needed to transport the tent and for the camp site expenses. The entire staff then gathered for a meeting, intending to bring a new proposal to me attempting to prove that based on our money, we were unable to run the camp that year. Our office treasurer reported zero money for anything but staff support, utilities, and the building program fund. They went on to conclude that it would be best to postpone the start for the coming year. However, I was not a man to give up a vision without a fight! I firmly said, "I don't think giving up is God's idea at all; besides, this scheduled camp has already been set and announced to our student body. And there is no turning back to cancel it – it's just too late as we'll lose our integrity. Plus, we'll be teaching our students the wrong lesson. They'll be prone to wonder if we'll keep our word with other promises."

The opposition bluntly asked me to produce the money that was needed. But I responded, "The better way is that everyone should go home and pray to our great Provider, and then let's meet in a few days to hear what the Lord has decided." I went home and asked Viorica to help us all in prayer. I prayed heartily and believed God would make a way for this money that we urgently needed. And, while praying before the Lord, I heard the still, small voice inside me saying, "John, you have the money with you." I thought perhaps the Lord might bring this money right here and now. But while waiting before the Lord with thanksgiving, I heard Him speak again, "John, don't you have the $1500 sent to you a month ago for the purchase of your family's airfare tickets, for the end of August, to America?" But I argued, "Lord isn't this money sent specifically from this church for our traveling expenses? And what if I use this money, and my speaking itinerary becomes compromised later?" Then I thought, "John, you are a man of little faith. Why not just trust God?" And I quickly said to the Lord, "Yes, I will correct myself here. I do have the money."

On the second day I asked to meet each one of the staff, and told them, "Hey guys, I have here all the money needed. Our cashier has come to pick it up. This is the camp fund – use it wisely! The Lord is our great provider." However,

I observed that whereas most of them were rejoicing, a couple of them didn't show much enthusiasm. For them, money was not the real excuse to postpone the camp this year. The real issue was their fear of a couple hundred young people coming together in the mountains, which could denigrate our good name.

The fact is, we all realized we were creating a precedent concerning faith for funds that, from now on, every camp would follow. But the Lord was *consistently* good to us. A couple weeks after the camp began, we received over $2000, which more than made up for the expenses needed to make our U.S. flight, and to cover the needs of that trip.

The First Youth Camp

Our first Tabernacle camp was on a beautiful western mountain range of Padis, called the Alps of Romania. This is a most beautiful tourist area, wild and wondrous, remote with nature all around. In those days asphalt roads were in bad condition, broken up with potholes being a very common thing in the country. So, it was not easy to make it to our destination; but once arrived, God's beautiful creation was clearly evident. We paid a truck service to carry our big tent, including the chairs, sound system, and all other equipment needed. And for the first time, our zealous students and brave soldiers set up the tent while teaching themselves how to do it! Our leading student, Petru Ropotica, did an amazing job along with the other brilliant men who helped with the construction, while also aiding in the evangelism outreach. Although we lacked the presence of the expert who constructed the tent previously, our daring young lions did their best to make it stand strong.

The time had come for our students to show up, and they were arriving with some of their family members and friends who were invited to attend the camp. Many more showed up than what we expected. The final gathering was somewhere between three to four hundred young people, hungry for God with the expectation the Spirit would fall upon them from heaven. Even before the camp meeting started, the atmosphere was thick with the presence of the Lord. Everyone present was witnessing the same wonderful experience and were speaking and rejoicing about it all over that place. It was like that territory was occupied only by the Lord's angels! And when the young people started to show up, the heavy presence of God overwhelmed us, revealing an almost visible, smoky white curtain hanging over the entire space.

The first service started with a heavy presence of God, so much so that we could hardly sing or speak, as people were just in tears, loudly crying in the joy of the Lord. Others were just smiling and rejoicing. People could hardly sit, as they lifted their hands and stood in spontaneous worship led by the Spirit. The power of God so penetrated our tent without us having to do much of anything. Some felt that they couldn't stand the strength of it, as it was like a dense, holy smoke weighing on them. Any song or prayer, exhortation or reading of the scriptures, was met with 'Hallelujahs!' Here we were molded into one heart and one mind. Any announcement or simple encouragement was laced with a prophetic message, which spoke of God's presence moving all over Romania. There was no exception; everyone had been used by the Spirit of Life and was met with powerful witness from the people. We all stood together as one person, praising God which could be heard a mile from the tent. The entire mountain area echoed, resounding praise through the valleys and the surrounding smaller tents, where the people were in awe that God was moving in this country.

Now, I was very sure that the Lord took over. There was no glory given to anyone but Him. I believe that this first night was God's way of dedicating this camp with the presence of an angelic team who were joining us to worship the Father. The Spirit was passing from one person to the next, each feeling a special touch with a heart and life change to show for it. The Lord stamped His approval on this youth camp and all future camps that would occur in this nation. He was doing this despite all the religious opposition we experienced.

My heart grieved as a few of our staff missed this first move of God. One of our teachers, Petrica, who couldn't stand camping outside, missed this event and was never involved afterward. Brother Nelu and Aurel came to preach only for one evening service, and then left for Timisoara. Brother Valer was required to spend a couple of days managing the construction team who was building the chapel. Brother Nicu Iliese had a personal problem, but then was with us for about half of the time. Traian Lazea and Nicu Gramesc, however, were with us from the beginning to the end – Nicu being an avid camper. Nicu stood faithfully over all the camps in Romania, not missing a single meeting.

The Tabernacle's National Fame

The next year, following the powerful camp at Padis, the event was moved to Moneasa, in Arad County. The entire staff was now convinced that no evil would befall us, and no denominational leader would shoot any poisoned arrows at us. Besides, no one got killed! For the second year's camp, we printed an official invitation and mailed it to other churches and some youth leaders around Romania. This camp took place in the year 1995 with approximately two thousand young people enrolled. We had a large youth team from Colorado called Resurrection Fellowship, who assisted us with this undertaking. And from here on forward, we had at least one team from America join with our Romanian team. We would minister together during the evening and morning services, with about twenty Bible seminars held each day taught by different members of our joint team.

The Tabernacle camp grew to have leader's representing about twenty European countries, and it became known as the "International Tabernacle Camp of Romania." In the following years it grew to astronomical numbers, reaching around six thousand people under a tent that contained about two thousand seats. But if people packed in, standing in the back and by the isles, it would hold about four thousand people. The other thousands would just stand around outside of the tent. As a result of the overwhelming interest, we became desperate to keep the number of people down, but it was almost impossible to keep people away. We posted signs at the gate entrance and put up barriers to stop people from entering the campgrounds. Our ushers apologetically asked people to return as there was no more space left. Here and there the government got scared about these large numbers gathering in one place. They were intimidated by these large crowds due to the fact that in Romania there was an undertone of opinion amongst some of the people that the second-level communists needed to be purged. A large and growing crowd of young people could make this national dream possible. Government spies were in the crowd too; But the spirit of the Lord was saturating these camp meetings – there was no politics at all.

Truly, this was a youth revival, and a church awakening that was happening all over Romania. As a result, the Tabernacle camp became known all over the country. Usually, the camps included both evangelistic and teaching ministries and a variety of Bible seminars, which all contributed to the spiritual growth of those who attended. For a full week, everyone had the opportunity to feed on the word of God. I could feel the wave of God's presence even when traveling the country. Wherever I stopped, at stores or gas stations, there were young people present and interacting with me. Some shared with me their personal testimonies of how the Lord changed their hearts, saved or healed them, or just helped them to mature spiritually. They would introduce themselves to me and then share their miraculous stories. Some of them spoke as though they had graduated from the Tabernacle Camps. Today many of those young people have become pastors and leaders. Indeed, this proved to me the value of such a challenging endeavor despite the hard circumstances, as these camps made it possible for people to grow in Christ. Looking back, it is clear that the camps became like Bible training centers that not only blessed those who attended but produced ministry outreaches to others.

As this ministry grew, we began to import shipping containers from Dallas and Van, Texas, that contained brand new tents, each one able to support up to five hundred seats. The Lord provided some special people who heartily supported this outreach, including Resurrection Fellowship, led by the missions Pastor Mark Lucks. He sponsored the purchase of our tents from a tent making factory – a Christian company in Oklahoma. If we didn't have this God-given opportunity when we did, our camps would have suffered a lack of Individual classrooms for all our Bible seminars. And over the years, all of us who had been a part of the original Padis camp, would remind each other of our humble beginnings, and how the presence of Jesus became visible among us. This we will remember for all eternity.

A Miraculous Healing Takes Place

We had hundreds of recorded miracles during these camps, with many people being delivered, saved, or healed in every evening service. Around one to two hundred people were baptized in the Holy Spirit, per camp. Most were delivered from their sinful lifestyles, while others had received spiritual gifts, being empowered to go forth in ministry. One miraculous story worth mentioning happened in the mountains of Paltinis. This area in Sibiu county was known as a center for witchcraft, Transylvania being the home of this evil.

On one of the afternoons, when people were gathered for the Tabernacle evening service, one of our girls crossed the main road going up from Sibiu city, to the main ski and hotel resort. There at the crossing, an Italian citizen drove the mountain highway at a high rate of speed and hit this girl head on. She flew over the car, several feet in the air, and was left on the ground unconscious and unable to move. The police and ambulance made it quickly to our location and transported her to the hospital in Sibiu. A couple of our people went to stay with her, as she was in the emergency room, still unconscious. We continued to stay connected with our representative at the hospital, though many saw this as a hopeless case. The police stayed with us and the driver of the vehicle stayed across in a nearby tent. The police began questioning our safety signs, to some degree trying to make us equally as guilty in this incident. In the tent, we began interceding for God to save her life.

Although the police and other civil investigators looked at us like we were a crazy cult (who could possibly plot to take over the country of Romania), they began to believe that the God these people were praying to might intervene and save this lady's life, based on all the prayers and faith declarations. After an hour, the hospital gave us great news: the girl suddenly woke up and started to speak clearly! She looked around and wondered why she was there, as she felt fine. The doctors then began to subject her to all possible x-ray tests from the top of her head to the bottom of her feet and all tests came up negative – no broken bones or body trauma. So, after a couple of hours in the hospital, she signed the release forms, along with our signature, and was taken back to our evening service.

Our night turned into an explosive time of celebration, thanking and glorifying the Lord, who heals us! The policemen and civil investigating team witnessed the same thing as we did. They were dumbfounded! The spiritual witchcraft zone was immediately defeated as the power of God took over the whole place, the city, and the entire region, for Christ.

Fierce Opposition in Suceava

The Tabernacle camp was moving to a new location each year, closer to those campers who faithfully came each year. At this time, we took the invitation of Nicu Gramesc, our Christ Commission for Romania director of Suceava, to have our next meeting in the mountains surrounding the little town of Voronet. This was a great tourist area with many monasteries and was also a religious stronghold within Romania. Whether it was Orthodox, Baptist, or Pentecostal, the traditional mindset reigned supreme in this region. For this reason, this was not the best place to have a large gathering. But lots of young people from Suceava city and the northern region faithfully attended previous camp meetings; so it would be a benefit to them that we would hold meetings close to their home. However, for the religious institutions of Suceava, our camp became a big problem. Once they heard that our Tabernacle would settle amid their sacred area, they responded like the Israelites did whenever anyone tried to take their land – with hostility! Some of the sternest Christian leaders, who were known around the country as the religious police, planned to show up to the camp at night, shut us down, and tear our tent to the ground. They wanted to come at us like the Moldovans who stood up to the Ottoman Empire. I just saw these people as zealous children.

However, God knew better than us, as about the same time this religious mob showed up, the police patrol car showed up too, patrolling around the tent. They also walked around among us to make sure we stayed safe and out of trouble. Somehow, these policemen stayed longer with us this time, and it's possible that they noticed that a large group of men were gathering near the tent. Indeed, the camp meeting had been approved by the city hall of Gura Humorului city, and once in their territory, were required to keep us safe. We didn't ask for any protection, but this was the rule regarding any legal gathering.

Now, these hostile men were talking about how they might descend upon us, just as the police showed up behind them. And of course, appearing like nice people and respectable pastors, they put on a show for the officers. However, when they saw how the police guarded us, walked among us, and were talking with them, they realized that getting arrested was a likely outcome should they choose to attack us. They changed their plan, and although they acted calmer, they still tried to disturb the main service by asking some of our leaders to shut this satanic meeting down, as it was a plan to destroy the true Christianity of Romania. We told them that if they wouldn't sit on the front-row seats we prepared for them, they needed to leave. But their next plan commenced, as they attempted to convince their regional evangelist – who was that night's main speaker – to not preach for us. However, Pastor Petrica Hututui from Botosani, had already preached one night a year in our beginnings, and was renowned all over the country for his evangelistic work. Still, the religious zealots surrounded him outside the tent and threatened to excommunicate him from speaking in their churches if he continued that night.

Petrica looked dizzy and bewildered after this encounter, as though he had been pushed and punched; but he stood his ground to preach the Word. We found out that they were threatening him before he was about to preach his sermon when we asked him to come and speak, so we then told the threatening party they needed to leave if they couldn't keep quiet. They were trying to threaten me as well, telling me that I would not be allowed to preach in their churches if I continued. I told them, "That is fine. I'm not trying to get into your churches anyway. That is your responsibility, not mine." They then told me to go back to other regions of Romania where there were backsliding and wayward people, and to stay away from this holy place. They complained that we were singing too loudly, not the way we should in church, but wildly like in a night club. Instead of sitting humbly before the Lord, we were raising our hands and making a joyful noise. And even worse, we were shouting Jesus' name in a loud voice which, according to them, was not honoring to God – They said we were acting as though we were making a commercial for some company.

However, they did actually have a reason to be nicer to me, as they knew I helped pastors put roofs over their church buildings. They were also not ready to give up our financial fellowship either. And amazingly, they treated Nicu Gramesc nicer, as he was a friendly man known for helping them with more things than I did. But Petrica, Iuliu and the Timisoara men needed to be harshly disciplined concerning their attitudes as they were the active members of the Pentecostal Union leadership, and as the Pentecostal leaders among our tent meetings, they were not active in helping these men financially at all. Finally, this religious band of men were convinced they were not able to harm us as they first believed, so they picked up their notebooks and pens, and walked down the isles like police inspectors and wrote down the names of any church member they observed in attendance. I escorted a couple of these "inspectors" out of the tent; however, a couple more stayed in the front, and continued to see what would happen. Unfortunately, they were writing names of those in the congregations who were attending, in order to discipline them later, and keep them from participating in any future ministry. Truly, persecution is crueler when it comes from your own family!

In conclusion, there were unsung heroes in this group, who pioneered these camps, and strongly backed them financially. Without this wonderful team of Iuliu Centea, Nicu Gramesc, Traian Lazea, and Nicu Iliese, we wouldn't have accomplished what was done for Romania. There were also faithful leaders who led the Tabernacle camps. Included were

Valer Uta, Nelu Filip, Aurel Avram, and Daniel Junc, who all supported and administrated while preaching and teaching. And there was also a strong student body and team presence where young people worked hard with various assignments. Because there are hundreds of names I could mention, I will refrain; but my highest appreciation goes out to all of them who ministered alongside me in these early revival times in Romania.

Endings & Beginnings

I intentionally but unexpectedly showed up at a few camps to see how they were being run in my absence, as other leaders told me that this ministry might go under if I failed to show up. I was not always happy with what I heard from the faithful supporters. Yet overall, there was solid leadership in place who just needed to mature in their ability to administrate the move of God. At one time during my absence, our main leaders – brother Nicu, Nelu and Aurel, had drawn up a fellowship covenant with the Pentecostal Union leadership, to become partners in the camp ministry. Their motivation was that it could be a safeguard for the future, like having a big brother to watch out for us. And this would help to strengthen our grip on controlling the thousands attending the camps, as at times, it could become a dangerous mob and cause us a lot of problems. They would be a scapegoat so that we wouldn't directly take the blame for anything nefarious happening in the future.

Joining with a denomination would empower us and create a State-approved covering so that we could be represented should we need legal help. However, I stood on the other side of the isle from this point of view, as I did not trust organizations that attempted to be more powerful than God. And for a couple of years I tried to deliver them from their intimidation, as I was certain this fear was trying to destroy us. The fear of men was a snare, especially when it caused people to trust in government or another religious institution for their protection.

This was the time that our Life Center ministry started, when the Life Outreach International team visited us in Romania, spending a day in the camp meeting with us. The following year, while still taking part in leadership, the Pentecostal Union people were present too. They commended this camp as the best youth outreach in Romania. Certainly, each one of the leaders preached strong sermons, praising and worshipping with us, witnessing the hunger of our youth for the Lord.

We agreed that for this camp to continue many years into the future, we should buy a larger tent so all of the crowd might gather inside. Then, a year later, I was led by the Lord to have Nicu Iliese take charge over the camp ministry, assisted closely by the Bible school's leadership. In fact, the main leadership pledged to stand with Nicu for many years to come. We all made a similar covenant with each other: if hungry young people came flooding in, we would stand together to feed them.

Only a couple of years after Nicu and Nelu took charge of the tent mission, Nicu's leadership was being subverted by a couple of Timisoara leaders who were pulling strings behind him. And soon after, this great camp was ended by both the Christ for Romania staff in Timisoara and the Pentecostal Leaders Union, while under Nicu's watch. The only reason given was because it had become too large and unsafe, with the impending government potentially restricting it due to the size of the crowds at each meeting.

I grieved over this news as I heard the leaders announcing to the people and their pastors that the camp was ending, and that they should look for another local camp to fulfill this need. After this news, I was called by a couple of camp leaders while I was in America who asked me, "John, did you approve the termination of camp?" I just sadly replied, "I heard this heartbreaking news for the first time, right as you told me." As I understood, the camp leaders did not want to ask me my opinion before pulling the plug, because they knew I'd say 'no.' They didn't want me to change the outcome.

But then I considered that for twelve years this Tabernacle camp had impacted the whole country and changed the minds and hearts of believers, leaders and pastors. And here I firmly believed, that from that point forward, many would start camps within their local or regional churches. At least our initial goal was accomplished – Romania had changed! I believe the Kingdom of God won here, and not merely our ministry camp. And in all of this, you can clearly see what my calling has been: to plant churches and ministries as a pioneer. And I'm thankful I've had these opportunities. I was programmed to start and to stay with projects until maturity is reached. Then, others would take these over and run them well. But bringing them to a successful conclusion is just not my strong suit; others may tackle this part of ministry development, which is between them and the Lord.

The camp continued through the hands of other visionary leaders all over the country, most of them graduates of CFR Bible schools, or straight out of the camps. I will here mention just a few of the outstanding leaders and their respective camps: Nicu Gramesc and Marcel Lelcu over the camp of Moldova; Cornel Bistrian over the camp of Transylvania; Milo Novacovici over Oltenia and covered the whole Wallachia region. There were also Pentecostal Union Pastors who picked up the vision of God's Tabernacle camps. These included Pastors Romulus Paraluta, Gigel Ignat, and Costel Gramada over the Urziceni area; Vicu Cruceru, Leonard Gurgas, Navodari, and Dorel Toma, who are strongly active today in the Muntenia region, and to the far east stretching all the way to the Black Sea. I also met with many pastors all over Romania and the Republic of Moldova, such as Pastor Victor who told me that they caught the summer camp vision for their own district churches. Not only these, but Pastor Alex's camp in Ukraine, as an example of other countries which caught the vision for camps while attending in Romania.

Pastor Nicu Gramesc in Bucovina, Moldova, ran a camp for orphaned children for about two decades, where thousands of kids were blessed and trained as men and women of God. Also, the Suceava camp is still running with youth camps in the Bucovina mountain area. This was a timely ministry in Suceava, as there were many orphans who needed to be reached, along with the entire society which was blessed by this ministry. Pastor Milo and Nina Novacovici, both graduates of the Timisoara Bible School, were leaders of a children's youth camp in the Oltenia region, after his time as regional leader for the Tabernacle of Romania camp. They, like so many others I've listed here raised their own children and families for the kingdom of God as well. What a blessing they have been!

I urge every reader not to despair because of how the national Tabernacle ended; the spiritual eaglets who were trained and matured during this time have not stopped flying, and have transmitted much of this spiritual journey to their children in Romania, and those around the world. Hopefully, those who were touched by this ministry can do an even better job, as they can learn from our mistakes. This inheritance was passed from fathers to sons, who will continue to pass on the legacy long after we're gone. I await the day I can see the fullness of what took place through this camp ministry.

Children & Orphan Camps Active Today

These camps are currently running, mainly for unprivileged kids who are coming from impoverished regions. Many are living under the poverty line, much like the gypsy kids. What preceded the development of these camps was a growing need to offer a week-long vacation for orphans in Romania. At the time that the Suceava and Timisoara Bible schools were in their beginning stages, the state orphans needed social interaction, including a nourishing meal as many were physically weak, pale, and sick. The truth was that these children's homes were in bad shape, lacking resources to properly take care of the children. The summer camps that were organized by the Suceava and Timisoara ministries were instrumental in building these orphan children up. Pastor Nicu Gramesc still continues to minister to the Falticeni orphanage, feeding and helping these kids as this orphanage is in full operation. Amazingly, the ministry team of Pastor Sam Thompson from Fullerton, California, is still sending support, and has been doing so since 1996. This is an example of how important it is to hear from the Holy Spirit, especially regarding who you should connect with in ministry; Thompson's church was literally picked out of an Anaheim post office phone book! And as a result of this special work, most of these kids from

Falticeni and the rest of Romania are now in their thirties and forties, many of whom are serving the Lord Jesus.

Expanding further, this ministry went into the spiritually barren regions of Romania where the Evangelical church was non-existent. We reached these kids with the gospel of love, mercy, and salvation, feeding them with snacks and meals, and using music ministry to present them with the entire Bible story. In some towns and villages, we established church plants, primarily for the kids, who were eventually followed by their parents.

In Oltenia, Pastor Florin and Janina gathered a few teenagers and children together, feeding them meals, and having fellowship time while maturing them in the message of Christ. They envisioned having a church building for these kids where their parents could attend as well. First, they named these gatherings "Children and Youth Community Center." Next, the Lord responded to their love and faith by providing a church building for them. Presently, we have a church there that is a mix of different ages, with children, teenagers, and adults, all standing strongly in the Lord. This is just one example of the many ways that churches were established in Romania. Sometimes, a few ladies or some older people would get together and start meetings. This has clearly shown us that if God is amid a group of people, they will surely succeed at advancing His kingdom!

Chapter Twenty

Passing the Torch

By the year 2004, the ministry of Christ for Romania spread its branches in many different places, our spiritual sons and daughters having given birth to multiple Bible classes and ministries around the country of Romania. And since 1997, I had been launching regional Bible seminars and national pastoral conferences all over Romania. My vision had always been to raise up new leaders in the ministry, as this was my special calling – creating disciples for Jesus. A very effective way of doing this was starting regional discipleship Bible schools.

From the very start, I knew that my leadership and presidency over the schools would be temporary. Before starting the Bible schools, I told CFNI leaders that my calling was not to remain administrating these groups. However, I would be used to start and pioneer them until established. I would then train someone else to pick up the baton. You see, I'm a simple missionary who pioneers new ministries, handing them to others so they can run with them. Mom Lindsay loved this, and said I was like her late husband Gordon. She gave me a short biography of his ministry, in which I could see the spiritual resemblance. The leadership of CFNI said they trusted me and would do nothing in Romania unless I would be involved.

This ministry of president requires a lot of administrative work, including vision-casting, and providing the tools necessary for everyone's success; however, my spiritual and natural wiring was not to be a boss. This required much of my precious time, and sometimes even holidays and weekends. I was becoming too busy to oversee and care for each school, including the generating of funds for our staff salaries. Nor did I have time to mediate between disagreeing team members. My heart was not satisfied, as I wasn't able to disciple leaders properly and felt somewhat helpless to move every member into the unity of the vision. Only occasionally did others seek for ministry outside of Christ for Romania. They were guided by the idea that "the grass is greener on the other side," which of course, is never the case.

Beside all this, I didn't see "presidential ministry" in the Bible, but I do believe in the pastoral and apostolic ministries.

For example, my first duties as a president was to assign managerial tasks for those working beneath me, as this position requires the same development of infrastructure as any worldly institution. Personally, I don't agree with the idea that someone should perform the duties as president, along with doing pastoral work, at the same time; the work accomplished would become superficial at best. However, we may institute deacons or administrators to help take authority over certain teams of leaders; It is a position with certain authority, but it's not a disciple-making job.

I would have sacrificed my speaking ministry to remain as president, if I knew I could help my team fulfill the vision from the Lord. And I would be fulfilled by simply helping my them do God's will on earth. I would have continued to support and lead my team as a manager, giving up my right to preach and teach, gladly supporting them behind the scenes. You see, it's vital to know how *you* are designed – what you are made for. My inner design made me desire to be on the front lines where the outreach happens. And If God's will is completed through me, and all the outreach necessary to fulfill my calling was done, then I would gladly concentrate my energies solely in multiplying our team so that more could get accomplished.

It is just clear as day that my birthright in Christ is pioneering ministries and missionary outreaches, while touching the spiritual side of people's hearts. And although I've had to fulfill managerial type positions within the ministry, I have never been attracted to corporate titles or institutional positions. In fact, I didn't like it when someone called me by my official title, 'Mr. President' or 'Mr. Director.' I'd usually ask these people to call me by my first name or just simply 'Brother John,' or 'Pastor John.'

When I gave up the presidency over all three Bible schools, each group had fully matured, with around one hundred students in each location. All our Bible school directors, leaders, and our best teachers had graduated from Christ for the Nations. These were well-educated men, qualified, and mature individuals, who took over leadership in each school. Moreover, they had followed my life-example and fatherly leadership for fifteen years, enough time to reproduce the inner changes in each man, as they had been molded into the image of Christ.

An Inheritance for the Next Generation

I trained and commissioned all our local Bible school directors, each one taking the leadership of the schools seriously. By now, they were all free from the Timisoara legal requirements, which for some time, made it impossible for them to branch out to work with competing schools. I encouraged them to keep communication open with their special sponsors who supported our Suceava, Cluj, and Timisoara locations. I told them to write, call, and report to our partners in Christ, continuing to invite them to visit, and bring their church teams to help school ministries as needed. Directors who resigned over one department would be encouraged to take their teams of supporters with them to invest in the next project. I encouraged all the Timisoara, Cluj and Suceava former supporters to continue serving in the same schools as they did in the past; but going forward, they would be connecting with the new directors I had appointed. I was officially giving up my leadership rights, entrusting my American friends and pastors, the churches I labored to locate and connect with, and all the support I raised for Romania, to the next generation of leaders.

It was especially difficult to learn afterwards that some directors failed to consistently communicate with certain sponsors. The result was that the schools lost some of their support due to these leaders regarding their own importance above their commission to keep donors in the loop. They were misguided in their belief that those giving money should support them regardless of consistent communication. In addition to losing donors, these leaders failed to pursue important student outreaches as we had done for more than twelve years. This was the backbone of our CCFR program, as many students became missionaries while still enrolled in school.

But I insisted that the school presidents reported back to me, their progress, testimonies, and special needs, so that I could intervene should there be an exceptional circumstance requiring additional assistance. I told them, "Moving forward, I turn the ball over to you, so you may administrate God's favors and grace to all those in your charge. I am commissioning you to develop what we built as a team. Because from this moment onward, you're not just a director managing the status quo; you are commissioned to expand! While caring for the needs of each person, you are responsible to lead and protect Christ's sheep. And from this moment on, each school will be run independently from each other – each director is freed to develop his own vision." Unfortunately, until all the legal issues were settled, any school that branched out from Timisoara suffered less development. This was because the laws in place for the extension schools were shrouded in unfavorable bureaucracy. This made it difficult to get new projects off the ground. It was challenging to buy and build what we needed for these new projects, until they had their own presidents and structure.

I continued to exhort my leaders by saying, "From now on, each director should maintain a healthy relationship with the brotherhood of Christ for Romania directors, as well as our sister schools. Encourage one another to hold to the initial vision of the Lord, until you've finished the race. And from this moment, everyone has the responsibility before God to uphold the covenant we all pledged to one another and to the Lord. Fan the flame of the anointing Christ has given you and keep moving forward!"

And with the full blessing of CFNI leadership and of our CFR staff in Romania, my position of president had ceased. I became known simply as the founder of the Bible schools and ministry. I told my people, "If you wish, you may treat me as your spiritual father, or as a stranger! But we all know it is *your* duty to act like mature sons, following in your parent's footsteps. Keep in touch with me; but don't be spoiled brats, expecting me to treat you like babies. No! You have grown up and are now responsible before God. So, honor your parents! This is the scriptural way to proceed in our relationship."

The Life Center of Timisoara

From previous chapters, you can see that the 1990's were a foundation-building decade for me. We pioneered Bible schools as well as the other Christ Commission for Romania ministries all over Romania. These were run by me and faithful disciples. Looking back, I often wonder, "How was I able to accomplish all of that?" I then correct myself by saying, "Hey there, the main Actor was not John, but the Holy Spirit moving me wherever God wanted us to show up." It seems true that when a young man is broken down, molded, and then built up again by his Creator, greater things can happen through his life.

What came at the tail end of the '90s was another visionary project. The Life Center of Romania was founded in the year 1999. It was created in partnership with Life Outreach International – founded by James and Betty Robinson of Fort Worth, Texas. Now, before this endeavor was birthed, we had already created several Bible schools, children's camps, and orphanage ministries. These outreaches kept me at the forefront of Christ's work, as we were able to reach people less fortunate. I was in America, working on some appointments and presenting ministry needs, and I had a special appointment booked in the Fort Worth area. I knew James Robinson from a distance, either from TV shows or the evangelism outreaches he did. And while I was a student at CFNI, he was invited to speak at a missions conference.

I called the general office, and immediately got an appointment to meet the missions director, brother Phil Caldwell. He had a burning desire for missions, and I could recall his tears during a few meetings in our past. He was an extension of Robinson's heart, and was a kindred soul to mine. He told me, "John, James visited Romania but didn't connect with anyone's vision there. But here, we are often visited by a Baptist pastor from Timisoara who has invited us to work with him. Honestly, my heart is more in sync with your ministry. Something tells me if we ever pick up in Romania, we will work with you. But let me present it to James and Betty and plan a trip to Romania. We will pray to have a Life Outreach International team visit first."

It is important to note that I didn't push any of our needs or current projects in this conversation, as I made a rule not to do so in any conversation unless first asked. Truthfully,

I never went around begging for money or asking for project funding, as it was important to establish relationships with people. I believed that if what I was doing was God's will, it would be funded. And if I couldn't provide for our projects, I believed it would come through others. I recall a Baptist pastor who missed the mark on this issue, immediately asking for his project to be funded. Some leaders might feel pressured to fund such a work, but over time, that support will likely diminish. I would rather rely on people's inward knowing to fund the works God gave to me, rather than appeal to them through outward emotion.

At last, Phil had won James over to our cause, and could bring a couple of Life Outreach International leaders to Romania. The team came to the Bible school and mission center, visiting a few orphanages around Timisoara. Our goal was to minister to the street kids and feed them on a regular basis. We took in kids over eighteen years old as well, this being the age at which they would be kicked out of the orphanages. This epidemic of homeless youth was aggravated after the communist regime fell, as no one was adequately trained to care for all these young people. This certainly made a big impression on the Life Outreach team, as they were able to interact deeply with these needy youth, teaching them songs as well as Bible verses. We also carried nutritional packs with us, along with clothing and small toys.

Another strong impression that was left on the Life Outreach members, was the reputation that orphanage directors were thieves. Indeed, this reputation followed many of the institutions in Romania, due to the previous rule of communism. You see, under the communist state, practically all institutions had issues with stealing from the government. This was done to survive. At one point, the Life Outreach team met with the director of a certain orphanage which had a reputation of staff members stealing from the kids, skimming from their small food portions. In this meeting, brother Phil asked, "What is your greatest need around here, sir? What needs to be fixed?" The director said with tears in his eyes, "Mr. Phil, many of these kids don't know where they came from. They have no native city, no relatives or parents, and nowhere to go. If we let them go, they will just wander around, lost. They will not be trusted by locals for employment, so they can't expect to find jobs. I expect that they will become street people with no roof over their heads. We've had many already come back to the orphanage, begging me saying, 'Father, have mercy on us! Receive us back. At least for a few days so we can warm up and eat a little. We're hungry and cold and we slept under the open sky. What can we do?'" The director continued,

"So, we take them back for a couple of weeks, but as we don't get state support, we don't have enough beds or food to provide."

This was enough to convince all of us what needed to be done. We needed to build a life-training center for these displaced kids, train and prepare them well before moving them out, and find good jobs for them before they leave. Phil left us with this mandate firmly upon his heart and mind and began looking for a home to begin this "Life Center." We would use this to take some of the overflow of orphans as well, those who were especially needy. Phil made sure that James and Betty's heart would stand with this timely project. He left me saying, "John, please, let's build and rescue these kids as soon as possible."

Just before the turn of the Century, this project came to fruition. Some of the heroes of this endeavor were our teacher, Daniel Junc, and business administrator Valer Uta, who both decided to come and help with this vision. Beside these two men, former Timisoara schools mission director, Traian Lazea, was also instrumental in combatting the Goliath of poverty and the orphan spirit left after the Fall of Communism. Daniel was our first Life Center director, and Valer took the business administration of the Center, while teaching classes on personal development to the young men and women. We ran this organization with kids coming from the State Orphanage for about a decade. In this time, hundreds of kids were educated, trained for work, and most of them today are married, working solid jobs, and are emotionally healthy.

Looking back to a time around the turn of the Twentieth Century, the European Union ordered the state orphanages to go out of business because Romania had become a stain over the proud Union. The kids were then moved into foster homes with families who would receive government support to raise them. But this radical change had a negative side effect, as many of these kids ended up in families who were looking for a monthly income instead of doing the work to raise them with love and discipline. On many occasions these kids were used in a kind of forced labor, working hard for their adopted caregivers. This caused some kids to run away and live out on the streets.

As of today, the Life Center changed its profile, and are now receiving kids from large, poor families who may be living in dire poverty. They mostly come from underprivileged regions where families are not able to support any further education for their children. These precious young ones were created by the Father to love schooling and succeed in life, who would have the potential to attend a university for a career.

And this is exactly the void that the Life Center is filling, with most of our kids graduating the program and attending high profile colleges.

Rise of National Leadership Seminars

The ministry of raising leaders through discipleship training became the center of my heart. This would bring a greater harvest of souls and truth-seekers into the Romanian church, as discipleship would create a multiplication of trained believers. This visionary idea was an offshoot of the Bible school programs. However, this time the focus would be on special leader seminars. It was understood that we needed to teach and train future leaders and pastors in Romania. Most pastors, who were in office, were not trained properly or prepared to handle their pastoral duties. Many would just preach basic evangelistic messages, but not have the knowledge to bring believers into the fullness of their identity and calling. This became the birth of the national seminars and pastoral conferences to raise up spiritual sons and daughters.

The first national Bible seminar was in 1997 and was held at Hot Waters Resort of Baile Felix. Iuliu Centea was my first partner in this vision, who was from the city of Oradea. Currently, Brother Iuliu was filling the position of youth leader over the Pentecostal Union churches. He was a renowned teacher in Romania and had yoked his vision with mine. We met for the first time at our second national youth camp at Moneasa, Arad, and we became good friends from the moment we met. Our team then grew to include Pastors Milo Novacovici and Costel Gramada who joined us. I knew Costel from before the Fall of Communism, as I had preached in his Urziceni city church plant. We then connected with Pastor Nicu Gramesc from Suceava, who was the director of our Bible school there. As a visionary group set on creating spirit-driven conferences, we expanded in every direction within Romania, taking the vision all the way to America.

We also dedicated our first national leadership conference in the city of Baile Felix, with our guest speaker and my spiritual father, Jack Dehart – known as Papa De, from Irving, Texas. And from this groundbreaking meeting, the training continued as we held at least two national conferences and a couple of regional conferences each year. Bishop Larry Pyle took up the speaking mantle after bishop Dehart. Within a short time, we had between three to five national Bible seminars per year. And these larger meetings were followed by a couple of local discipleship seminars as well. This ministry has become so instrumental in building ministry that it has progressed for more than two decades and is the longest running Christ Commission for Romania ministry. And my hope is that the baton will continue to be passed from one generation to the next.

Church Planting & Building Development

I love the church of Christ. I love people gathering with the eternal purpose of God in mind. And I really love church meetings when the people are gathered in a circle, rather than in hundreds of rows where all you can see is the back of someone's head. I love small churches where the members can know one another and fellowship closely with one another. This is the best way to grow relationships, to the point that each member can exhort, counsel, and witness to his or her neighbor. I desire all Christians to exhibit a living faith, speaking life to one another. On the other hand, I don't like the spectacle assemblies where it is more like attending a show than a church service; the people go their way and are never able to implement anything in their day-to-day lives.

From the first year of our Suceava and Timisoara Bible schools, we had a church planting program. We would call it evangelism, sharing, or fellowship; but we were making sure that the true seedling church could be grown, matured, and expanded. And when we did the youth camps, we focused on creating a life-purpose church for the future. The way this worked was that a few believers would get together somewhere, whether it was a few children, some single teenagers, or just young people in general. We would then start with street preaching, mostly to the homeless and to burdened nursing homes, where the leaders' objective was to try to create regular church meetings. You see, the Church is meant to be like a family reunion, with Jesus standing between heaven and earth, wanting to connect the two as a united front.

Later, our focus became raising disciples and leaders all over Romania, with the Christ Commission for Romania, European and American Fellowships, all helping to accomplish this goal. Included in our mission was to build Bible schools, church outreach plants, followed by the Bible training centers. We had graduates like Pastor Milo who, along with his ministry team, planted at least twenty churches in the Walachia area. All total, our graduates have planted hundreds of churches in Romania. This was done in conjunction with continual support – ministerial, financial, and logistical – from our partners and supporters like those in America.

Before the CFNI Bible schools in Dallas started, founder Gordon Lindsay started and pastored dozens of churches. After they were established, he would put in place leadership development so that local disciples were raised up, eventually taking his spot as church leader. Well known in the 1950s and 1960s, Apostle Gordon helped to pioneer the apostolic teaching movement. As a young man, though I didn't know ministers like Gordon Lindsay, I was blessed to be guided into the apostolic ministry by the Lord. In time, I would eventually relate to Apostle Lindsay's vision, and ultimately be considered a friend of Freda Lindsay, who took up the leadership mantle of her husband after he passed away and became like a mother to me.

Along with his many projects, Gordon Lindsay started the Native Church Roof ministry. This was begun about the time I started working with CFNI in 1988. The first roof project I oversaw was that of the Elim church in Timisoara. Before defecting from Romania, I was a member of Elim church beginning in 1971, and I lived there until 1980 after which I left the country for good. Looking back, it was a great privilege for me to raise money for a ministry that provided spiritual sustenance in my earlier years. From this church project until a few years ago, I have personally overseen the covering of forty-eight church roofs, getting around $100,000 in funding. Indeed, in order to successfully fulfill this type of ministry, I needed a team. Under my name, I authorized nine other leaders from Romania who were certified to do this special work, including Nicu Gramesc who helped with most of the roofs I worked on. And under the supervision of these nine men, we watched another 101 church projects come to completion. To date, the total funding for Romanian church roofs is $336,580, providing for a total of 149 church roofs. This was a joint venture between CFNI's Native Church Program leaders, and those selected from Christ for Romania ministry.

Remember, that the apostolic ministry Jesus has in mind is to reach out to other people, building them up both spiritually and naturally, as opposed to just building our own natural institutional kingdoms. We fulfill Christ's vision for His family when we bless those around us – whether we are giving out food, homes, or roofs. And when others grow stronger, than we are growing stronger. Only then will we fulfill Christ's mandate to manifest the unity between heaven and earth.

424

Chapter Twenty-One

Miracles part 1

This book has been an account of the miraculous and historical way God has moved in and through my life. We've looked at the miracles of protection, as I was divinely led out of a country hostile to anything that threatened its communistic regime. We've seen the miracles of relationships that came into my life at the right time for a specific purpose. I've recounted the miracles of provision, as the Lord always brought forth resources for all the projects that He called me to do – whether Bible schools, churches, or the Life Center. Truly, these miracles were the *favor* of God which is poured out over all those who walk as His friends on the earth, who are submitted to His will.

Overall, the miracles which God brought into my life came before I even knew to ask for them. He knows our hearts and therefore the things that we need. Moreover, He is a loving

Father and will provide more perfectly than any father on earth. And it is His desire to give us the very best, so that we prosper in Him, and in everything else which aligns with heaven's design.

In this chapter, we will look at four specific miracles that built up my faith, and that of my team's. These accounts will undoubtedly provide wisdom to those trusting God for miraculous provision; for it takes wisdom to reveal God's kingdom on the earth, and faith to courageously display that wisdom through our everyday lives.

Oltenia Camp's Lottery Miracle

After the Tabernacle Camp of Romania concluded its mission, the children camp began on the southern side of Romania. While our graduates of Timisoara Bible School moved out to do mission work in Oltenia, we were in desperate need to continue providing a summer camp for the youth. Many of the younger generation were freshly converted to faith in Christ and needed further spiritual maturity. Pastor Milo took this time to scout out the mountains of southern Pades by Closani village, for a plot of land for sale.

Now, there was already a land developer who wanted this property and was offering a higher price than we were. But the favor of God was upon us as the seller was aware of Christ for Romania, and all the charitable work we were doing for the orphans, the poor, and destitute. He felt strongly that we should get this land, as we would use it to take care of society's most needy. As a result, the seller drove the price down for us, a good thirty-five percent! There was a condition to this sale; a deadline was set for a couple of weeks, at which time we needed to pay the entire amount in cash, or else he would be forced to sell to the real estate developer.

Pastor Milo called and told me the situation. He said, "Papa John, can we produce $6000 in less than two weeks before the deadline?" I told him, "If we're able to do it, it will be a miracle, as the Christ Commission bank account doesn't have any money to spare. But two weeks is a long time for a miracle to happen. Let's just pray and believe that if it's God's will, it will be done." Because I was in Romania at this time, I wrote an email to present this urgent project to our supporters. It was an inconvenient time, as I was doing missional work and was not able to make it to America. Because Romanian banks were not yet able to have money wired to them, money had to be physically brought into the country. It was as if we needed a second miracle – just getting the money to our country! If we did happen to get the money in our Florida bank account, someone would have to fly it over. But with God, all things are possible.

About three days later, after I had written the email, I heard back from Robert and Betty Alexanders, announcing to me that their local grocery store had offered lottery tickets to their most loyal customers. They said, "John, we are among hundreds of people competing for it. But when we filed the store ticket, we promised the Lord to do whatever He wanted us to, should we win it. We even said, 'We'll give it to John's ministry in Romania to cover one of his valuable projects.' And John, by a miracle, we just had the winning check mailed to us! How should we send this money to you?" I replied, "My dear faithful servants of God, please wire it today to Lowell and Sally in Florida." Then, I asked Lowell if they might know someone coming to Romania. Of course, they found a trustworthy brother who just happened to be leaving in a few days for our country. So, the money was wired immediately, and by the second day, the minister got the money and carried it to Timisoara a couple of days before the deadline. I happily drove to Oltenia and paid for the land. Although we bought it for $6000, the same land today is worth $100,000! And since that day, there have been hundreds of youth delivered, saved, and healed there. God always causes us to triumph in Christ Jesus!

$15,000 From Across the World

Another miracle happened for the Christ for Oltenia Christian center in Motru, led by Pastors Milo and Nina Novacovici. As my spiritual son, I've had the opportunity to see Milo pull off some amazing deals in a short amount of time, which would certainly be hard to do if God was not intervening. This just seems to be the way with him, as a man ordained by God.

Brother Milo planted many churches in smaller towns and villages, in places where there was complete darkness prior to him coming, as the curse of witchcraft was deeply embedded in the culture. People would trudge around, hopelessly looking for something to fill their empty hearts. And so, all of us prayed about planting a church in Motru, which is a small city surrounded by the towns and villages where smaller churches were already planted. There were some believers in Motru who attended, as well as a few ministers serving other churches around the city. And while planning and praying for it, a large piece of land close to the downtown area had opened for sale.

The sale price for this plot was $15,000. The owner was not a Christian but sympathized with anyone involved in charitable deeds, and because this was a central piece of land, it was coveted by businesspeople looking to build their portfolio. But brother Milo presented the Life Center project, explaining the goal of creating a ministry that would require the land for all the charity work to take place. He spoke of a home where deprived children and poor people's needs would be met. Again, the landowner was moved and convicted by the Lord that he should offer this property to God, with the risk of losing money. And so, he gave us a short window of time to buy at a lower price. If we missed the deadline, the sale would immediately be given to a businessman willing to pay the normal rate.

This agreement was valid till the last day of that month – a three-week period. I told Milo, "As you know, this is not a convenient time to be raising money, with the multiple local and national projects that have not all been accounted for monetarily. Asking our sponsors for more money would not be a good thing. It would be embarrassing to present yet another need to them. However, let us pray and believe, and I will take some time to think more on who I can present this project to." I then recalled being introduced to a man named John Stoker, who was a pastor from Resurrection Fellowship, in Loveland, Colorado. He came as a guest speaker while our Romanian students were still at CFNI. I was introduced to him by Freda Lindsay. From that time forward, his church assisted our summer camps both financially and by sending ministry teams to help in Romania. He also decided to pledge a monthly support to my family, as he was supporting a host of worldwide missionaries. His church was the most dedicated to missions of any church I had been to in America.

Now, the missions pastor of Resurrection Fellowship was a man named Mark Lucks, who visited Romania a few times. He had a loving heart for world missions, one of the most compassionate pastors I had ever met. I emailed him with this emergency project, indicating our needs. One day later, I received an email with the subject: "John, the Lord answers our prayers before we tell them." I knew immediately that this would be a divinely inspired correspondence. He wrote, "Hi John! I'm glad to let you know that a couple of days ago, a lawyer who is a member of our church came into my office, pulled out a check from his wallet, and laid it on my desk. The Lord had impressed upon him to write it for a country in Eastern Europe – I do believe it was for Romania. I picked up

431

the check to see the amount, and to my shock, it was $15,000. What wonderful generosity for missions! This man was willing to give this money without knowing any specific needs. And, I was just about to write you an email asking if you had any current needs. But you beat me to it! And here is the provision!"

Mark continued, "John, the Spirit of God is over us, and our requests, projects and needs are on His table before we even know what to pray or ask! Now, I'm mailing this check today to your Florida office, and I will ask Sally to send this money to you right away. Be blessed and prosper my friend!" What a conclusion to this story! The full payment was given on time, and the property was acquired. Today, the value of this land is at least $150,000, not including the home that was built on it where the ministry of serving the needy was being accomplished.

Following these miraculous provisions, Pastor Morris Sheats of Hillcrest Church gave $10,000, which became the first faith-seed to be planted for the foundation of Motru Christian Center. Next, Pastor Mark Duke of the Rock of Brentwood church came with building materials for the walls, floors, and ceiling. CFNI's Native Church Program built the roof. There were also American donors who, along with many Romanian locals, donated money and made the building gorgeous. It has been our hope that this ministry would grow until the building is filled with disadvantaged people who need to be cared for. Moreover, the goal is to use this facility as a convention center for all the local churches and the surrounding ministries. And going forward, Pastors Milo and Nina have been responsible to make this Life Center a great blessing for the central region of Oltenia.

Led by the Spirit in a Phonebook

From the early days of my U.S. ministry until today, I've done everything as upright as possible, without becoming religious or politically correct. This can be seen in the first part of the decade of the '90s, when for a couple of weeks I was in Anaheim staying with my friends Nicu and Rosy Crihalmean. I was scheduled to speak to a Romanian church's Sunday evening service, pastored by Lazar Gog. My morning was free, however, as my ministry was still small with an unformed mailing list. The night before, I felt like picking up the city phonebook that was laid on the family desk, to check out who I should visit the next morning in the Anaheim area. I felt a joyful quickening in my spirit when I saw a church called

Christian Life Fellowship. This was evidence to me that God was leading me to check out church names and to make contacts.

I attended the morning service as the pastor spoke on living an earthly life guided by the Spirit. I introduced myself to him at the end of service, and he was visibly happy to see me. He even gently rebuked me for not introducing myself before the service, as he would have gladly let me greet the church. He wanted to know how I found out about them. I said, "No one told me except the Lord, who guided me through a phonebook until I landed on your name and church." He was impressed with how I was led there, and then said, "John, I've had Romania on my heart for some time. I've even thought about planning a mission trip there, and to make it our mission field." From that initial meeting, we decided to meet up throughout the week and talk about the future.

Since then, Pastor Sam and his wife Gloria have visited us several times in Romania, their church teams ministering there as well. Their church got heavily involved in building homes for the poor with the summer camps for the orphans of Suceava, as well as supporting the Falticeni State Orphanage. And since my first encounter at Christian Life Fellowship, they have contributed over $100,000 to various needs in Romania. Wow! It seems to me that all we need to do is listen to the Spirit of God. He is the grand alternative to killing ourselves with stress and pressure, trying to raise money and working the people around us to death. His will is worth discovering on earth, as He will always provide a better way for us!

A Five-Minute Phone Call, Ten Years of Support

In that early part of the '90s, when the ministry in Romania was really flourishing on every side, I was traveling quite a bit in the States, visiting people and churches, regardless if I knew them or not. It was a time to present the ministry outreach opportunities in Romania. And while driving from Texas to Arizona, I had a casual conversation with a friend on the phone who told me it would be good to contact a from Tempe, Arizona. However, knowing I would spend just a short time in the Phoenix area, I called the church while still on the road to see if I might get an appointment with the Pastor, James Roam. I caught him at the tail end of his day and told him about my ministry and asked if we could meet the following week.

Brother James said, "John I'm sorry. I'm just leaving for a leadership conference and will not be home for another week. I will not be able to meet with you. But starting next month you will receive a regular monthly check of $50.00." Confused, I asked him why he so quickly decided to support me not knowing who I was. I said, "Did you hear about me and Christ Commission for Romania already?" He replied, "Not at all John. I heard of your ministry for the first time in this conversation. But no need to wonder any further John on how I decided to help you, even though it's been only a brief introduction. Because Jesus is with me, and plainly told me, 'Jim, you should support John right here and now, whether or not you meet him.'"

"So, you see," he continued, "you were confirmed by God and not man. And I'm sure you have been called to reach Romania for Jesus. And for this reason, I hope to connect with you later in the mission field. But until then, look for the first $50 check coming from Christ Life Church of Tempe. Please, just provide me with your mailing address and expect to receive this month by month. Also, join me in prayer so we may acquire more missions funds, and increase it to $100 a month. Bless you and the ministry you're doing for our Lord. Now, I must run! I'm already a little late, but it was God's plan that we should meet before leaving the office."

Truly, Pastor James did this without wavering. And soon after, the check doubled. For more than a decade, he sent it month by month, until he passed on to His eternal home. And his wife, sister Sharon, took over the helm of this ministry of giving, until she joined with her husband in heaven. Then Pastor Phil Goldsberry continued it until the church merged with Gate Church, after which support had ended. It is true that everything on earth is temporary. But surely doing the will of God will have an eternal impact which will last forever.

Chapter Twenty-Two

Miracles part 2

America was not only home to my family and me, but a home to numerous miracles. While ministering in churches around the U.S., many believers saw me as a missionary in my ministry to them, to them, as they saw major shifts in their lives, and exalted the Lord. But Satan was looking to hinder my path, trying to block Christ Commission in Romania and America from finishing our race.

Angels & Gas Stations

The first evil attempt of note happened with our car. Viorica and I were newly married and starting fresh in America. We were working hard to build up the ministry of medical aid for Romania, as well as smuggling Bible materials into the country. We were driving a large, white, Mercury Cougar – our original car when we first came to the States. For a long time, I would hear a little ringing bell noise that would sound off in the engine like drumbeats. As an experienced driver, I knew a bit about the mechanical side of vehicles, and I figured this to be a cylinder problem, which raised doubt about the reliability of our car – we might go another mile or another hundred miles. Either way, we were tight on money, so rebuilding the engine or buying a new car were not options.

We started our drive early in the morning from Dallas, and by 11 p.m. we were looking to take a few hours to rest. We were scheduled to connect with someone the next day to set up new locations for shipping containers coming from Romania. Our travel route was to pass through Virginia, and then on to Pennsylvania, Ohio, Illinois, and then back to Dallas. But just as we passed the border of Virginia, I heard a loud bang in the engine which shook the car. I knew what had happened, but still didn't want to believe it. Saying nothing, I just lowered our speed and drove slowly while praying. To her surprise, Viorica was wondering why I was not stopping to see what had happened. "Perhaps it is a flat tire?" she asked. But knowing what was going on, I said, "No. But since it is dangerous to stop here, let's be praying. I will drive a little more." But the car went slower and slower. Besides, I didn't like the idea of stopping in the middle of nowhere. Thankfully, around the corner was a big gas station. With the engine bumping around and us slowing down, I pulled into the parking lot.

Right after we parked the car, a member of the gas station staff came out to see who it was with the noisy vehicle. And once parked, I pushed on the gas pedal for a few seconds just to hear more clearly what the engine sounded like. The attendant heard this as well. But once I released the gas pedal, the engine made a bellowing noise and then died. I tried to start it up again, but to no avail. I told the man what had happened just a couple of miles down the freeway. Then he said, "Beside my job here, I am also trained as an auto mechanic, and based on what I just heard from your engine, it was a miracle you were able to drive it this far. The bad news is this engine is finished. Until you fix it, you will not be able to start or drive it from this spot. It will have to be towed. But we have a mechanic shop here too." He pointed toward the large, closed doors, and continued, "But ours is not for heavy engine work like what your car needs. However, tomorrow, you may ask the manager and maybe he will accept it." Then, looking disappointed, he said, "We might need a week to get the necessary parts and rebuild it. But let's just wait till morning to see what we can do."

In this newly developing situation, I knew we'd be losing the Friday appointment, the Sunday services, and maybe the whole trip. Moreover, we were short on cash to rebuild the engine, and we didn't have credit cards. The only viable option was to leave our broken car there and continue our trip on foot. However, not to panic Viorica, I didn't express any of these alternatives to her. I was certain that the only way out of there was a miracle from God. Then she asked me, "What are we going to do from here?" I simply told her, "My dear, you know what, we're already tired and hungry and a little confused. So instead of planning anything now, let's wait till morning for the solution. Let the Lord speak first what will be the best course of action for us."

We ate some light food in our bag and slept in our car. I took the front seat and Viorica took the back, which was a lot more comfortable because of how much room these eight-cylinder Mercury's had. I then told her, "While we sleep, let's stay in meditation and prayer so that by the morning, we'll get the right answer." Now, I went to sleep while quietly praying. Somehow, I slept soundly till the morning. But as I woke up, I heard a voice speaking to me from the driver's side window, in Romanian. I could barely see his figure through the window, although I was mainly listening and not trying to see who was speaking.

"Good morning John and Viorica! Now, when you have awakened and are ready to go, bring your thanksgivings to the Lord, eat breakfast, and thank the Lord for it. Then, make sure you fill up the gas tank and just continue your trip. Have a good day and journey." And then, everything went silent. When I turned around to see who was talking, there was no one there! I looked through both windows, front and back, and realized that they were all closed. It was early in the morning, so no one was moving around the station. I then turned to Viorica, wondering why she wasn't listening to the same voice. All I could do at this point was thank God for sending a Romanian speaking angel to me.

My first thought was to test the engine, but then I reconsidered. "This might not be an act of faith," I thought. Also, I didn't want to wake up Viorica too soon. Now, after she woke, she asked me again, "What should we do? Do we have a plan?" I replied, "Yes, we have one!" I then repeated the same words the angel had told me. "We will pray and thank the Lord, clean up a little, eat breakfast, and then get back on the road." She just looked at me as though I had two heads. But she trusted me, knowing that I was speaking like a faith-man, so she knew she could follow my lead. All I could think was, "Viorica married a crazy person!"

We did exactly as I said, started the car, filled it with gas, and took off. The engine started right away; in fact, it went more smoothly and stronger than it did before. And while driving, I told her the story of the mechanic angel who fixed our car while we slept. Excitedly, I told her that this angel spoke perfect Romanian. We drove at least another 3000 miles for a few weeks in a row, having no more problems. But after a few weeks, when we took off from Chicago headed to Dallas, the engine noise came back. We were then several miles onto the Chicago freeway loop. I decided to stop in the emergency lane and check our location on a Chicago map. I found out that we were less than a mile away from the Lungu family, who emigrated from Suceava to Chicago. We got out on the freeway again and in just a few minutes we made it to their home. While we were with them, we told them about our car issues, and discovered that they had a car just sitting their driveway, not being used. The car was a few years younger than our car and an expensive sports car that had brake light issues. They had given up on it as they figured the problem was electrical and not a simple fix.

The Lungu family advised us to leave our car with them and use their sports car to drive to Dallas. They cautioned us to be aware that the brake lights were not signaling correctly. They told us if we liked it, we could keep it, and they would just keep ours. We decided to take them up on this offer, as we had some appointments to make in Dallas. After getting back on the freeway we stopped at a gas station to fill up the tank. Close by was a parts shop, where I got a second opinion from one of the mechanics there. I already knew something about electrical wires, and the man confirmed that I was correct. We detected the problem, put the necessary parts in, and in a few minutes all the car lights were fixed.

What is fascinating is how God chose to supernaturally fix our old car, and then gave us a newer car soon instead, which by itself is another miracle. Over the next few years, we kept the sports car, and the Lungu family kept the Mercury, and everyone was happy! Sometime later we bought another car and gave the sports car to a CFNI graduate as a blessing. Later, he went on a South American mission field, which left many other young men earnestly desiring his state-of-the-art vehicle! The Lord is truly amazing.

Highway Miracle of Protection

After about a month living in Dallas, Viorica and I were driving to Los Angeles when we passed Van Horn going to El Paso. Driving up the hills there, something happened to our cooling system as the engine got hot and the water began steaming through the hood. We stopped to look, cool off the engine, and check and refill the radiator if necessary. But while we were stopped on the side of the freeway, a car drove by filled with young Spanish men. When they saw we were having a car problem, the stopped their car and asked us what was going on in broken English. I then had a spiritual insight that they were likely illegal immigrants in the country, and the fact that we were close to the border of Mexico, this made sense. I then perceived that they weren't there to help us but rob us instead. I also saw them eying my beautiful wife. In what I could understand in Spanish, they were encouraging each other to harm us and were trying to figure out the best way to do it. I trusted God to help us get out of this spot, but their bodies were blocking our ability to move forward.

Just then, a police car coming toward us from the opposite direction stopped another driver who had pulled over parallel to us. When the suspicious men had seen the cop car, they hurried away, quickly climbing into their car and sped off. Now, on that deserted freeway with only a few cars passing by, what were the odds that a police car would pull over another vehicle right across the road from us, at that exact time? God will do miracles in our lives to keep us in His safe keeping, because He cares deeply for us!

Spinning in the Smokey Mountains

Near the end of the '90s, we were now a family having three kids – Alina, Nadine, and Nathan, their ages ranging from four to eleven. We were continually traveling back and forth between Romania and America, as we were often in need of funds to be raised in the States for various projects. And so, Viorica and I packed our family luggage into our large Plymouth van, ready to take off for about six weeks on a northeastern American itinerary. But just before leaving, Randy Bozarth asked me to stop in front of the main offices to pray before sending us off. After we prayed, he said to me, "John, please stay safe as Satan is after your life, and we still need you here! I will keep praying for you too." After saying goodbye and driving off, I found it odd that I had never heard Randy speak such a cautionary word.

But in the same moment I was pondering what was said, I reminded myself about a dream I had the night before. My whole family was traveling somewhere together in an unknown mission field, and while we were walking between these white buildings to find our appointment, there appeared a tall, thin man dress in black clothes behind us, with a gun in his hand. He began chasing us with the gun pointing at us. He followed closely with the purpose of shooting me first, as I knew his intention was to kill me. But just as he attempted to take a deadly shot, he missed us again and again. After we kept turning one corner after another, like running in a circle, we finally escaped our aggressor. As my recollection of this dream ended, I told Viorica and the kids that we needed to pray as Satan wanted to kill us; but as God was with us, we would avoid Satan's grasp.

On that same day, just after 11 pm, we were driving over the Smokey Mountains of Tennessee, and I was just thanking the Lord for keeping us from any evil incident so far on our journey. We drove on that day and began to feel we were ready to stop and stay the night in the next motel we saw. And just as I was thinking that any possibility of peril had passed, and while driving up a mountain road, our van suddenly lost power steering, and the car began to spin out of control! It seemed worse than if we were driving on a sheet of ice. We were going about seventy-five miles an hour when the power steering failed and the van started to spin around, colliding with the left safety rail and then with the right. The only thing I heard was Viorica shouting "Jesus!" and praying in tongues. Our kids were in the back doing the same thing. We became a bona fide church in that car!

Now this miracle was significant in scope, because big trucks were passing by us as we were spinning in the road, missing our vehicle to the left side and to the right. It felt like we were in a game of human ping pong! Then suddenly, we found ourselves parked perfectly on the right side of the road and out of harm's way, where I put the emergency lights on. Looking in the backseat, no one was hurt at all! My wife said they piled one upon the other, holding tightly to each other down on the right side of the car floor. We were all fine and the car had some minor dents, but was also basically fine, and no one was complaining. About ten minutes later, we saw the flashing blue and red lights of a police car pulling up behind us. With a tremor in his voice, the policeman approached the car window and asked, "Is everyone alright here? Does anyone need a paramedic? They will be here shortly." I replied, "No sir, everyone is fine. God kept us safe!"

I then asked him, "How did you arrive so quickly? We're surrounded by these mountains with nothing but blackness around us." He responded, "We got calls from several truck drivers telling us a white van was spinning out of control, and likely went over the edge into a gorge......that people are likely severely hurt or dead. When I got the message, I was patrolling not far from here, just a few miles away. I sped over here thinking the worst, that I'd encounter hurt or dead people everywhere. But you say everything is fine? That's unbelievable. I mean, are you sure?" He then checked Viorica and the kids and agreed with my assessment. He pulled up a Catholic cross from his shirt and thanked God for making his night. He signaled the paramedics to turn around and go back to where they came from.

How do you go from spinning seventy-five miles per hour on the freeway, with trucks on every side, and make it out okay? And in just ten minutes, he filled out a short accident report stating that the driver was not at fault, but just caught an oily spot on the road. Smiling, he said to me, "Maybe a midnight evil spirit was here to get you, but God's angels just dropped down and saved you!" I replied, "You are so right sir! It's exactly that. Satan wanted to kill us, but we have a mighty God!" Then, with his lights still on, he went on ahead of us and allowed us to follow him to the first motel. Waving goodbye to us he said, "The Dolinschi family has a great God who truly protected you, and we're all happy! Have a good night!"

Where Transmissions Fail,
The Church Succeeds

This van that we had was an older Plymouth model which we drove hundreds of thousands of miles around America and became like a second family home to us while ministering. When ministering in churches, I considered myself to be a missionary for both America and Romania, so I would preach a combination of messages that spoke to both cultures. We mainly stayed in homes with Christian families who were hospitable and loving toward us – some American friends and some Romanian families as well. I was especially welcomed in homes when I was with my family. The friends we made over the years would plead with me to bring Viorica and the kids back with me. It was generally reliable with the exception of some occasional electrical glitches. The problem was that these glitches would cause the engine to shut down. I brought the van to have it fixed but there were no mechanics who were able to correctly diagnose the problem it was having. And then on its own, the glitch would resolve itself and the engine would start up again.

On one itinerary in particular we were headed for the northeast part of the U.S. Typically, our travel would take about six weeks, seldom reaching three months at a time. Now, we made it all the way to North Carolina, up to Pennsylvania, and all the way to Michigan. However, I felt the transmission begin to make more noise, sluggishly shifting as we drove. And about fifty miles before we reached a church in Lansing, Michigan, the transmission began to fail, and the speed diminished to around ten miles per hour. I spotted a small entrance into a parking lot area where I parked and began my inspection of the engine. There were no oil leaks or any other fluid leaks for that matter, and it seemed that the issue was confined to the transmission. The church service was about to start in an hour, and I hadn't missed a service so far. So, I felt frustrated that I was being forced to miss it especially since it was my first time in the church. We prayed and believed that we would make it, even if we were a little late, as we were fine with getting there before it ended. I just put the key in the ignition to start the car again, and amazingly it started back up. As I drove it, the speed increased to 50 miles per hour with the transmission running more smoothly. Although I didn't appreciate the many stop signs along the way, we made it to the church only twenty-five minutes late. Everyone was just happy that we made it, not knowing the reason for the delay.

When I got up to speak, I shared the van story: "Hey church! If we are here it is because of a miracle." Then I told them about the issue with the transmission, "We made it here, but I'm not sure if we will be able to move this van out of the parking lot!" At the end, all the people were curious to see if the van would be drivable. But this time, we couldn't get it to move an inch forward or backward – it was dead. This gave people a reason to wonder, "How were you even able to get it to the church parking lot?" Of course, we know that with God, *all* things are possible. And He will make a way for us to arrive exactly where we need to be.

We stayed with the Fighter family in Lansing, while praying and thinking about our next move. The following day, we hauled the van to a transmission service. Here the manager told us that a new transmission would cost at least $1500. Because the total value of the car was less than the repair, he said it would better to save our money and buy another vehicle. Now, Georgia Fighter was a feisty girl. On Thursday, she asked the pastor to come to her home for a chat. We didn't know what was in her head yet. But when the pastor arrived, she bluntly told her, "Our family will put at least $2000 toward the purchase of another, newer van for the Dolinschi family. But the church must put the other half to make the down payment now. We should not let this sweet family leave the way they came to us; they should be sent out blessed! As for us, we'll not let them out of our home without the best possible van in Lansing."

The next day, we went to a dealer with both new and used cars. The salesperson showed us several vans to choose from. My whole family eyed the same one – a new, red, Montana Pontiac. This was just two years old, with thirty thousand miles, and in great condition. The sales rep was generous too, giving us $3,000 less than asking price. The total expense was $14,000. With the down payment coming from the Fighters and the church, we were able to put $4,000 into our purchase. What a blessing! God knew where our old car should break down, the people who should generously bless us, and the reward which would be given to us and to those who gave of their treasure.

It was amazing to discover how much emotion we had when parting from our old van. We spent over ten years making memories in this vehicle, from near accidents, to many fruitful ministry trips. Viorica and the kids had tears in their eyes at the thought of leaving the Plymouth behind. But the

Lord was faithful. And I was jubilant as this marked a new season for us, one which I could hardly wait to discover.

Leaving the blessed Michigan state behind us, we still had about $10,000 left to pay for this new vehicle. But less than three months from that point, a money miracle occurred. I was ministering at Good Shepherd Church in Christian, Missouri. And on one Sunday evening, while being housed in a hotel near the church, Pastor Mike Barbera came by our hotel bringing some unexpectedly good news. "John and Viorica," he started, "You have been blessed again! We have a car dealership owner in the congregation who was moved by your story. Late this afternoon he called me to inform you that by tomorrow, he is going to pay your car payments in full! I just need your car information, and the bank account, and you will be all set." It's profound that we call these sorts of blessings "miracles"; and yet, to God, this is simply His nature. It's as though He reminds us in the miraculous provision, "This is who I am!"

This miracle van is still with us today. It's drivable and in good condition, with all the electronics working perfectly. And like our old van, we have great stories that could be told with this new one. If you're wondering why vehicles seem to pop up quite a bit in my story, it's because they have helped to not only transport me and my family, but the gospel message all over the country!

Home Sweet Romanian Home

When we moved from Austria back to Romania, we found ourselves living in a crowded apartment with Petru and Maria Sarbu, my sister and brother in law in Timisoara, as well as with other friends. There was no real privacy which meant that I didn't have the focus I needed for the work I was doing. We started to pray for our own home and office, a blessed place where we could launch our ministry around the world. Furthermore, we needed a correspondence and communication center that would keep us connected with our people in Romania and America. And so, after the first year of living back in Romania, it was time to pray and envision a new life in our home country.

During this time of prayer and travel between Romania and America, we met with sister Lindsay who asked about our living arrangement in Romania. And then in time, several other pastors asked me the same question. In response, we made a simple plan to buy an apartment or a little home in Timisoara, with an approximate price based on our knowledge of the value of homes in Timisoara. Before leaving the States, we got about half of the total fund from two churches, and half from CFNI. We also received a couple thousand dollars from offerings and donations. When we made it back to Timisoara, we began looking at apartments for sale. But it was a challenge to find anything of value, as the real estate market had gone bankrupt after the communist regime. This caused a freeze on the sale of apartments and houses due to the uncertainty of banks and sellers. There was still a large swath of people who doubted that the communists left for good. Instead, many were looking to escape the country, and settle under freer governments. Therefore, prices did not rise too high, because of the panic and uncertainty, people were afraid to sell too cheap or to buy and then lose family members leaving the country. Sometimes there was an emergency sale for families moving out for good. And this is when we found the Czech family, who were citizens of Romania, but decided to move back to their native land of the Czech Republic.

We found this family's house in an advertisement paper, where it was listed as an apartment because it was a split home with two little units. We really liked the home as it was well maintained and the price was about the same as what we were prepared to pay; however, we could buy it in our names as we were still citizens of America. In those times, any foreigner needed a Romanian citizen as a partner in order to purchase Romanian property. So, we decided that our partner would be Valer Uta, our Bible school administrator in Timisoara.

This home needed a lot of remodeling, as the house's water supply was illegally connected to the city water through the underground pipes running through the back yard and garden of the neighbors. This was a common practice of Romanians, in order to make a decent living in the communist era. So, we connected the water to the correct city pipe, brought the sewer line down our street, and brought the gas pipeline from the main street into our street. We did this using the money we had saved, as the city didn't provide any help at all. Keep in mind, all of this took place over a ten-year period, as we used whatever money we could set aside for the next project.

The price today is incomparable to then, as we paid about $12,000 for the home and a few thousand to bring utilities in. But the same home price now is over ten times that much. As always, we considered this to be the Lord' s provision for our lives, helping us get what we needed at the lowest possible price with only a little money saved up. And as for the controversial issue of communism returning in Romania, I never believed it. In fact, the Lord told me five years before its fall that this evil system would totally collapse.

Home Buying in the U.S.

The Lord continually directed us to step out in faith, trusting in His providential guidance and miracles. Otherwise, many of these projects would never have begun. While spending part of our time in America, we used to stay on the campus of Christ for the Nations International, in an apartment which my family considered to be a home. We could feel the godliness of this area, even though there was much ungodliness in the greater area of Dallas. And as far as buying a house here, the Lord told us the same thing He instructed us concerning marriage – "Take care of my sheep and I will take care of your home." And by God's providence, we met a good friend, Pastor Paul Greer, a pioneer of faith who along with Dennis Lindsay, visited Romania in the early '90s. We developed a strong relationship, sometimes speaking together in the Ambassadors for Christ Church in Bertram, Texas.

Our friend Paul was assisted by a pastoral assistant named David Humphries, who also owned a few pharmacies around the Burnett area. While we ministered one Sunday, brother David came to us with good news. "John and Viorica, you have a wonderful family, and you do great work for the Lord. Linda and I have decided that through the pharmacies we own, we want to support you with one thousand dollars a month. Also, Linda and I were discussing your situation, and we would love to see you get your own home. We know that your family is the priority, and moving from one place to another is hard, especially since wives need to feel stability, a place where they can put their clothes and other valuables away, and not worry about having to ruin or lose items." David was not wrong, as at least two times we lost most or at least part of our things in the moves we made. One time, we left our belongings with a Romanian family, storing it in their garage. Our good brother Cornel forgot about our things being stored there, and while his wife was away from home, he cleaned out the entire garage, sending everything to the local Good Will store! I don't fault him for this; God is in control!

David continued, "John and Viorica, Linda and I strongly advise you to save this money we will be giving you, so you can get that blessed home for you and your family. We are aware of the ministries of the many missionaries who visit us in this small church; but we prayed and prayed as to where to give our support, and at last, the Lord moved us to choose *you*. And along with you, we'll help two other missionaries, each one of you receiving the same support." I then called Sally Senitz who kept track of our Florida bank account, and told her, "Please, don't use this monthly support for anything, even emergencies. Set it aside in a special account as it is not ours."

And after a few years, the need arose for us to buy a home, as many other CFNI staff were moving out of apartments and doing the same. Sister Lindsay and brother Dennis encouraged us to believe God for a home around the CFNI campus. By this time, we had already saved over $50,000. And from this point, we started to look for a home to buy; and of course, before long we found the right one. Despite not having credit cards and virtually no credit built up, we had such a large down payment that we got approved for a low interest loan.

This was the year 2001. And from this year on, we continued to buy and sell homes, always making money on each sale. As in the case of our latest house purchase in Arizona, which has doubled in equity, we have likely lived for free in each house. We've also been able to bless missionaries and immigrants from Romania who have stayed with us in our various homes. You see, when God oversees our endeavors, even our little investments and finances, our homes and cars, everything becomes a blessing to us and to those in our lives.

The Handbag, the Beggars, & the Angels

In the early '90s, when the first two Romanian schools were in full operation, CFNI president Dennis Lindsay and Pastor Paul Greer of Ambassadors for Christ Church taught in both the Timisoara and Suceava Bible schools, as well as in a few city churches. To travel and minister with Dennis is much fun, because he is a happy, humorous person to be around. I am reminded of the time Dennis, Paul, our ministry administrator Valer, and I were driving the ten-hour drive from Timisoara to Suceava. While stopped at a rest area, Dennis grabbed the keys from me without me knowing it. While on the way to the bathroom, I realized the keys were not in my pocket. When we all got back to the car, I was expecting the one who took the keys to unlock the doors. Dennis decided to fake us out! He said, "John, you must have lost them" putting all the responsibility on me. However, I had a feeling he was playing games with me as he usually did, so I was not fearful that we lost the keys. I played along saying, "Look here my friends. If the car keys are lost, then there is no option left except that we hitchhike to Suceava! After all, it'll take days till the locksmith can get here, and we don't want to mess up our schedule. Wouldn't it be fun for everyone to see two poor Americans and two Romanians hiking up the road, with little money in their pockets? This adventure would be remembered forever! So, let's get to the highway – we don't have time to waste!" Dennis could hardly hold back his laughter as he said, "Thanks, but no thanks! I'm a true American. Besides, the Lord just found our keys for us!" I replied, "Sorry, guys! It looks like our grand adventure failed. I guess we'll have to drive from here. Dennis, thanks for your faith in God, as mine was too weak!"

We continued driving on the road for several hours, with certain traffic delays and bad road conditions as we passed over the Carpathian Mountains and toward the Ukrainian border. Just before reaching the Suceava School, two policemen pulled us over in the middle of nowhere. The traffic police were still operating with communistic era rules, randomly stopping cars for no reason. I asked Valer to hand me my handbag, however, there was no handbag to be found. I had everything in there, thousands of dollars, and personal identification like my passport and driver's license. Everyone looked around but couldn't find it anywhere in the car. Then we remembered that I did something in a Deva city restaurant that I don't normally do. I took the bag with me just in case we needed more money than what was in my pocket. Now, we ate upstairs by a window table next to big curtains. Although it seemed safe enough to hide the bag near the curtains, it was not a good idea, as it could be easily forgotten. And sure enough, when we left the restaurant, everyone was joking and having fun, but I forgot to take the handbag with me.

While I told the policemen that I left my handbag in a Deva restaurant, I noticed that they seemed happy that they were going to be able to fine these rich Americans, or even arrest me for driving without a license. So, I said, "Let's go to the police station so I can call the restaurant manager and ask about the bag I left." It would be a close call, as it was late, and the restaurant was likely closing. Suddenly, two beggars came up to our car window, aggressively asking for money and beginning to shove the officers out of the way. In fact, the policemen seemed to lose all authority as they told the two to shut up and go away; but the beggars became indignant and kept shouting at us for money. Not knowing what else to do, the policemen said, "Goodbye!" and drove away, leaving us free to depart.

As we left that spot, Dennis exclaimed, "Oh man! Did you see how those two angels showed up out of nowhere? I mean, their faces looked different. And although they were dressed in rags, they were well-built and looked strong. They appeared to have so much authority over the policemen; once they showed up, the officers had no more control over us. What a miracle we just got!" Right away, Pastor Paul Grier started to prophesy, "The handbag left in Deva is in a restaurant safe, untouched, with everything still inside. John, you will get it back, without any question. I'm one hundred percent sure of it! Stay happy!"

When we got to the hotel in Suceava, we immediately called the Deva restaurant and spoke to the manager who was still there, despite the place being closed. Then the good news came, that the handbag was in fact in their office safe, and it would be there safely until we returned to pick it up. Now, this was highly abnormal in Romania, as in those times of crisis, it would have been expected that something so valuable would have been stolen. But as the manager had said, we recovered the bag to find everything still there, not even one dollar missing. Although we wanted to give the manager some money as a reward, he refused saying, "What I did should be a normal thing. Besides, I fear God and believe that He expects us to do these things for others." I then asked Dennis, Paul, and Valer, "Guys, didn't we look for adventure on this trip? The Lord is good! He has given it to us; this one should be remembered forever."

Assistance Angels Arrive (AAA)

Several years ago, my whole family was returning home from an American, West coast itinerary, visiting Colorado, Washington, and Oregon. While driving through the dry areas of southeastern Oregon, on Interstate 5 to Phoenix, our back tire picked up a nail and flattened on us. As I stopped to look for our spare, I saw that it was also flat, and the little tire air-pump was broken. In this situation, I couldn't do more than trust God, pray, and wait for some merciful person to stop and help. After praying in the back of the car with the family, I got back into the front seat believing for a miracle before nighttime.

After a while, a little pickup truck stopped behind us with two men coming toward us with tools in hand, both looking like mobile mechanics. I stepped out of our car and asked them, "Are you going to help me here?" They said, "Yes, we came to fix your tires." I blessed them for doing it so quickly without having to contact anyone. I told them I would pay them for their generosity, but also that I would pray for them as a missionary and pastor, and while doing their job, they said, "Great! We receive your prayer, but no money is necessary – we're missions pastors like yourself." Then I asked them, "What church do you serve, here in Oregon?" They said, "Many international churches, Spanish, American, European, or Asian, it doesn't matter. We have all sorts of people in our congregations."

I asked for a church card or business address, so they went over to their truck and brought me a card with the inscription, "Serving God on the Highways." It had the address and phone number on the card too. Then, as they left us, we blessed each other, and told them to keep in touch as we would contact them soon. But our greatest blessing in this situation was that both tires were repaired. After about a month, I tried calling the number a few times, but no one answered. I wrote to the address, but no one ever gave a response. Then, I looked closely on the GPS map and found no such city or church ministry in Oregon or California. It seems that we had a couple of international angels assigned to us, to help us in our time of need. It might just be that these were the two angels who helped us while driving with Dennis, Paul, and Valer to Suceava!

The Gang & the Airport Official

I recall in the early nineties when I needed to pay our contractors and workers, that I carried a handbag filled with money to the Timisoara tram. At that time, the cities and public transportation systems were filled with robber gangs. And here on this tram with the bag in my hand, I discovered that there was a gang with four men in it. I kept my eyes on them, sternly checking all their moves, and at least one of them was watching me as well. But after a while, somehow my gaze scared them off. I was dressed in a nice suit which could have given them the idea that I was someone with governmental authority checking them out or ready to call the police. But I knew that the authority of God was upon on me and that was what caused them to run off the train; otherwise, I would have been an easy target.

Another time in the Washington airport, a governmental agent came inside the waiting room an hour before boarding the plane to Munich. He asked us how much money we had with us? Now, we were a family of five at that time, all the kids were with us. I asked him, "So we look like a family who has a lot of money? I mean, sure we'd like to have more in our pocket; but we have just enough to take care of our visit. We have somewhere around $6,000." Besides our personal money, we carried money for the building fund and ministry, which totaled over $30,000. But I didn't speak of this money as technically, it wasn't our personal funds. These funds belonged to CFNI and CCFR. This man was satisfied with my humorous reply and moved on to other people. But with them, he performed a thorough search. This took place in the '90s when the Romanian banks were not yet connected to the U.S. banking system. Everything was harder, took longer, was more expensive and unsafe to transfer money through the former communist banking system. Thankfully, now we have safer banks where the system is secure, and all our ministry money is transferred by wire, through the banking system rather than taken over the border by hand. In a way, this has been like a miracle for the nation, and has especially helped missionaries bringing financial support to what God is doing in Romania.

Conclusion

The term "apostle" in the Scripture speaks of a "sent one," as this is what the Greek translation of this word actually means. Other translations use the words "special messenger" to describe this ministry. Still others use the term "missionary." But one thing is certain: God is the one who commissions those who have this calling. This is not a ministry that everyone agrees on, as some believe it has passed away with the last apostle mentioned in Scripture. Others believe that it functions today but have extra-biblical ideas as to how a modern-day apostle operates.

Indeed, I have not endeavored to use the term "apostle" lightly when referring to my calling. But one thing is certain: a person either has the fruit of apostleship, or they don't. And besides church planting, pioneering ministries, and working in places where Christ has not been named, there is a depth of constructing that Christ must do on the inside of those who have this ministry. There is a road that every "messenger for Christ" must walk down, which is full of hardships, uncertainties, and warfare, as well as unimaginable blessings, miracles, and results. And one of the main ways we will be tested, is in the area of provision.

For those of us who have been called into apostolic ministry, we should accept the fact that our beginnings will likely be a test for us, as we are relying solely on God's commission, not the wallets of other believers. This means that we often start with little, because our faith must be tested for it to grow. Unfortunately, many people graduating ministry schools today are expecting lofty pulpit positions, with large congregations that have been gathered by another – some pastor or apostle who already did the work to bring the people in. What a mistake! Now these graduates have a degree, a diploma to hang on their wall, and a lot of theological theories. But the real testing happens outside the classroom.

The way of the Lord might be slow, but it is a sure way to the blessings that will last long after we pass into eternity. You see, the Lord blesses us based on *who we are*, and not based on degrees or the corporate growth of our ministries and churches. We might not become recognizable figures in this life, but our obedience will pay off in heaven – every minute spent obeying His word and every dime spent furthering His kingdom. It is true that God will bless us on earth as we bless others; however, we will ultimately receive the crown of eternal life, in the heavenly kingdom where we will receive eternal dominion to reign over cities. We really don't deserve god's generosity, but the Lord is just gracious. And you know what?

While we are here, we should be reaping heavenly fruit which is love, joy, and abundant peace, regardless of the storms around us, even despite those hardships that have been with us for a long time.

For special messengers sent by God, there is a ditch on both sides of the road we have been called to walk. On the one side, you have people who believe that missionaries should be poor. In fact, the poorer he or she is, the more they are right with God! This is the mentality that thinks holy saints should look like any of the monastic images of religious expression – where the minister is considered as holy if he is poor, without possessions, and without any material desires. On the other side of the road you have the idea that a Christian should be radically prosperous, and that a believer who is not, or does not aspire to be a millionaire, has something wrong with his or her thinking.

The truth is both beliefs stem from a lack of faith. The two extremes are human-focused, believing that human performance is the key to a holy life – on the one hand, the man who only has a little is more righteous than the one who has a lot, and on the other hand, the man who has a lot is holier than the one who has a little. However, the Christian road we must walk down recognizes *Christ* as our only sufficiency, not our self-righteous acts. He may want us to walk our road with little for a time, or with abundance; but either way, we must see that it is Christ who determines what we possess.

It strikes me as important to recognize that many who are poor expect everything to come into their lives for free. This is a wrong frame of mind and keeps people in a cycle of poverty. The truth is that many of these people have made wrong choices. Moreover, we may find these people in good mental and physical shape, yet are never making progress in their lives, because everything they get is spent selfishly on themselves. I'm not including those who have certified disabilities where obtaining a good job is an impossibility. And yet another group of people who are stuck in the poverty cycle are those who are single parents, especially those who have multiple children. They may be making a very minimal income per month. Still, regardless of a person's economic condition, everyone can give to someone else who is less fortunate then themselves.

Now, the ones who are giving the little they have, are sure to reap a harvest very soon, and the rewards will be a multiplication of whatever was sown. Usually, the same people who faithfully sow their seed are those who appreciate any gift, regardless if it is large or small. Also, we should honor the giver without expecting a second offering to come from the same person; otherwise, our attention becomes fixed on what is in man's hands as opposed to God's hand. We should see every small gift as valuable, even as the poor widow in Scripture who gave all she had but was esteemed by God as having given much. Besides, no one is required by law to give or help us – this is a free response of the human heart. And as the recipient of a gift, we should only be thankful, unless we want to be an offense to the generosity of God. Think of it this way: the giver heard the voice of God and is being faithful to deposit the gift into my hands. How then should I respond? As though God was the one giving me the gift! We ought to pray and offer thanksgiving for everyone who has blessed us in obedience to the Father.

This certainly applies to pastors, missionaries, and any other minister of God's Word. None of us should demand anything for the ministry we have been given by God; it wasn't men who commissioned us, but Jesus! If we fall into the trap of expecting our ministries to grow the way a business grows, we will slowly become another religious, human institution, and will rely on others to be our benefactors.

In our case, God didn't make us to beg for the good things we obtained from other people. Missionaries are not beggars! And yet, this is how a lot of Romanian pastors in America were presenting the ministry. The pastors would get up and introduce us to the congregation, saying, "Hey people!

This is not an easy job to be a missionary, having to ask and beg for money from strangers." Of course, I never asked for an offering from any church for the needs of Christ Commission for Romania. But this is the perception so many have had – if you are a missionary, you must be a poor beggar! I took these churches off my itinerary as I wouldn't speak in places that perceived me as someone who had his hand out. I just happen to believe that Jesus is Lord of the harvest, and every tool, building, vehicle, article of clothing, and dollar, belongs to Him.

And so, to conclude this chapter and my life's journey presented within these pages, I'm beseeching you my reader, my partners, my sons and daughters, to continue walking this path of consecration, faithfulness, and obedience to Christ, who we so dearly love. It has been the highest honor to have all of you share in my life, many of whom appear on these pages, and others who have silently sown your finances, your kind words, and your material possessions into the work of the Lord. Regardless of where our physical address might be – whether in America, Romania, or anywhere else – we are one! My prayer for you is that you go in peace and run to the end of your race. Jesus' loving eyes are always on you, waiting for you to receive the crown of life! My desire is that your eyes are ever on Him, the Author and Finisher of your life.

Made in the USA
Monee, IL
31 January 2020